AMERICAN FOREIGN POLICY
IN THE MAKING
1932–1940

A STUDY IN RESPONSIBILITIES

By

CHARLES A. BEARD

NEW HAVEN
YALE UNIVERSITY PRESS
1946

PREFACE

THE nature and limitations of this work are described in Chapter III, entitled "Problems Posed by Charges of War Guilt," pp. 43–46. This volume deals with public statements of foreign policy (1932–40), not with pronouncements on international morality, or with secret negotiations, offers, and promises in foreign affairs.

To Miss Louise Powelson and Miss Susanna Small, both students of exceptional competence, I am deeply indebted for invaluable assistance in research.

With characteristic generosity, Professor Edwin Borchard, whose mastery of international law is everywhere acknowledged by scholars, has aided me in the assembly of materials, read the entire manuscript, and given me critical counsel such as any student might covet. No mere line in this preface can discharge my indebtedness to him.

For the privilege of quoting many passages from Thomas A. Bailey's *Woodrow Wilson and the Great Betrayal*, I am under special obligations to the publishers, The Macmillan Company, of New York City.

CHARLES A. BEARD

New Milford, Connecticut,
Summer, 1946.

CONTENTS

CHAPTER I

"Evil" Senators Responsible for World War II

ON January 15, 1945, shortly after President Roosevelt had delivered his annual message on the state of the Union and the world, a memorable debate on American policy occurred in the Senate of the United States—that great national forum for the free and uncensored discussion of public affairs. In the course of the debate Senators reviewed the historical backgrounds of the global war then raging, referred to the actions and ambitions of foreign governments, including Russia and Great Britain, and drew into question some of the principal foreign projects advocated by President Roosevelt. Throughout the controversy, the tension which usually marks blunt exchanges of views in the chamber was kept taut by a realization of the fact that in the coming months the Senate would be compelled to act upon the treaties and laws designed to fix the policy of the United States in and for a world of contentious nations.

On this occasion, the task of upholding the Administration in respect of certain issues was undertaken by Senator Claude Pepper of Florida. Mr. Pepper had long been a defender of President Roosevelt's domestic and foreign policies, if sometimes a dissenter in matters of detail. A graduate of the University of Alabama, trained in law at Harvard University, an experienced debater, with nearly ten years' service in the Senate behind him, Mr. Pepper ranked high among his Democratic colleagues in learning and dialectical skill. Moreover, he was a vigorous supporter of the internationalism to which President Roosevelt was committing the

1. Here and in the following pages the term *internationalism* is used as meaning: World peace is desirable and possible; it is indivisible and can be secured for the United States only by entering into a positive connection with a league, or association, of nations, empowered to make pacific adjustments of international conflicts and to impose peace, by effective sanctions or by force,

Government of the United States and he assumed the burden of championing it amid a cross fire of sharp criticism.

In his efforts to sustain his cause against challenges from the opposition, Senator Pepper arraigned the Senate itself at the bar of moral judgment: "It was not on the battlefields of Flanders that the last war and its victory of peace were lost, but in this Chamber."

Immediately after Senator Pepper had launched his indictment, the following colloquy ensued:

Mr. Millikin [of Colorado]. Mr. President, I challenge that statement, and I should like to have a demonstration of it.

Mr. Pepper. History demonstrates it.

Mr. Millikin. Mr. President, I do not care about the Senator's notions of history. I think that is a terrible accusation to make against this country and against this Senate. . . . In what way was the peace of the world lost on the floor of the Senate? Let us have a demonstration of it.

Mr. Pepper. Very well. It was because, in my humble opinion, the Senate failed to ratify the Treaty of Versailles and to provide for our part in the League of Nations. . . .

Mr. Millikin. . . . Will the Senator demonstrate how, if we had been in the League of Nations, any decisions would have been different than those which were made?

Mr. Pepper. I will tell the Senator how I think they would have been different. I think the United States at the conclusion of the last war had the moral leadership of the world. . . . I believe the United States in a world-wide organization would have brought to its councils not only great moral leadership, great physical power, and great natural resources and their strength, but a moral elevation, if you please, and personal disinterestedness which the nations of the Old World do not have. I think we could have brought to bear upon those councils influences without which they disintegrated into a bickering, fighting lot of Old World powers, as they have always been. . . .

After the Senate failed to ratify the Treaty of Versailles, including provision for the League of Nations, it did not even

on aggressors or peace breakers; the United States cannot maintain neutrality in case of any major war among European and Asiatic powers.

take up the pact to make secure the frontiers of France. We abandoned our allies. We abandoned our objectives. We abandoned our dead. We waited for the next war to come.

That is why I say that if America had taken an affirmative part, at least the probability is that we might have avoided the war which has come to curse this generation.

MR. MILLIKIN. Mr. President, will the Senator agree with me that the war might have been prevented had France, which had the best and largest army in the world, repelled the German aggression in the Rhineland?

MR. PEPPER. It might have. . . . I am not at all sure that France has any greater obligation to keep a would-be world conqueror in check than we have. . . .

MR. MILLIKIN. . . . The Senator cannot demonstrate that had we been a member of the League of Nations the course of history would have been any different.

MR. PEPPER. Mr. President, I will leave the Senator to argue with history. . . .

Thus in the development of the controversy, Senator Pepper's original assertion had been reduced to the level of a mere probability and his appeal to history had been questioned. Certainly it had been clouded by ambiguity. But his unequivocal declaration stood firmly in the record: "The last war and its victory of peace were lost . . . in this Chamber."

Later in the year, July 23, 1945, when the Charter of the United Nations came before the Senate for ratification, Senator Tom Connally opened the full-dress debate and, in the manner of Senator Pepper, called history to support his arguments. He reminded his colleagues of the treatment meted out to the League of Nations twenty-five years previously. While he refrained from ascribing World War II to the defeat of the League, he laid the blame for that defeat on the Senate; and in a warning tone lamented that "many representatives of foreign nations are still doubtful as to what the vote on the charter will be here in the Senate. They remember 1919."

Then in a florid style all his own, Senator Connally declared to the Senate that these representatives of foreign nations "know how the League of Nations was slaughtered here on the floor. Can you not still see the blood on the floor? Can you not see upon the walls the marks of the conflict that ranged [*sic*] here in the Chamber where the League of Nations was done to death. They fear that that same sentiment may keep the United States from ratifying this charter. Our ratification of it will instill hope into the hearts of the peoples of the earth. . . . I trust that the Senate . . . will ratify this charter by a vote so overwhelming as to carry the conviction over the earth that the United States expects to assume its obligations for the purpose of keeping them, for the purpose of living up to them, for the purpose of supporting a world organization for peace with all our spirit and with all our hearts."

The charge that the peace at the end of World War I had been lost in the Senate was an old doctrine which had been repeated with almost endless reiteration by advocates of internationalism, at home and abroad, since the final vote of the Senate on the Treaty of Versailles in 1920.[2] In one form or another, during a quarter of a century, it had been proclaimed by members of Congress, publicists, educators, journalists, and radio broadcasters and reasserted on innumerable occasions as if it were an absolute truth. Often it had been narrowed in such a way as to place the responsibility not upon the Senate as a whole but upon a small group of scheming, willful, evil Republican Senators led by Henry Cabot Lodge, who has long been characterized by enemies as a bigoted, ignoble, deceitful, and dishonest politician.

Indeed the thesis that a little band of Senators, mainly Republicans, mainly inspired by party malice, wrecked the peace in 1920 has appeared in a veritable flood of "literature."

2. On the nature of the Treaty of Versailles see William Bullitt, "The Tragedy of Versailles," *Life*, March 27, 1944, p. 99. W. D. Herridge, former Canadian Minister to the United States, said that "Versailles was not a treaty of peace but a declaration of war." Herridge, *Which Kind of Revolution?* (1943), p. 23.

Amid the plethora of such assertions it is difficult to choose the most typical document to illustrate the accusation. But from the embarrassment of records may be taken as a fair example an article by Joseph H. Baird, entitled "Will the Senate Hamper the Peace?" published in the *American Mercury* for June, 1945. This article not only stated the case of senatorial guilt in stark simplicity; it also pilloried with the customary severity the wicked minority of willful men. The author, Mr. Baird, had once been chief of the United Press Bureau in Moscow, had previously "covered" the State Department, had served as a member of the United Press in London, and had held a post of night foreign editor in New York City. With good reason it could be supposed, therefore, that Mr. Baird's reporting deserved serious consideration by the public.

Mr. Baird opened his account of senatorial obstruction by recalling the famous words of John Hay: "There will always be 34 per cent of the Senate on the blackguard side of every question." He declared that "the Senate fight over the League is too well known and its deviations are too tortuous to be outlined here"; so he ventured to summarize the long controversies and negotiations in a few words: "In February 1919, Senator Lodge told Senator Borah of Idaho, later to succeed him as chairman of the Foreign Relations Committee, that 85 per cent of the Senate was for the League. He then went on to explain to Borah and to Senator Watson, Republican, of Indiana, who said that 80 per cent of the public favored the League, that adherence could be defeated by a skillful campaign of reservations. . . . As a result of endless reservations and political maneuvering, when the resolution of adherence was finally balloted upon on March 19, 1920, it failed by seven votes to obtain the necessary two-thirds majority. Forty-nine votes were cast for the League and 35 against it. Thus a plurality of fourteen Senators favored it." [3]

3. For the multiplicity of facts that utterly demolish this oversimplification, see the findings of Thomas A. Bailey, below, pp. 7 ff.

For the view that the leaders of the opposition to a ratification of the Treaty without reservations were petty and mean partisans, writers in 1945, such as Mr. Baird, could appeal to the authority of a person no less distinguished than President Wilson. Shortly before the final vote on the Treaty of Versailles, with reservations, was taken in the Senate, the President said to Ray Stannard Baker that the reservations demanded by the Lodge group "are not made by thoughtful men to improve the Covenant; they represent a dishonorable attempt, on the part of leaders who do not speak for the people, to escape any real responsibility, so far as the United States is concerned, for world peace in future years. They are essentially partisan political devices. If I accept them, these senators will merely offer new ones, even more humiliating. These evil men intend to destroy the League." [4]

Another stark declaration of the evil men's responsibility for the second World War was made by "T. R. B.," nominally a regular correspondent for the *New Republic,* in his "Washington Notes," June 18, 1945. Without referring to the files of that journal and its own hostility to the Versailles Treaty and accompaniments, the author of the Notes named several of the "evil" men of the Senate in 1919–20: Borah, Lodge, Knox, and La Follette, for example, and then placed the terrible burden of war guilt upon them: "They had joyously hounded Woodrow Wilson to his grave. . . . They had riddled the League with reservations till its own friends couldn't support it. They had hidden behind the two-thirds rule, killed Wilson, restored Normalcy, erected tariff walls, snubbed Russia, rejected a world court, and then had the last say after all, by writing the Johnson Act. . . . And the cost was little enough; only a Second World War." Here is a succinct statement of the theory that the war woes of the terrible years from 1939 to 1945 lay on the heads of a few "dishonorable" and "evil" Senators of the United States.

A version of the formula relative to senatorial guilt for World War II made it less personal and partisan: the "cause"

4. Baker, *American Chronicle* (Charles Scribner's Sons, 1945), p. 474.

of the defeat administered to the Treaty of Versailles was the archaic and undemocratic rule in the Constitution which made the concurrence of two thirds of the Senators present necessary to the approval of a treaty. If it had not been for this two-thirds rule, if treaties could have been ratified by a mere majority of the Senate or of the House and Senate combined, the United States would have joined the League of Nations and World War II would have been warded off. As far as the theory of American responsibility is concerned, however, this version was in upshot the same as the first statement of the case: scheming Senators, mostly Republicans, took advantage of the two-thirds rule, kept the United States out of the League, and hence made it impossible for the other members of the League to stop the coming of World War II.

That the world and the peoples thereof were victimized when the Senate of the United States rejected the League of Nations is the theme of a substantial work by Thomas A. Bailey, *Woodrow Wilson and the Great Betrayal*,[5] published in 1945. This volume presents a stinging bill of moral indictment; but it is no mere defense of party or cause, sustained by avoidance, emphasis, and special pleading. It was written by a scholar of high standing in the historical profession. Although Professor Bailey admits to the record solid evidence which contradicts his own thesis, he files fourteen charges of infidelity against the United States, under the head of "betrayal," an unequivocal term of accusation and guilt.

The term "betrayal" stems from the same root as the word "traitor"—the Latin word *tradere*. To betray is to give up to or place in the power of an enemy a person or thing by treachery or disloyalty. Betrayal is a treacherous surrender to a foe, a violation of a trust or confidence, an abandonment of something committed to one's charge. A betrayal is commonly regarded as a human and moral act of the lowest and vilest kind.

5. Published by The Macmillan Company.

Such an act of necessity involves two parties. The party that commits the act of betrayal is bound to the second party by a solemn pledge, promise, or loyalty, which by express language or clear implication forbids the performance of, or participation in, such acts of treachery. The second party, the one that is betrayed, of right has indefeasible grounds for trusting the first party—the betrayer—and for expecting that the trust will never be forsworn, dishonored, or broken.

As a prelude to his indictment under the head of "betrayal" (Chapter XXII), Professor Bailey contends that President Wilson had authority to make the commitments on behalf of the United States which were incorporated in the Treaty of Versailles, that his commitments were in harmony with his public addresses to the country and the world, and that the people had "warmly applauded or had seemingly accepted" his proposals. Such, it appears, were the elements of a solemn contract entered into by the people with President Wilson—a contract binding on the people in good conscience and in honor. If the President made any mistake in the transaction, Professor Bailey says, it was not so much in giving the pledges at Paris as in assuming that "the same high degree of wartime idealism would continue indefinitely after the signing of the peace."

In other words, according to this particular passage in Professor Bailey's volume, a solemn obligation in respect of world peace and an association of nations in some form was assumed by President Wilson and the American people while World War I was raging, and the President afterward made commitments at Paris in keeping with this obligation. But the American people allowed their wartime idealism to decline. They repudiated the commitments made by the President with their authorization. This they did heedlessly, for, presumably, the terms of the Versailles Treaty conformed to the specifications laid down in the public addresses of President Wilson which the American people had applauded during the war—conformed to the stipulations of the contract between the President and the people. And, presumably also,

the other powers that participated in the drafting of the
Treaty agreed to this meeting of minds in the obligation
undertaken by the President and the people.

Immediately after offering his brief recital of the way in
which "the great betrayal" came about, Professor Bailey became cautious about fixing the blame for the defeat of the
Versailles Treaty. In the simplification he places the blame
on the people—on the decline in their wartime idealism. But
at once he introduces uncertainty by saying: "whoever was
at fault, the unwillingness or inability of the United States
to carry through the promises made in its behalf was catas-
trophic"—resulted in "the great betrayal."

This is one of the most puzzling sentences in the history of
etymology, syntax, grammar, logic, and philosophy. On its
face it seems to declare that *whoever was at fault* the United
States was at fault, for it was unwilling to carry through the
promises made by President Wilson. Yet Professor Bailey
does not say just that, for he couples with the word "unwillingness" the words "or inability." He thus destroys all the
force of moral guilt inherent in the word "unwillingness,"
by adding that it may have been the "inability" of the United
States which led to "the great betrayal"; for inability means
in this case the lack of ability, physical, mental, or moral, the
lack of the power, capacity, or instrumentalities necessary
"to carry through" President Wilson's promises.

Having in fact declared uncertain the issue of *who* was at
fault and having admitted that perhaps the United States was
after all lacking in ability to carry out President Wilson's
promises at Paris, Professor Bailey proceeds as if the betrayer
were actually known and as if the United States were the cul-
prit. For, in Chapter XXII, he lists "the results" of "the unwillingness or inability" of the United States to fulfill the
commitments made by President Wilson in the Treaty of
Versailles:

1. . . . a betrayal of the League of Nations.
2. . . . a betrayal of the Treaty of Versailles.

3. . . . a betrayal of the Allies.

4. . . . a betrayal of France.

5. . . . a betrayal of Germany.

6. . . . a betrayal of liberal opinion the world over.

7. . . . a betrayal of American boys who had died, and of American boys yet unborn.

8. . . . a betrayal of the masses everywhere.

9. . . . a betrayal of our humanitarian, missionary, and educational interests not only in Europe, but particularly in the Near East.

10. . . . a betrayal of the legitimate interests of American merchants, manufacturers, bankers, and investors.

11. . . . a betrayal of America's responsibility to assume that world leadership which had been thrust upon her.

12. . . . a betrayal of the nation's plighted word and of good faith in international dealings.

13. . . . a betrayal of our clear moral obligations to finish the job.

14. . . . a betrayal of the American people.

After presenting this list of "betrayals" which constitute "the great betrayal," Professor Bailey makes a generous gesture toward his country by saying, as a qualification, that the great betrayal did not "necessarily" mean that "our withdrawal was solely, or even primarily responsible for all the ills that befell Europe from 1919 to 1939." It did mean, however, he added, that the United States "cannot escape a very considerable share of the blame for what happened." Thus the amount of guilt justly ascribable to the United States is made indefinite.

And a few pages later in this volume Professor Bailey introduces more uncertainty. By joining the League of Nations, he says (p. 367), "we had very little if anything to lose . . . ; and everything to gain—possibly a preventing of so-called World War II"—just "possibly," not even "probably."

Then Professor Bailey asks a question that cuts right into

the validity of his betrayal theory: "Would the results[6] have been essentially different if we had joined the League?" On this issue so crucial to the validity of his whole argument, Professor Bailey remarks that "conclusions here must of course be more speculative" (than in the case of whether the United States had anything to lose by joining the League of Nations). Thereupon, after confirming the speculative character of his thinking on the subject, he makes the statement: "it may legitimately be doubted whether, when the pinch came, the United States [if a member] would have provided adequate support for the League of Nations."

One explanation of the "speculative," or inconclusive, character of Professor Bailey's conclusions may lie in his findings in the twenty-one chapters which precede his Chapter XXII entitled "The Great Betrayal." In preparation for writing his volume, he had studied with meticulous care the debates on the Treaty in the Senate, articles in the press, the unpublished Woodrow Wilson papers, papers of distinguished contemporaries, and indeed a documentation impressive in its range and authenticity. On the basis of this study, he made the following positive statements:

Senator McCormick was "uncomfortably close to the truth" when he said that President Wilson had "stacked the Peace Conference with Democrats" (p. 73).

"It would have been better if he [President Wilson] had been willing to . . . compromise enough to save the pact [Versailles Treaty]" (p. 100–101).

"Wilson's physical and mental condition had a profoundly important bearing on the final defeat of the treaty" (p. 145).

"It is hard to understand how Wilson could have insisted that the fourteen Lodge reservations, ten of which concerned the League only, completely nullified the whole treaty" (p. 166).

"Having made up his mind that he was right, he [President Wilson] saw evil in any other course. Personal pride and in-

6. It should be noted again that Professor Bailey called the fourteen betrayals "results" of the unwillingness or inability of the United States to join the League of Nations. Above p. 9.

grained stubbornness partially blinded him to the public weal" (p. 169).

"Some apologists for Wilson claim that if he had not collapsed he would have compromised with Lodge. Perhaps so, but there is nothing to support such a view in his public utterances, in his private papers or in his character" (p. 173).

"If he [President Wilson] told the Democrats in the Senate to vote for the treaty with the Lodge reservations, most of them undoubtedly would do so, and the two-thirds majority would be won" (p. 174).

"Senator Hitchcock . . . privately confessed to Colonel Bonsal, the day before the November vote, that *he and most of the Senate Democrats favored getting the treaty ratified 'in almost any form'* " (p. 177).

"Wilson bluntly told Hitchcock on November 17 that the Lodge reservations were a 'nullification' of the treaty, and that if they came to him he would pocket the whole thing" (p. 179).

"It also seems reasonably clear that by this time [November] public opinion favored either the Lodge reservations or something rather closely akin to them" (p. 180).

"Wilson's communication to Hitchcock, dated November 18 . . . told the Democratic majority how they should vote, and it spelled the difference between ratification and non-ratification of the Treaty of Versailles" (p. 185).

"If they [the Democrats] had voted for the treaty with the Lodge reservations, *instead of combining with the 'irreconcilables'*, the Senate would have approved the pact (on the first vote) 81 to 13, or with 19 votes to spare" (p. 195). [Only thirteen or fourteen Senators were "irreconcilable."]

Important French newspapers favored a ratification of the Treaty even in spite of some of the reservations: "The powerful *Temps*, which often spoke for the Foreign Office . . . believed that the Lodge reservations merely set forth restrictions which would in practice exist anyhow" (p. 205).

Colonel House advised President Wilson that Democratic Senators be instructed to vote for ratification with reservations. "Neither of House's two letters was answered or acknowledged" (p. 210).

December 14, 1919, President Wilson authorized an official statement that "he has *no compromise or concession of any kind in mind*" but intends to place the whole responsibility on the Republican leaders of the Senate (p. 212).

In his Jackson Day letter, President Wilson declared that if "there was any doubt as to the views of the people," the way out was "to give the next election the form *of a great and solemn referendum*" (p. 217).

William Jennings Bryan, on Jackson Day, branded the "solemn referendum" idea as "folly" and urged working out a compromise on the Treaty (p. 218).

"An impressive number of Democratic newspapers" supported Mr. Bryan's proposal in favor of a compromise with the opposition (p. 221).

"An appeal from the League of Free Nations Association urged the President to accept the necessary reservations and get the treaty into operation" (p. 225).

"A committee representing twenty-six organizations, with a total membership of fifty million memorialized both the President and the Senate to compromise their differences" (p. 226).

Viscount Grey, after trying in vain to see President Wilson in Washington, published in England a powerful article in which he favored the entrance of the United States willingly with limited obligations as preferable to unwilling partnership with unlimited obligations (pp. 234–237).

Mr. Lloyd George, British Prime Minister, publicly expressed willingness to accept the United States with reservations, provided the other powers were not expressly required to agree to the conditions (p. 240).

In February, 1920, President Wilson told Senator Glass that if the Treaty was approved with the Lodge reservations he would pocket it (p. 256).

The day after the final vote on the Treaty, Senator Hitchcock wrote to President Wilson, saying that it required the "most energetic efforts" on his part to prevent a majority of Democrats from surrendering to Senator Lodge—and thus effecting ratification (p. 271).

"The evidence is convincing that Wilson wanted the issue cast into the hurly-burly of politics"—the election campaign of 1920 (p. 275).

"Minds no less acute than Wilson's . . . denied that the Lodge reservations completely nullified the treaty" (p. 277).

"By his action, he [President Wilson] contributed powerfully to the ultimate undoing of the League, and with it the high hopes of himself and mankind for an organization to prevent World War II" (p. 277).

"Many elements entered into the legislative log jam of March, 1920. . . . No one of them was solely responsible for the pile-up. *But as the pile-up finally developed, there was only one lumberjack who could break it, and that was Woodrow Wilson*" (p. 278).

"Wilson gave orders that the treaty was to be killed in the Senate chamber. And there it died" (p. 281).

In dealing with the influences which may have induced in the minds of Senators a hostility to the Treaty of Versailles, Professor Bailey, however, minimizes a large amount of information respecting the "inside history" of World War I and the settlement at Paris, which reached the American public between 1918 and 1920. Most startling of all was the publication of various secret treaties and understandings entered into by the Entente Allies preparatory to the war, or in relation to the distribution of the spoils at the close of the conflict.

After the Bolsheviks came to power in Russia in 1917 they opened the hidden archives of the Tsarist regime and spread broadcast many documents which gave to the political and moral aims of the Entente Allies an aspect wholly different from that expounded in their war propaganda from 1914 to 1918. Particularly significant for its effect on opinion in the United States was the publication, in January, 1918, of certain secret treaties drawn from the Russian archives[7] and later the dissemination of other documents bearing on the transactions of the governments with which President Wilson carried on negotiations at Paris when the terms of the Versailles Treaty and the Covenant of the League of Nations were being drafted.

Nevertheless, without carefully estimating the influence

7. In the *New York Evening Post* under the editorship of Oswald Garrison Villard.

of such revelations in arousing American hostility to the Entente Powers and the Treaty, Professor Bailey, in apportioning blame for the rejection of the League of Nations, makes the Senate carry a burden of guilt. Whatever may be the degree of responsibility he ascribes to President Wilson, Professor Bailey leaves the impression that the Senators whom the President characterized as "evil men"—especially Senator Lodge and the "bitter-enders"—are at least to be regarded as among the culprits in the "great betrayal" which brought World War II upon humanity.

In the foregoing expressions of opinion that make the responsibility for World War II in some way turn upon "obstructionists" in the Senate of the United States are exhibited both the assurance and the ambiguity that have attended the exposition of this particular thesis. For some time President Wilson attributed the obstruction to "evil men" in the Senate and this view has widely prevailed. Senator Pepper and Senator Connally located the blame *in* the Senate without naming or characterizing the Senators to be held accountable. Professor Bailey represented President Wilson as eternally right in regarding isolation as a mirage and believing that "the next war would surely drag us in"; and, while holding that the President was impolitic in methods, Professor Bailey also portrayed the Senate "oligarchy" as an activating force in "the great betrayal" which eventuated in the second World War.

CHAPTER II

The American People to Blame for World War II

A WIDER view of culpability in respect of the woes that befell the nations of the earth after 1919, involving them at length in World War II, places the blame upon the American people as a whole, upon the "public," or upon "the country" at large. This view does not exclude from responsibility the "evil men" of the Senate, or the two-thirds rule for ratification of treaties to which the nation had clung. Indeed, all the Senators, "good" and "evil" alike, are among the offending persons covered by the all-embracing indictment of the American people as the guilty party. While the wider view of culpability takes various forms in actual statement, it generally comprises certain features which, collectively, amount to a thesis: that the American people are responsible for the foreign policy that led in effect to World War II.

Rallying to the leadership of President Wilson, as "the farsighted statesman" of his times—the thesis runs—the American people had waged World War I for the purpose of destroying German militarism, making the world safe for democracy, imposing a liberal program on backward nations,[1] realizing President Wilson's Fourteen Points, putting a final end to war, and ushering in the age of permanent peace. While the battles of that war were raging, the American people cheered his projects for a grand association of nations to carry out the aims of the war; and at the Paris Peace Conference the League of Nations was projected in

1. According to Ray Stannard Baker, "Wilson meant to change the world, not by changing the system, as was the proposal in Russia and by radicals in Western Europe, and 'so shaking every foundation in order to dislodge an abuse,' but by administering it uprightly according to traditional liberal principles of America and Great Britain and with the guarantee of a league of nations founded upon those principles." *Woodrow Wilson and World Settlement* (Doubleday, Page & Co., 1922), II, 64.

fulfilment of the President's pledges to the American people and to all "peace-loving" nations.

But—the thesis continues—soon after the war the American people forgot their noble professions and resolves, let their war idealism "slump," grew weary of hearing about the woes of the world, turned selfishly to their own affairs, and sank into the mire of "isolationism." [2] In heroic efforts to marshal the people in support of his policy as against the "evil men" in the Senate, President Wilson toured the West in 1919. He begged the people to remember the war aims he had announced in their name. He asked them to remain faithful to the cause for which he said American soldiers had died, warned them that another world war would come if the United States rejected the League of Nations, and told them that only under the League could adequate outlets be found for American goods in foreign markets. On this tour President Wilson, worn out by his arduous labor, was overcome by a desperate illness. Disregarding his pleas and misfortune, the Senate refused to ratify the Treaty of Versailles.

It is true that in 1920 the Democrats in their national convention endorsed the League of Nations and nominated two ardent supporters of the League, James M. Cox and Franklin D. Roosevelt, for President and Vice-President, respectively. But at the "solemn referendum" the American people swept the Democrats out of power in an avalanche of votes. Then, under Republican leadership, they turned to isolation with a vengeance. They remained obdurate in their narrow vision, even after the Democratic party recovered supremacy in 1933; they clung obstinately to the traditional doctrine that the United States should not become entangled in the age-

2. *Isolationism* is used in this volume as meaning: Rejection of membership in the League of Nations; non-entanglement in the political controversies of Europe and Asia; non-intervention in the wars of those continents; neutrality, peace, and defense for the United States through measures appropriate to those purposes; and the pursuit of a foreign policy friendly to all nations disposed to reciprocate. An isolationist may favor the promotion of good will and peace among nations by any and all measures compatible with non-entanglement in any association of nations empowered to designate "aggressors" and bring engines of sanction and coercion into action against them.

long quarrels of Europe and Asia; they selfishly wanted peace, neutrality, and defense for the United States in a warring world.

In vain—the thesis concluded—did Franklin D. Roosevelt, after he became President in 1933, warn the American people that peace could be maintained only by collective action of "peace-loving nations," by putting a "quarantine" on aggressors. In vain did he tell them that the United States could not defend itself against victorious aggressors if Great Britain fell. In vain did he beseech Congress for adequate measures of defense against aggressors. The American people remained adamant. Congress "stifled" the President's calls for preparedness. Even after Hitler's hordes had overrun France in 1940, the people still demanded peace for the United States. For years the people blocked President Roosevelt and the Secretary of State, Cordell Hull, in their efforts to enforce a policy designed to restrain aggressors and prevent outbreaks of war in Europe and Asia. The people insisted on holding fast to their "ignorance," "smugness," "indifference," and "isolationism," until Japanese bombs blasted Pearl Harbor on December 7, 1941. Not until then did the American people see that President Roosevelt had been right from the beginning, rush in a solid body to the support of the war, and display a willingness to assume the moral responsibility to the whole world which they had surrendered and spurned almost immediately after World War I.

The widening of responsibility from the "evil men" in the Senate to include the people as a whole began before the Senate had acted on the Versailles Treaty. As early as the autumn of 1919 experienced editors in New York City informed Ray Stannard Baker, President Wilson's confidant and aide, that "the American people were 'fed up' on the Peace Conference; they didn't want to be bothered any more with the woes of Europe." [3]

Apparently President Wilson himself finally came to the conclusion that it was the people, not merely the "evil men"

3. Baker, *American Chronicle*, p. 463.

in the Senate, who actually defeated the ratification of the Versailles Treaty at the end of World War I. According to a statement given to the press in May, 1945, by his daughter, Mrs. Eleanor Wilson McAdoo, Mr. Wilson said within his family circle a short time before his death in 1924: "It was right that the United States did not join the League of Nations. . . . I've been thinking about this for a long time. If we had joined the League when I asked for it, it would have been a great personal victory. But it would not have worked, because deep down in their hearts the American people didn't really believe in it. The time will come when this country will join such a league because they will know that it has to be. And then and then only will it work." [4]

From year to year after 1920 the thesis of popular responsibility in the United States for the world's woes and wars was set forth in articles, books, pamphlets, and leaflets. Illustrations of it were as thick as autumn leaves in the literature of the period from 1920 to 1945. Professors, preachers, editors, publicists, columnists, and propagandists repeated it with a determination that increased in intensity as World War II approached and rose to fury after war broke in 1939.

The thesis of popular ignorance and responsibility was incisively presented many times, for instance, in the voluminous writings of Frederick L. Schuman, Woodrow Wilson Professor of Government at Williams College. In the professor's opinion it was the American people, or the "public," who demanded neutrality legislation and estopped President Roosevelt from leading or joining Great Britain, France, and Russia in a movement for "collective security" that would have prevented the war in Europe.

Speaking early in 1936 of the neutrality legislation then pending, in the *Nation*, February 12, 1936, Professor Schuman described it as "one part lunacy, one part stupidity, and one part criminal ignorance of diplomatic and economic realities." The bill in question as slightly modified passed the House on February 17, 1936, by a vote of 353 to 27. In favor

4. *New York World-Telegram,* May 8, 1945.

of the measure were 273 Democrats, 78 Republicans, and 2 Farm-Laborites; opposing were 11 Democrats, 9 Republicans, and 7 Progressives; the Senate passed the bill the following day without a record vote; and the President signed it on February 28. Judging by the action of Congress it is evident that "lunacy," "stupidity," and "criminal ignorance" —to use Professor Schuman's epithets—were widespread among representatives of the people in the Government of the United States.[5]

Writing after the war had broken out in Europe in 1939, while President Roosevelt was assuring the American people that every effort of the Government would be directed to keeping the United States out of the war, Professor Schuman was again harsh in characterizing the American public and placing on the American people the failure to check the aggressors. In his *Night over Europe*, published early in 1941, the professor said: "No one knew better than he [President Roosevelt in 1940] that passive defense of the United States or of the 'Western Hemisphere' would become a strategic impossibility, mathematically certain to insure defeat, the moment that Britain surrendered." Why was it that President Roosevelt "could say none of these things openly lest he be accused of 'war mongering'?" The professor answered in language not quite so mathematical: President Roosevelt "knew that the public would flee, as from the devil, from any suggestion of belligerent participation [in the war], and that a motley crowd of pacifists, appeasers, isolationists, enemy agents, and muddleheads would seize upon his every move to impede the march of the aggressors as a basis for charging him with aiming at dictatorship and scheming to send American boys to die on foreign soil." [6]

While Professor Schuman castigated the American public for adhering to a foreign policy of isolation and nonintervention, he did not entirely exculpate President Roose-

---

5. Vote in *American Year Book* (1936), p. 27. Charles A. Beard, *The Devil Theory of War* (Vanguard Press, 1936), p. 112.
6. *Night over Europe* (Alfred A. Knopf, 1941), p. 553.

velt. On the contrary he described the President, then facing an election campaign, as "a leader who preferred to follow his followers, as a prospective candidate who felt obliged to march behind the electorate rather than in front of it." [7] But this characterization of the President as less than ingenuous in no way softened Professor Schuman's condemnation of the American people as guilty of criminal ignorance in matters of foreign policy.[8]

Another exposition of the popular-responsibility thesis by a distinguished citizen was set forth in an article entitled "America's Faith—a Call for Revival," published in the *New York Times* Sunday Magazine on July 18, 1943. The author of the exposition was Robert N. Wilkin, judge of the district court of the United States in northern Ohio. A loyal Democrat, appointed to his post by President Roosevelt in June, 1939, Judge Wilkin could write on foreign policy with warm feeling and in a tone of authority.

After placing "the chief responsibility for our nation's default" in 1919–20 on the senatorial minority and after ascribing its opposition to animosity toward Woodrow Wilson, Judge Wilkin represented President Wilson as finally betrayed by the people. That "great intellect" had voiced the aspirations of humanity but could not maintain "the unity of his own people." "That courageous and patient soul who had gained the acceptance of our faith from all the rest of the world [9] had to witness the loss of that faith at home." The President believed that "the people's relapse would be followed by a revival." Yet, declared Judge Wilkin, "the American people cannot be absolved from the doom of his prophecy."

Having brought the American people to book and con-

7. *Ibid.*
8. For Professor Schuman's later views and doubts, see "The Dilemma of the Peace-Seekers," *American Political Science Review*, XXXIX (February, 1945), 12–30.
9. For what "the rest of the world" demanded at the hands of President Wilson, see Baker, *op. cit.*, pp. 324, 330, 331, 336, 350, 354, 363, 365, 372, 398, 405, 411, 413, 415, 421, 423.

victed them of a terrible sin against the aspirations of all humanity, Judge Wilkin asked how "we" could be redeemed. "What can we do to rectify our mistakes and minimize the consequences of our error? What retribution can we offer for the wrongs we have done? What can we do to be saved?"

Judge Wilkin offered his plan of salvation: "We must confess and repent. . . . There can be no spiritual health or strength in us until we are cleansed of our wilful error." The people must support measures in Congress looking to the establishment of a new world organization; they must demonstrate to American soldiers that their hopes are not in vain, "that we have forestalled another relapse into isolationism; that we have solemnly consecrated ourselves to the fulfilment of their sacrifice. . . . If we will give up our national irresponsibility and assume our share of international responsibility . . . we will be able to fill, with gratification to ourselves and benefit to the world, the position to which we have been deputized by destiny."

The thesis of American responsibility for wrecking the League of Nations was partly if not fully underwritten by Carlton J. H. Hayes, the American Ambassador to Spain, in his *Wartime Mission to Spain, 1942–1945*,[10] published late in 1945. On the first page of this volume Mr. Hayes says: "I was henceforth [after 1918] a convinced and outspoken advocate of the League of Nations and of any agency or measure which might forward the cause of collective security and lessen the danger of another World War in which many more millions of Americans were sure to be involved. It seemed to me then, and it still does, that we who were decried in the partisan strife of 1920 as 'idealists' and 'dreamers' were far more realistic than those 'realists' who wrecked the League of Nations and pursued narrowly nationalist ends. Unfortunately for the present generation, there proved to be more 'realists' in those days than 'idealists.' "

Here in a brief passage are the presuppositions so com-

10. Published by The Macmillan Company.

monly taken for granted without analysis, namely, that the
contest in the United States over the League of Nations was
a "partisan" strife; that it was a struggle between idealists
who were realists and alleged realists who did not know what
they were doing; and that the United States was "sure" to be
involved in the next war, in other words, fated to be involved in that war, as if it made no difference what policy
other than internationalism was pursued by the Government
of the United States. Leaving aside the problem of ontology
implicit in the Ambassador's assumptions as to realists and
idealists and as to fate, here also is the clear intimation that
American partisans, presumably Republicans on the whole,
"wrecked the League of Nations" and were in some measure
at least responsible for World War II.[11]

One of the accompaniments of the thesis that the United
States or the American people were responsible for World
War II is the proposition, often associated with it, to the
effect that the same American people who betrayed their responsibility to the world in 1920 or thereabouts were and
still are capable of asserting superior moral leadership. Senator Pepper gave voice to this idea when he laid the blame
for World War II on the Senate of the United States. In an
address before the New York City College alumni on November 17, 1945, Abe Fortas, Under-Secretary of the Department of the Interior, declared: "We are the one nation
in the world that can successfully assert the moral leadership
necessary to guide the world to peace and civilized living." [12]

11. In respect of his own party views, Mr. Hayes wrote, on p. 7: "though I
had voted for him [Mr. Roosevelt] in 1932 and 1936 and again in 1940, I had
never taken an active part in politics, and my adherence to the Democratic
party had been more 'independent' than regular. At no time then or after-
wards did he or any other official of our Government ask me about my
'politics.'"
12. *New York Times*, November 18, 1945. Mr. Fortas also warned his auditors that there was danger of another world war and added: "The burning
question before us is whether we have the ability . . . to change the world
sufficiently to avoid this disaster. The answer is so largely dependent upon the
people of the United States that every one of us shares an immediate and com-
pelling responsibility." About the same time Dr. Max Lerner, formerly a professor in Williams College, likewise indicated the way for exculpating Russia

An official document that in effect lent support to the thesis of popular responsibility for World War II, without mentioning it, was issued in March, 1942. It was presented in the Senate by John H. Overton, of Louisiana, and printed as Senate Document Number 188. The volume is entitled *Development of United States Foreign Policy* and embraces "Addresses and Messages of Franklin D. Roosevelt compiled from official sources, intended to present the chronological development of the foreign policy of the United States from the announcement of the Good Neighbor Policy in 1933, including the War Declarations." Sixty-nine pages of the volume are given to addresses from 1933 to 1940 inclusive, and the remainder of the pages (70–150) to the years 1940 and 1941.

This official collection of pronouncements which purports to represent the foreign policy advocated by President Roosevelt from 1933 to 1942 contains only selected addresses and messages. With few exceptions, such as the Chautauqua speech of August 14, 1936, the selections showed consistency in President Roosevelt's foreign policy and revealed him as pursuing a substantially unbroken course from 1933 to 1942. The editor of the volume, whose name does not appear on the title page, not only confined the selections almost entirely to official messages and addresses; he omitted all of President Roosevelt's campaign speeches in which the President's foreign policy was repeatedly proclaimed to the people, from 1932, when he was seeking the Democratic nomination, to and including his campaign speeches of 1940; unless the Chautauqua address of 1936 be characterized as a campaign speech. In net result this exercise of the selective principle foreshadowed other statements of the thesis of popular responsibility, semi-official and official, which were to follow the publication of Senate Document Number 188.

and putting the blame for coming troubles and wars on the American people. Appealing to workers, farmers, businessmen, scientists, teachers, preachers, fathers and mothers, Dr. Lerner said on November 18, 1945: "The stakes are yours. The victims will be yours. The final decisions must be yours." *PM*, Sunday, November 18, 1945, p. 3.

The verdict that the American people, or at least a dominant portion of them, were afflicted with smugness and ignorance in matters of foreign policy, hampered President Roosevelt in pursuing his own policy, and were responsible for the catastrophe that marked the opening of the all-out war for Americans at Pearl Harbor was given semi-official confirmation by Forrest Davis and Ernest K. Lindley in their volume, *How War Came: An American White Paper*, published in the summer of 1942. This work, if not officially inspired in a strict sense, was written by two well-known journalists who had easy access to the White House and the State Department.

In fact, both Mr. Davis and Mr. Lindley had what was called by reporters "an inside track" with the Roosevelt Administration. Mr. Lindley in particular had long been in sympathy with New Deal policies and had written extensively in defense of them even while he was connected with an opposition newspaper. His work of this nature had been duly appreciated by President Roosevelt. Although, like many New Dealers, Mr. Lindley had once been actively opposed to foreign entanglements and had favored concentration on domestic measures of reform, he later changed his mind and became a vigorous exponent of collective security. As an acknowledged supporter of the Administration's foreign and domestic policies, Mr. Lindley was in a strategic position to secure inside information on the views and designs of the Executive Department.

The subtitle of the Davis and Lindley volume, *An American White Paper*, was so framed as to convey the impression that it had at least a kind of official *imprimatur;* for the words "White Paper" mean, in diplomatic usage, a government document containing selected papers on foreign affairs issued presumably for the information of the public. Hence in the case of *How War Came* the clear implication was that it constituted an official account of the war's origins.

It is true that the authors in their Foreword declared that the book was "unofficial" and that they alone were "accountable." But other statements in the Foreword, innumerable passages in the book, advertisements of the work, and various circumstances connected with its preparation and publication demonstrated that the volume was more than an "unofficial" report by two journalists who had at their command only the ordinary information available to all their colleagues in the profession.

On the jacket of the book the publishers were permitted to say: "This book tells the inside story of American foreign policy from the fall of France to the attack on Pearl Harbor. . . . Never has such a job been reported in such intimate detail, so soon, and with such authority. *How War Came* abounds in news scoops and off-the-record revelations. It tells how President Roosevelt negotiated the destroyer-for-bases-deal with Ambassador Lothian . . . tells who wrote which phrase in the Atlantic Charter and gives the historic circumstances in colorful and intimate detail. It discloses that Churchill, not Roosevelt, favored an immediate break with Japan. It explains why the Germans called Admiral Leahy the real ruler of unoccupied France. It lifts the veil on the Kurusu–Nomura conferences with Secretary Hull. . . ."

In an advertisement in the *New York Times*, August 25, 1942, the publishers of the Lindley-Davis volume said: "This book is a report to the American people, based on official records and the confidences of the men who made and are making American history. It is the first uncensored story of what has been going on in our own country and in our government from the fall of France to Pearl Harbor."

In their American White Paper, Davis and Lindley emphatically presented the view that President Roosevelt, in 1940 and 1941, was committed to a foreign policy at variance with the policy to which the American people in general were committed. The conclusions of the authors in this respect may be summarized in the following statements:

1. President Roosevelt believed that a strong policy in the form of active intervention was necessary during the entire

period under consideration, but was obstructed in his proceedings by the sentiments of neutrality, peace, and isolationism all but universally cherished by the American people (p. 317).

2. The American people were afflicted by a "trancelike unawareness of peril" in 1941; and their attitude toward the Japanese peril in particular "may be attributed to a national sense of sufficiency, a smugness based on a continental state of mind, an indifference to and ignorance of the world about us" (p. 316). Davis and Lindley attributed this attitude in part to the "simple, kindly" and "optimistic" nature of the American people, given to ignoring "evil"; but they put smugness and ignorance in their catalogue of American characteristics.

3. Furthermore, Davis and Lindley said, during the prewar months the isolationists "helped to disarm the American people psychologically." Forces "personified by Wheeler and Lindbergh"—two marked men on the White House list —"dinned the public's ears with assurances of our immunity from danger" (p. 317).

4. It might have been better if "we" had "gone to war earlier, on our own volition," instead of waiting for "the physical attack" (p. 317).

Here, then, in *How War Came*, is what purports to be the official view of President Roosevelt's Administration on responsibility for the making of foreign policy and on war guilt: the American people in their "smugness" and "ignorance" insisted on a policy of peace and neutrality, and so prevented the President from effectively pursuing the correct line of strong action in conjunction with other powers arrayed against "aggressors," until the Japanese attacked Pearl Harbor. In other words, the President was convinced that collaborative intervention in the conflict of Europe and Asia was the right policy but the American people, with contemptible stubbornness, clung to an opposite doctrine—nonintervention and neutrality despite the wars raging in Europe and Asia.

The Davis and Lindley formulation of the theory that the American people's sentiments of isolation hampered President Roosevelt in the correct conduct of foreign affairs was given a certain official confirmation by the State Department, with caution and circumspection, in its edition of *Peace and War: United States Foreign Policy, 1931–1941,* published in July, 1943, Chapter I, entitled "The Fateful Decade."

In its statement the Department declared that, while the powers of the President and Secretary of State over foreign affairs are very great, they are nevertheless constrained by public opinion:

The conduct of the foreign relations of the United States is a function of the President, acting usually through the Secretary of State. The powers of the Executive in this field are very broad and sweeping. Yet the President and the Secretary of State have by no means entire freedom in matters of foreign policy. . . . They must closely approximate the prevailing views of the country.

Although the State Department did not, like Davis and Lindley, speak scornfully of American "ignorance of the world about us," it referred to the superiority of the Executive in matters of knowledge and to the duty of the President and Secretary of State to explain to the public "the forces at work." It said:

In the history of our country situations have arisen in which the Executive, with wide access to many sources of information from abroad, has known of or foreseen developments in foreign relations of which the public had not yet become aware. In such cases the President and the Secretary of State have exercised such executive powers as they possess and have endeavored to explain to the public the forces at work and the probable course of events and to outline the policies which need be pursued in the best interest of the United States. In such cases, if and as legislation has been needed, the executive branch of the Government has as soon as practicable asked of the Congress legislation to make possible the pursuit of the proposed policies.[13]

During a large part of the period between 1931 and 1941, the State Department revealed, the President and the Secretary of State differed from the thesis respecting foreign affairs that was accepted by "much of public opinion," and held views relative to foreign policy in conflict with this popular thesis:

During a large part of the period with which this volume deals [1931–41], much of public opinion in this country did not accept the thesis that a European war could vitally affect the security of the United States or that an attack on the United States by any of the Axis powers was possible. In this respect it differed from the President and the Secretary of State, who early became convinced that the aggressive policies of the Axis powers were directed toward an ultimate attack on the United States and that, therefore, our foreign relations should be so conducted as to give all possible support to the nations endeavoring to check the march of Axis aggression.

Our foreign policy during the decade under consideration necessarily had to move within the framework of a gradual evolution of public opinion in the United States away from the idea of isolation expressed in "neutrality" legislation and toward realization that the Axis design was a plan of world conquest in which the United States was intended to be a certain, though perhaps ultimate, victim, and that our primary policy therefore must be defense against actual and mounting danger. This was an important factor influencing the conduct of our foreign relations. Of determining importance also was another factor, namely, that in many nations outside the United States a similar complacency of view had originally prevailed and likewise was undergoing a gradual modification.

13. The President and the Secretary did not call for an abrogation of the Neutrality Act in principle when, in 1939, they asked for the repeal of the clauses laying an embargo on the export of munitions. On the contrary they both agreed with the opposition that the maintenance of neutrality was the great objective. They contended then that the supreme issue was merely one of the *method* most likely to achieve the objective of neutrality. See below, Chap. IX.

The pages which follow [of text and documents] show the slow march of the United States from an attitude of illusory aloofness toward world-wide forces endangering America to a position in the forefront of the United Nations that are making common cause against an attempt at world conquest unparalleled alike in boldness of conception and in brutality of operation.[14]

The interpretation as to the course of foreign affairs and policies between 1931 and 1941 thus given by the State Department is difficult to analyze in concrete terms of time (years, days, and moments) and of relevant facts and events which occurred in that decade. Yet a microscopic examination of the passages quoted above from the State Department's explanation and of the several sentences which make up the paragraphs yields some definite conclusions, while leaving unanswered many queries immediately pertinent to what the Department said.

The State Department's exposition declared that the President and Secretary of State were, in some measure, controlled in the conduct of foreign affairs by public opinion: "They must closely approximate the prevailing views of the country." The word "country" is abstract. The country holds no views: persons hold views—American people. The views which the President and Secretary had to approximate were "prevailing views," that is, views held by so many people, or by so many people of noteworthy influence, that the President and Secretary felt bound to "approximate" the said views.

In this sentence the President and Secretary are represented as if standing outside the public whose views they must approximate in conducting foreign affairs. Since the word "approximate" means "approach" or "nearly conform to," the sentence is to be understood as stating that the President and Secretary had some freedom of action in forming foreign policies and maneuvering under them, but not much.

14. *Peace and War*, pp. 2–3.

Or to put it in another way, their conduct of foreign affairs, whatever their own views, was in the main or on the whole determined by views prevailing among American people—views that came into being by some process beyond the control of the President and the Secretary.

In the third paragraph quoted above the State Department says that during "a large part of the period" from 1931 to 1941 "much of public opinion" in the United States accepted a "thesis" of foreign affairs which was not held by the President and the Secretary of State.

What was the thesis with regard to which much of public opinion differed from that of the President and the Secretary? Summarily, the thesis was this: a European war could not "vitally affect" the security of the United States and an attack on the United States by any of the Axis Powers was impossible.

It would be difficult to prove by an examination of the available evidences of public opinion from 1931 to 1941 that this was a correct formulation of the thesis held by "much of public opinion" against the view of the President and the Secretary of State; but the formulation by the State Department must be taken as it stands, as the State Department's formulation.

Some other questions are immediately pertinent. Where among the available evidences of public opinion was this conviction as to immunity from danger of European war impacts on the United States so frequently proclaimed that it had to be accepted as truly or even fairly representative? Who among the people furnished much of the public opinion in support of the conception of the war's meaning for the United States? What Senators and Representatives, what party platforms, what journals of opinion, what makers of opinion expounded the foreign policy of "isolation" from which the President and the Secretary dissented or began to dissent "early" in their official careers? In short who joined issue with the President and the Secretary over this "thesis"?

The State Department proffers no answer. Nor does it indicate by what process of inquiry, analysis, and documentation it arrived at its statement of the thesis.

This "thesis," however judged as a statement of fact, evidently did not form the whole of the issue over which much of public opinion differed from the President and the Secretary of State. For in the next paragraph the State Department makes it clear that its first statement of the "thesis" was not entirely comprehensive. In that next paragraph it says: "our foreign policy" during the period, as shaped by the President and the Secretary, "necessarily had to move within the framework of a gradual evolution of public opinion in the United States away from the idea of isolation expressed in 'neutrality' legislation."

It would seem, then, that the difference between "much of the public opinion" and the official policy of the President and the Secretary was over the idea of isolation or neutrality; for the purpose of the neutrality legislation was to "isolate the United States from war," to preserve the neutrality of the United States in case of war. Therefore it must be inferred that what the President and the Secretary of State had to do in shaping foreign policy was to move gradually away from isolation and neutrality in an opposite direction.

The language of the State Department's explanation yields with difficulty to the tests of etymology, philology, and grammar, but it appears to say that "early," some time in advance of much of public opinion, the President and the Secretary privately came to the conclusion that isolation or neutrality for the United States was incompatible with "the best interest of the United States" [15] and that some policy other than isolation or neutrality was desirable and necessary.

15. For an attempt to discover the meaning of "interest" as used in the diplomatic language of the United States from early times, see Charles A. Beard, *The Idea of National Interest* (The Macmillan Company, 1934). This study, which occupied about a year and a half, was made with the collaboration of two competent investigators, George H. E. Smith and John D. Lewis, with valuable assistance from experts in the Government of the United States. What the State Department meant by "best interest" of the United States from 1933 to 1941 is nowhere made plain in *Peace and War*. Nor is the process

What was that other policy which the President and the Secretary "early" decided was in the best interest of the United States? Judging by the State Department's exposition it consisted of two features: (1) the President and the Secretary "early became convinced that the aggressive policies of the Axis Powers were directed toward an ultimate attack on the United States and that, therefore, our foreign relations should be so conducted as to give all possible support to the nations endeavoring to check the march of Axis aggression"; and (2) that our primary policy . . . must be defense against mounting "danger" and must take the form of a "slow march . . . to a position in the forefront of the United Nations that are [1943] making common cause against an attempt at world conquest" by the Axis governments.

In sum and substance, assuming that all the sentences of its exposition have meaning, the State Department says: the President and the State Department "early" became convinced that the isolationism represented by neutrality legislation would have to be discarded; that "all possible support" would have to be given to the powers aligned against one or more Axis governments; and that the United States would have to take a position at the forefront of the nations engaged in conflict with one or more Axis governments. For, "all possible support" necessarily involves measures of war as well as measures short of war, and taking a position at the forefront of nations at war necessarily involves going to war.[16]

In any event, it would appear from the State Department's explanation, at some point in time between 1933 and 1941 President Roosevelt and Secretary Hull reached a great decision; namely that the policy of isolation, neutrality, and non-intervention in European and Asiatic conflicts must be

by which the President and the Secretary learned that isolation or neutrality was not in the best interest of the United States set forth anywhere explicitly in that volume.

16. If the statement of the State Department does not mean this, then just what does it mean?

discarded and an opposite policy pursued by the Government of the United States, despite "much of public opinion" in the country arrayed against this policy. When was this great, indeed revolutionary, decision reached by the President and Secretary Hull? The State Department merely says the decision was reached "early." How early? In 1934, 1935, 1936, 1937, 1938, 1939, or 1940? As to the exact year, or even the approximate time, the State Department's exposition gives no hint.

On what grounds was this decision reached at some time during the period in question? The State Department provides its answers: the Executive had access to information from abroad through special sources and thus had knowledge of developments with which the public was unacquainted.

But the public, according to the State Department's report to the nation, was not kept in ignorance of the course of affairs abroad which warranted a reversal of the previous policy—neutrality, non-intervention, and peace for the United States—in favor of a different, or opposite, policy. On the contrary, to use its own words: "In such cases [of special knowledge pertaining to foreign affairs] the President and the Secretary of State . . . have endeavored to explain to the public the forces at work and the probable course of events and to outline the policies which need be pursued in the best interest of the United States."

Taking these words as commonly understood, the President and the Secretary of State endeavored to explain to the people the nature of affairs abroad which called for a reversal of the foreign policy, then generally held to be sound, and endeavored to outline to the people the other policy which they deemed it necessary to carry out in the best interest of the United States. This version of the controversy is clear and intelligible. The only pertinent question left unanswered is: When and in what public documents did the President and the Secretary "outline" to the people the particular foreign policy upon which they had decided?

A little more than two years after the State Department's

pièce justificatif appeared in 1943, President Harry S. Truman, more tersely, more bluntly, confirmed the thesis of popular responsibility for adherence to the wrong foreign policy prior to December 7, 1941. This confirmation he made at a press and radio conference on August 30, 1945.[17] The immediate occasion of his remarks on this subject was a discussion of the reports on the Pearl Harbor catastrophe issued by the War and Navy Boards during the previous day, August 29, 1945; but his statement was broad in scope. It ran as follows in full:

I have read it [the Pearl Harbor reports] very carefully, and I came to the conclusion that the whole thing is the result of the policy which the country itself pursued.

The country was not ready for preparedness.

Every time the President made an effort to get a preparedness program through the Congress, it was stifled.[18]

Whenever the President made a statement about the necessity of preparedness, he was vilified for doing it.

I think the country is as much to blame as any individual in this final situation that developed in Pearl Harbor.

Terse and blunt though his statement was, President Truman exhibited doubts in his own mind as to where the war guilt lay. His first sentence makes "the whole thing . . . the result of the policy which the country itself pursued," but his last sentence apparently divides responsibility: "I think the country is as much to blame as any individual in this final situation that developed in Pearl Harbor." Even so, taken in connection with the exposition of foreign policy given in *How War Came* by Davis and Lindley and in *Peace and War* by the State Department, President Truman's statement conforms to the thesis of popular responsibility for the course of affairs that eventuated in war.[19]

17. Official White House "Immediate Release," dated August 30, 1945. Paragraphing supplied in the above quotation for emphasis.

18. See Appendix to this Chapter.

19. On an earlier occasion Mr. Truman had said: "I am just as sure as I can be that this World War is the result of the 1919–1920 isolationist attitude." McNaughton and Hehmyer, *This Man Truman*, p. 167.

Appendix to Chapter II

PRESIDENT TRUMAN's statement that "Every time the President made an effort to get a preparedness program through Congress, it was stifled," deserves technical consideration here. It is true that in loose conceptions of public affairs foreign policy is often treated as standing apart from "preparedness," from the appropriations of Congress for military and naval purposes; but in fact foreign policy and preparedness are inseparably linked in any wise and efficient administration of the national government. Foreign policy, whatever its nature, bears an intimate relation to the military force that can be brought to support it; and expenditures for military and naval purposes are in themselves, if rationally determined, expressions of actual or potential foreign policy.

In the financial practices of the United States Government the regular proposals for preparedness, for military and naval expenditures, are formulated in detail by the War Department and the Navy Department respectively, often in consultation with the President. These formulations are reviewed, approved, or modified by the Bureau of the Budget under the immediate direction of the President; and the final results in the form of "estimates" for military and naval appropriations are transmitted to Congress by the President in a regular message or in supplementary messages in case of special requests to Congress. These "estimates" from the President's office are used as the basis for "appropriations" by Congress, which may increase or decrease the amount of the expenditures proposed in the Executive's "estimates."

The "estimates" for military and naval expenditures for each year, therefore, represent the President's "preparedness program" at the time; and the actual "appropriations" by Congress for such expenditures show whether or how far Congress "stifled" the President's particular "preparedness program."

Both the estimates and the appropriations are matters of public record in the official documents of the United States. Thus indisputable mathematical data are at hand for testing the accuracy of President Truman's declaration that "Every time the President made an effort to get a preparedness program through Congress, it was stifled."

The essential facts bearing on President Truman's allegation are set forth below in a table which was compiled by the Legislative Reference Library in the Library of Congress. In column 4 appear the estimates for military and naval expenditures presented to the session of the Congress indicated in column 1; and in column 6 are given the appropriations made by Congress after its consideration of the estimates. A comparison of the figures in these two columns shows how much Congress in its actual appropriations decreased or increased the amounts requested in the Executive estimates.

During five of the eight years under review Congress failed to grant to the President all the money he requested for preparedness but in no year was the reduction so drastic as to "stifle" his preparedness program.[20] In three of the eight years Congress appropriated more money than was requested in the Executive estimates. And in the grand totals for the eight years, it is evident, Congress exceeded Executive estimates by $1,874,513,033. Indeed as war approached Congress became more lavish than the President in conceiving the needs of preparedness. At all events the figures in gross and detail show that President Truman's statement on August 30, 1945, was lacking in the accuracy that becomes a declaration by the President of the United States, at all events in denouncing Congress, a coordinate branch of the national government.

A special incident often associated with the alleged congressional "stifling" of President Roosevelt's preparedness proposals involved a scheme to fortify Guam, that came up early in 1939 and has frequently been cited as an example of the way in which Congress refused to heed the President's requests for additional military and naval appropriations in the interest of national defense. It was said at the time and later that President Roosevelt actually called for the fortification of Guam. But records of his press conference in January, 1939, dispose of that contention.

Asked at his conference on January 17, 1939, about a report from Tokyo to the effect that the Japanese fleet would smash the American fleet if an attempt was made to fortify Guam, the President said: "Has an appropriation been asked of this Congress

20. In some cases there were legitimate grounds for differences of opinion as to the need and utility of specific items in the list of requests, particularly when the Navy Department had not started the construction of ships already authorized and provided for in appropriations previously made.

MILITARY AND NAVAL APPROPRIATIONS, 73D CONGRESS, 2D SESSION—77TH CONGRESS, 1ST SESSION (1934–1941)

Estimates and Appropriations

1 CONGRESS AND SESSION	2 DEPARTMENT	3 ESTIMATES	4 TOTAL ESTIMATES	5 APPROPRIATIONS	6 TOTAL APPROPRIATIONS
73d, 2d	War	261,562,150		256,436,089	
	Navy	288,052,030	549,614,180	286,389,389	542,825,478
74th, 1st	War	328,062,481		361,741,408	
	Navy	492,403,750	820,466,231	485,628,330	847,369,738
2d	War	388,230,740		393,410,089	
	Navy	553,728,233	941,958,973	530,695,092	924,105,181
75th, 1st	War	417,486,461		416,263,154	
	Navy	568,141,167	985,627,628	518,479,266	934,742,420
2d & 3d	War	470,235,710		463,123,129	
	Navy	618,152,697	1,088,388,407	590,857,328	1,053,980,457
76th, 1st	War	848,086,705		813,744,715	
	Navy	838,540,852	1,686,627,557	817,437,229	1,631,181,944
2d & 3d	War	5,274,456,883		5,722,202,419	
	Navy	2,696,096,662	7,970,553,545	2,680,122,556	8,402,324,975
77th, 1st	War	23,686,371,995		24,889,267,588	
	Navy	7,692,912,088	31,379,284,083	8,071,235,856	32,960,503,444
TOTALS:			45,422,520,604		47,297,033,637

for the fortification of Guam? Answer yes or no. Let's stick to facts and brass tacks. . . . When the Navy goes up on the Hill, I will be able to say whether an appropriation is to be requested."

At a press conference three days later, January 20, 1939, the President was asked to say whether he favored the appropriation of $5,000,000 for the fortification of Guam. According to a stenographic record, he "turned back the question to inquire whether it had been proposed to 'fortify' the island and explained that the money was largely for dredging the harbor." He then explained to the reporters the fundamental difference between an "authorization" by Congress and an "appropriation." Asked whether there need be any confusion in anyone's mind as to where he stood on the proposed fortification of Guam, the President said: "I don't think there is any confusion; I am in favor of deepening the harbor at Guam. . . ." Asked whether he favored the other appropriations for Guam including a million dollars for a landing-field improvement and the same amount for barracks, the President said he favored the whole appropriation because the barracks were in bad shape and were inadequate to house the small number of marines who were sitting on the islands. In other words Congress was not called upon by President Roosevelt in January, 1939, to appropriate money for the *fortification* of Guam.

It is fair to say that President Truman later changed his mind about the way Congress stifled President Roosevelt's preparedness programs. August 30, 1945, he said: "Every time the President made an effort to get a preparedness program through Congress, it was stifled." In his Jackson day address, March 23, 1946, President Truman said: "At that time [before the United States went to war], our isolationists were still debating, and *almost* defeating, *most* efforts of Democratic leaders to improve the national defenses." (Italics supplied.) *Congressional Record*, March 25, 1946, p. A1682.

According to this version, the isolationists almost, but not quite, defeated, not all but most of the preparedness measures advanced by Democratic leaders. It would seem that President Roosevelt's preparedness program was not stifled every time, but *almost* defeated in *most* cases, that is, not defeated or stifled. So, at least it appears in President Truman's latest redaction of his preparedness history.

CHAPTER III

Problems Posed by Charges of War Guilt

WHETHER the guilt of bringing on the second World War was in fact attributable to the "evil men" in the Senate, to the "undemocratic" provision of the Constitution which requires a two-thirds vote in the Senate for the ratification of treaties, to the refusal of President Wilson to accept reservations to the proposed Treaty of Versailles, to his resolve to make the matter of ratification a partisan issue, to the "ignorant" and "smug" adherents of isolationism among the people at large, to "much of public opinion" which opposed renewed entanglements in European and Asiatic quarrels, to the "country," to the "United States," or to "America," a multiplicity of charges certainly lodged the culpability somewhere in the United States after 1919.

Here is a conjuncture of allegations relative to the making of foreign policy and the conduct of government unparalleled in the history of great nations: a multitude of people within a great society ascribe to that society or to some persons, some things, or some events in that society the responsibility for bringing on a world war. Being an unparalleled historic phenomenon intimately related to the fate and fortunes of the American Republic among the nations of the earth, it presents to American citizens a question of origins and meanings with intellectual and moral ramifications that run to the very roots of constitutional government. How did it happen, how could it happen, that so many American citizens looked homeward for the sources of this evil doing? How did it happen, how could it happen that they fomented or accepted a thesis which, in upshot, acquitted foreign nations of guilt, put the burden on or in the United States, and set the American people at variance with their own representative government? Here is posed a primary problem in history and political science that calls for a searching examination, if the matter of how we are governed under the Constitution continues to deserve consideration.

Owing to the profusion and, in some instances the vagueness, of the charges involved in the indictment, it is difficult to present the thesis with precision. The matter is further complicated by the introduction of partisan interpretations into the allocation of guilt. For example, Walter Johnson, historian of the battle against isolationism, says: "The Republican party during the interval between the two wars was predominately isolationist. A few notable exceptions, like Secretary of State Stimson, Elihu Root, Nicholas Murray Butler, and William Allen White, were internationalists. . . . However, the isolationist attitude of such men as William E. Borah dominated the Republican party. When the Democratic party came back into power in 1933, it was still the party of Wilsonian internationalism. From 1933 to 1939 the United States Government followed a policy of attempting to improve international relations and thus prevent the collapse of world peace. . . . President Franklin D. Roosevelt and Secretary of State Cordell Hull were avowed internationalists. . . ."[1]

Another difficulty encountered in efforts to formulate the thesis with precision is due to the fact that many critics, who located the responsibility for World War II in the United States, at the same time brought charges of guilt against the "aggressors," namely, Germany, Italy, and Japan. It was these offenders, they said, who first disturbed the peace of the world after 1919; while the overwhelming majority of nations were in fact "peace loving" all along. If, then, a share of the war guilt must be assigned in truth to Hitler, Mussolini, and Hirohito, the whole responsibility for the second World War can scarcely be placed on or in the United

1. *The Battle against Isolation*, pp. 10 ff. On the jacket of Mr. Johnson's book, published by the University of Chicago Press (1944), the following judgment is expressed: "Isolationism, which here stands condemned by its own lies, must not have another chance."

States. In this case the thesis of war guilt is made more complicated for seekers after the truth of the business.

Should the thesis of responsibility for World War II be so formulated as to lay a share of the blame on other nations[2] or on the three aggressors, an examination of its validity would assume Herculean proportions. It would involve, first of all, an informed judgment on the most perplexing questions of historical interpretation, including the issues connected with "causation" and "free will" in the making of history, national and universal.[3] It would also raise special questions of challenging intricacy; for example, at what point in time should history of the "blameworthy" nations be taken up in search for the characteristics to which war guilt is to be ascribed? Or again, for instance, how did Japan, after clinging to a hermit-like foreign policy for more than two hundred years, rather suddenly acquire, near the end of the nineteenth century, the propensities of a rabid imperialism and crusade against "white" supremacy in the Far East? Moreover, an inquiry so broad in scope would call for a mastery of languages, documentation, and philosophic thinking which few, if any, students of history or political science command.

Undoubtedly the matter of the responsibility attributable to other nations has a direct and great relevance to the problem of responsibility in general; and unless it is seriously considered, the discussions of the subject are not likely to rise above the level of mere clichés, empty abstractions, and partisan or sectarian slogans. Relevant also to the larger view

2. The State Department, while attributing much of the difficulty encountered by the Roosevelt Administration to isolationist opinion in the United States, also lays some of the blame on other peace-loving nations: "Of determining importance also was another factor, namely, that in many nations outside the United States a similar complacency of view had originally prevailed" during the period in question. *Peace and War* (July, 1943), p. 3.

3. As to the complications of historical interpretation and efforts to determine "causes" in human affairs, see R. Aron, *Introduction à la philosophie de l'histoire;* especially sections on *la pluralité des systèmes d'interprétations, le déterminisme historique et la pensée causale,* and *les limites de l'objectivité causale et de la causalité historique.*

is the question as to how the American people originally acquired a tenacious attachment to the doctrine of hemispheric independence on the one side and non-entanglement in the conflicts of Europe and Asia on the other side. But an investigation of these broader phases of war guilt is beyond the scope of the present volume.

Another limitation on this survey is to be emphasized. It is responsibility for *foreign policy* that comes into purview; and foreign policy is to be carefully distinguished from *foreign affairs*. A policy is a rule, plan, or program to be followed in practice, to be implemented by actions, affairs, deeds done under its direction and control. Policy is also to be distinguished from ambiguous pronouncements respecting peace, good will, friendly relations, promotion of commerce, encouragement of cultural intercourse, adherence to international morality, and approval of universal philanthropy, such as the State Department issued with profusion between 1933 and 1940.[4] Policy is a definite design which has meaning in the concrete terms of the actions necessarily signified and conveys to common understanding the practical purport of the language used in expressing it.

Whatever may be said of responsibility for foreign policy, in general, the thesis that locates in the United States the responsibility for the policy that eventuated in World War II[5] is the thesis that has the most immediate relevance to

4. For example, Secretary Hull's peace manifesto to the world on July 16, 1937, the "principles" of which were quickly accepted, with apparent cordiality, by the great powers that were soon to be at war. Portugal alone raised issues. It joined the other governments in approving what it called "the assertions, advices, or wishes" of Secretary Hull but filed objections against "the habit of entrusting the solution of grave external problems to vague formulae." State Department press release, September 18, 1937.

5. The contention that World War II would not have occurred if the United States had joined the League of Nations is, of course, a mere matter of opinion, informed or uninformed. The hypothesis cannot be tested by repeating the events and conditions of 1919–39, with the United States in the League, and thus proving the case the one way or the other. If the United States had been a member of the League after 1919, would it have quickly recognized Russia as a make-weight in Europe or would it have cooperated with Great Britain in the rehabilitation of Germany and the appeasement of Hitler from 1934 to

American character and the conduct of government in the United States. Insofar as this thesis applies to the period from 1933 to 1940, it involves the following features:

1. The country or, to use the State Department's language, "much of public opinion," insisted that the President and the State Department must pursue the policy of "isolation expressed in 'neutrality' legislation"; that is, the policy of neutrality, non-entanglement, non-intervention, and peace for the United States in the presence of conflicts and wars among European and Asiatic powers.

2. At some point in time—"early," according to the State Department report—President Roosevelt and Secretary Hull adopted and endeavored to outline to the American public a policy at variance with "the idea of isolation." If they had been permitted to carry it into effect, they would have served due notice on all aggressors and, in collaboration with the peace-loving nations, prevented the outbreak of World War II—that is, maintained the peace of the world.

3. But the country or the people or much of public opinion or the isolationists blocked President Roosevelt and Secretary Hull in pursuing their policy effectively, stifled the President's preparedness program, kept the neutrality legislation on the statute books, lulled the country into a false security, and hence must bear the responsibility for the progress of aggressors in Europe and Asia which finally and inevitably "drew" the United States into the war in spite of President Roosevelt's warnings and his efforts to maintain peace.

In any attempt to test the validity of the thesis of popular responsibility for foreign policy formulated in this manner, certain questions become self-evident. Under whose influence or sponsorship did the policy of non-entanglement, peace, and neutrality for the United States in a warring world secure and maintain so strong a hold on the people or the country, especially between 1933 and 1940? Did Presi-

1939? The best of answers can be nothing more than calculations of probabilities.

dent Roosevelt and Secretary Hull or the Democratic leadership with which they were affiliated consistently oppose the development of the isolationism expressed by this policy? Or did they contribute in any material way to the strength of the grip which that policy had upon the people or the country? At what point in time during these "fateful years" did the President and the Secretary decide that the policy of neutrality and isolation cherished by the people of the country was untenable and announce to the public that another foreign policy—one opposed to it—was in the best interest of the United States? In what addresses, speeches, or statements did the President and the Secretary present to the country their fateful decision and their outline of a foreign policy adverse to isolation, neutrality, and peace for the United States?

These questions point to matters that are public in nature and answers to them are to be sought in the public speeches, addresses, papers, and other documents of the time, which are available to all citizens. The questions are questions of plain historical facts. A search for answers calls for no special powers of insight or cognition, and conclusions having at least a high degree of relevance and sufficiency can be easily drawn from public records strictly germane to the problem under consideration. It is to an examination of these records that the following pages are devoted.

Although the inquiry thus undertaken is historical in character, it is concerned directly with the making of American foreign policy—with methods, personalities, parties, interests, and tactics involved in the process. At the same time it has a distinct bearing on the conduct of foreign affairs by the Government of the United States; on the responsibilities of officials and party leaders to the people of the United States; on the relations of the Executive and Legislative Departments in practice and with reference to measures best calculated to assure the fulfilment of the obligations assigned to each Department by the Constitution; on the procedures of diplomacy appropriate to a country dedicated to popular government, freedom of the press, and the education of the people in matters of the public interest; and, finally, on the fortunes of constitutional and representative democracy in the United States and also in the world, to which, many Americans urge, this system is both fitting and applicable.

CHAPTER IV

Preliminary: Attitudes of Democratic Leadership in 1924 and 1928

JUDGING by party platforms in 1916, surveys of editorial views, and other indices of public opinion, a large majority of the American people then agreed in principle that the United States should join some kind of league or association of nations in the hope of preventing another great war. After President Wilson presented to the country in 1919 the Treaty of Versailles, with the Covenant of the League of Nations incorporated in the text, many Americans, however, shrank from just that type of organization and expressed unwillingness to approve the Treaty without reservations, minor or major. Nevertheless, in the campaign of 1920 the Democrats endorsed the League, while allowing for limited reservations, and the Republicans advocated an undescribed form of "agreement among nations to preserve the peace of the world." Hence it could be reasoned, with historical justification, that, despite the Republican landslide which overwhelmed the Democrats in the election of 1920, internationalism had not been definitely rejected by the people of the United States at the polls.

Not until 1924 did the Republicans put into their platform an official declaration that appeared to reject the League Covenant once and for all: "This government has definitely refused membership in the League of Nations or to assume any obligations under the Covenant of the League. On this we stand." But as against this categorical assertion, their platform also hinted at the desirability of cooperation with the League in certain limited respects. At all events numerous distinguished Republicans still clung to internationalism, and hoped that the United States would gradually move in the direction of closer "cooperation" with the League of Nations, and perhaps at length enter it formally.

As the Democrats assembled in New York for their convention of 1924 they found themselves sharply divided over internationalism in the specific form then presented—the League of Nations. One group, including Thomas Taggart, national committeeman from Indiana, stood out against incorporating in the platform any plank that tied the party to the League.[1] Another group, associated with William G. McAdoo, an aspirant for the nomination, was conveniently vague on the issue, for it was claiming, or at least seeking, the active support of William Randolph Hearst, a persistent foe of the League. In an address to delegates who were supporting his candidacy, Mr. McAdoo avoided endorsing the League but declared that one of the real tasks before the country was "to end the era of isolation and to begin the era of cooperation in foreign affairs; to promote peace and further reduce the burden of both land and sea armaments to the lowest point compatible with national safety."[2] This may not have been entirely satisfactory to Mr. Hearst, but it was more politic than an explicit approval of the League.

A third group of Democrats at the New York convention of 1924, led by Newton D. Baker, favored a straightforward endorsement of the League and American adherence to it, with moderate reservations. With this group of delegates various propaganda organizations, such as the League of Nations Association and the Foreign Policy Association, cooperated in the hope of pledging the Democratic party once more to internationalism.[3]

To the aid of Mr. Baker's group came the *New York Times*. In an editorial on June 23, 1924, it criticized those Democrats who were inclined to sidestep the League issue and asserted that they now had even better reasons for

1. *New York Times*, June 23, 1924.
2. *Ibid.*
3. *Ibid.*

espousing it than they had in 1920. "It is at such a time," the editorial went on, "that Democrats are advised to soft-pedal the League in their platform! The League does not need endorsement from them, but they need to associate themselves more positively than ever with its advancing success. Of little use will be vague and pious platitudes holding out the hope of cooperating with Europe in restoring peace and stability, ways and methods not mentioned. If we honestly mean to cooperate, how is it possible to shut our eyes to the one great cooperating agency already in existence and functioning well?"

In stating his own case for a positive commitment to the League Mr. Baker said that he would work out a modified plank on the League of Nations; that he would not be uncompromising in his position but would be willing to accept a League platform with reservations which would satisfy those who were opposed to Articles X and XVI. Mr. Baker was obliquely supported in his strategy by Col. E. M. House who sent the following suggestion to Cordell Hull: "The Democrats should declare in their platform that if successful at the polls next November they will pledge the President to ask Congress by joint resolutions to authorize the United States to become an associate member of the League of Nations, without in any way committing the country to the covenant. Thus the fears of the timid could be dispelled regarding a superstate and an entangling alliance. . . ." [4] Colonel House also declared that it was not enough for the United States to adhere to the World Court without making use of the machinery of the League of Nations.[5]

When the resolutions committee of the Democratic convention was organized on June 24 to hear proposals for planks in the platform, the pro-League forces, headed by Mr. Baker, then advocated the adoption of a plank identical with that incorporated in the 1920 platform. In presenting the

4. *Ibid.*
5. *Ibid.*, June 24, 1924.

plank of the Woodrow Wilson Democracy, Judge Westcott declared that Woodrow Wilson would have succeeded had it not been for the betrayal by Henry Cabot Lodge, "the Judas Iscariot of humanity," and wanted to know whether there were any Henry Cabot Lodges in the Democratic party.[6]

A fourth group of Democrats at the convention, while expressly favorable to the League of Nations, urged that the commitment of the United States to the League could be hastened by taking the question out of party politics. The foremost leader of this group was William Jennings Bryan, who in 1920 had pleaded with President Wilson to make terms with Republican Senators, secure a ratification of the Treaty of Versailles with reservations, and avoid making a strict partisan issue of the League in the election campaign of that year. In 1924 Mr. Bryan was still convinced that by removing the League from the arena of partisanship many Republicans would be won over and that with their help the two-thirds vote might be obtained in the Senate. As head of the subcommittee of the Resolutions Committee, Mr. Bryan was able to effect a substantial agreement on a plank which reaffirmed President Wilson's faith in the League, declared for adherence with reservations, and proposed an independent referendum on the question, free from personalities, candidates, and party interests.[7]

Mr. Baker refused to accept the proposed plank and announced that he would offer a minority report to the full committee advocating immediate entrance into the League.[8] The full committee, however, rejected Mr. Baker's project by a decisive vote in favor of a plank including a provision for a referendum. Thereupon Mr. Baker resolved to carry the fight to the floor of the convention.[9]

Mr. Baker's impassioned plea for the League of Nations

6. *Ibid.*, June 25, 1924.
7. *Ibid.*, June 26, 1924.
8. *Ibid.*, June 27, 1924.
9. *Ibid.*, June 28, 1924.

proved to be one of the most dramatic events of the convention. Of the majority's scheme for a referendum he spoke scornfully:

. . . what does the majority report do? With praiseful and perfumed voice it praises the League of Nations as a lover would address his sweetheart. Everything that fanciful words and artistic and cunning expressions of praise can do is done to express the admiration and approval of the majority of the committee for the League of Nations. . . .

. . . after having said that there is no substitute for the League of Nations, that the world will be a wreck unless war is prevented, that the only path to peace is the League of Nations . . . there is not one syllable in this that proposes that we shall go into the League of Nations until after a fanciful, illegal, unconstitutional, revolutionary referendum shall have been called, operated either by postal cards or through the Census Bureau or in some other way, for there is neither constitutional basis for a statute nor a statute which provides for a national referendum.

I know what my associates on this committee thought as they sat over and drew that. They said the people who will be in that convention at least are people who four years ago were willing to have died for the ideal of the League of Nations. We must speak well enough of it to satisfy their devotional affection for it, and so they have spoken, and then after having marched through the dictionary with all these superb epithets of praise and approval, they give it their confidence, but promise it no aid of any kind. . . .[10]

Mr. Baker also maintained that those who favored a League only after a referendum had been taken were, in effect, following the method Lodge had adopted to defeat the League.

In the contest Mr. Baker lost. The convention adopted the plank which the majority of the Resolutions Committee presented. As it finally appeared in the platform the plank affirmed the desire of Democrats to see the United States

10. Text of debate on League, *New York Times*, June 29, 1924.

resume her place of "moral leadership" in the world, and then added:

There is no substitute for the League of Nations as an agency working for peace; therefore we believe that, in the interest of permanent peace, and in the lifting of the great burdens of war from the backs of the people, and in order to establish a permanent foreign policy on these supreme questions, not subject to change with change of party Administrations, it is desirable, wise and necessary to lift this question out of party politics and to that end to take the sense of the American people at a referendum election, advisory to the Government, to be held officially under act of Congress, free from all other questions and candidacies, after ample time for full consideration and discussion throughout the country, upon the question, in substance, as follows:

"Shall the United States become a member of the League of Nations upon such reservations or amendments to the Covenant of the League as the President and the Senate of the United States may agree upon?"

Immediately upon an affirmative vote we will carry out such mandate.[11]

By separating the League of Nations from the political contest the Democrats, in effect, divorced their party from a definite pledge to take the United States into the League if victorious at the polls in November. In other words they now repudiated the tactics which President Wilson had insisted upon in 1920 and refused to put the fortunes of their party at stake on any such turn in American foreign policy.

The disaster which overtook the Democrats in the election of 1924 was even greater than the landslide that crushed them in 1920. When they brought their shattered ranks together in convention in 1928, they decided to give internationalism a cold shoulder and let it drop into innocuous desuetude; while the Republicans toyed with a brand of limited international cooperation all their own.

Before the platform was formally presented at the Demo-

11. *New York Times*, June 29, 1924.

cratic convention in 1928, Newton D. Baker, who had led a forlorn struggle for the League four years previously, announced that he would not oppose eliminating the League issue from the party's obligations. "I do not plan," Mr. Baker stated publicly, "to try again for a plank favoring immediate entrance into the League. I do not think this is the time for it. I would favor a plank urging sympathetic and effective cooperation in the task of preserving the peace of the world. I will not oppose the dropping of the League of Nations plank from the 1928 platform, but I wish to say that I have not changed my mind as to the desirability of the United States joining the League and taking its place as one of the leaders in this movement that developed as the result of the war." Mr. Baker also assured his Democratic colleagues that he approved membership in the World Court; and while American sentiment was not yet ready for joining the League, in his opinion, it would eventually endorse such a step when the League showed its effectiveness.[12]

In their platform of 1928 as finally drawn, the Democrats charged the Republican Administration with having no foreign policy, applauded the outlawry of war, expressed abhorrence for militarism, conquest, and imperialism, denounced interference with the purely internal affairs of Latin-American countries, favored international agreements for the reduction of armaments, and asserted that in our foreign relations "this country should stand as a unit." The platform made no reference to the League of Nations. It did endorse "full, free, and open cooperation with all other nations for the promotion of peace and justice throughout the world, and approve international conciliation, arbitration, and conference." But it countered this clause of convenient vagueness by committing the party to that central principle of isolationism: "freedom from entangling political alliances with foreign nations."

In his numerous campaign speeches reported in the *New York Times* the Democratic candidate, Alfred E. Smith,

12. *Ibid.*, June 26, 1928.

dealt only twice with foreign policy at some length; and a careful search of the *Times* files for the year reveals no reference in his speeches to the League of Nations by name or indeed any statement which even a vivid imagination could construe as expressing any sympathy with the contention that the United States should then consider joining it. Although at one point Mr. Smith appeared to approve the idea that the United States should be willing to attend "any meeting where fifty-five nations come together," by no verbal adroitness could this remark be interpreted to mean an appeal to the country for a rally to internationalism, particularly in view of all that Mr. Smith said to the contrary.[13]

On August 22, 1928, in his address accepting the nomination, Mr. Smith said:

I approve the effort to renew and extend the arbitration treaties negotiated under the Administration of President Wilson. But the usefulness of those treaties as deterrents of war is materially impaired by the reservations asserted by various nations of the right to wage defensive wars, as those reservations are interpreted in the light of President Coolidge's record. Defending his policies he announced on April 25, 1927, the doctrine that the person and property of a citizen are a part of the national domain, even when abroad. . . . Our unwarranted intervention in internal affairs in Latin-America and this specious reason for it constitute the basis upon which other countries may seek to justify imperialistic policies which threaten world peace and materially lessen the effectiveness which might otherwise lie in the multilateral treaties.

The real outlawry of war must come from a more substantial endeavor to remove the causes of war, . . . I am neither militarist nor jingo. I believe that the people of this country wish to

13. The results of an independent search of the *New York Times* files mentioned above are confirmed by an authority in the field of international affairs, Arthur Sweetser, *American Year Book* (1928), p. 71. As a member of the League of Nations Secretariat, Mr. Sweetser was always on the lookout for any political utterances that indicated a tendency toward internationalism on the part of candidates for the presidency and the Government of the United States. He had to report that in 1928 the Democrats omitted even the name of the League from the platform and that in his campaign speeches, Mr. Smith "avoided specific reference."

live in peace and amity with the world. Freedom from entangling alliances is a fixed American policy. It does not mean, however, that great nations should not behave to one another with the same decent friendliness and fair play that self-respecting men and women show to one another. . . .

I believe the American people desire to assume their fair share of responsibility for the administration of a world of which they are a part, without political alliance with any foreign nation. I pledge myself to a resumption of a real endeavor to make the outlawry of war effective by removing its causes and to substitute the methods of conciliation, conference, arbitration and judicial determination.[14]

At another point in his acceptance address, Mr. Smith assailed the practice of making Executive agreements with Latin-American governments, subject to no action by the Senate:

To no declaration of our platform do I more heartily commit myself than the one for the abolition of the practice of the President of entering into agreements for the settlement of internal disputes in Latin-American countries, unless the agreements have been consented to by the Senate as provided for in the Constitution of the United States. . . .[15]

It was only at Baltimore, October 29, 1928, that Mr. Smith gave a full exposition of his views respecting correct foreign policy for the United States; and these views, to say the least, afforded no more comfort to internationalists than had the orotund phrases of Warren Gamaliel Harding in 1920.

. . . in my speech of acceptance I said that any foreign policy finally adopted by this country had to spring from the majority will of the rank and file of the people and could not be handed down to them from the head of the Government.

I could go a step further and amplify that for you just a bit by

14. *New York Times*, August 23, 1928.
15. *Ibid.*

calling your attention to the fact that the Constitution of the United States provides for a two-thirds vote in the Senate for a ratification of a treaty with a foreign power.

It unquestionably was the intent of the forefathers, when they put that provision into the Constitution, to raise treaty making above the level of mere legislative or of partisan politics, and to make the vote of the Senate express the overwhelming majority sentiment of the American people. . . .

At times I found it difficult to escape the conclusion that in the handling of our foreign affairs it is largely the personal equation; plus that, the desire behind it to do the right, fair, square thing; plus that, I regard it as necessary that we have an administration of our public affairs that will adhere to a definite policy as far as one can be enunciated. . . .

Now, we are all prepared to agree with the declaration that it is the foremost duty of the Government to protect the life and property of the citizens of our country, but at the same time we must subscribe to the undoubted and indisputable theory that we have no right to meddle in the internal affairs of any other country. . . .

I believe just as firmly as a man can in the great brotherhood of man under the fatherhood of God, and I am satisfied that the American people are prepared and ready to do their full share in the administration of a world of which they are a great part.

In that belief, and with that in mind, it would be the duty of the Democratic Administration to make every effort and every endeavor to make the outlawry of war an effective thing.

And this, we hold, can be done by removing the causes of war and substituting the methods of conciliation, arbitration and judicial determination. . . .

Only by executive leadership, only by Congressional cooperation and only by public support can we hope or even think of a solution of the problems that lie before us. . . .

Only by that method can we hope for arbitration and conciliation and a peaceful settlement of all disputes. Only by that method can we hope for an agreement between the great naval powers that will lift from all the backs of the people the crushing burden of naval armament. . . .

The Democratic Party, in its platform and in its declaration of principles, promises . . . an open, an honest, a fearless and an unprejudiced approach to every one of these questions absolutely on the basis of their merit.[16]

One of the major events of the campaign in 1928 was the return of Franklin D. Roosevelt to active political life after a heroic battle with a crippling illness. Before that affliction forced him into retirement, he had risen rapidly in the councils of the Democratic party. In 1910 he had been elected to the Senate of New York and was serving there when President Wilson called him to the post of Assistant Secretary of the Navy in 1913, which he held for about seven years. In 1920 he had accepted his party's nomination as candidate for Vice-President and made an extended campaign, giving ardent support to the party's position in favor of the League of Nations, with minor reservations, and the type of internationalism represented by that association. Shortly afterward he was laid low by a stroke of paralysis and not until 1928 did he resume his political career. In that year he championed the candidacy of Alfred E. Smith; he placed Mr. Smith's name before the Democratic convention as an aspirant for the nomination; later, on the insistence of Mr. Smith, he became the Democratic candidate for Governor of New York; and he entered enthusiastically into the campaign, state and national.

During the period of his political inactivity Mr. Roosevelt had taken little or no part in the internecine conflict among Democrats over the League of Nations and internationalism, and with considerable expectancy the warm advocates of the League awaited from him a statement of his position on the subject in 1928. But he failed to satisfy that interest. Not once in his speeches reported in the *New York Times* did he endorse or even mention the League of Nations by name. In only two of his reported speeches during the campaign did he make any material reference to foreign affairs; and after

16. *Ibid.,* October 30, 1928.

the tariff issue became "hot" he lent support to Mr. Smith's position on that controversial theme.[17]

In calling upon the Democratic convention to nominate Mr. Smith as the party's candidate for the presidency, Mr. Roosevelt said: "If the vision of real world peace, of the abolishment of war, ever comes true, it will not be through the mere mathematical calculations of a reduction of armament program, nor the platitudes of multilateral treaties piously deprecating armed conflict. It will be because this nation will select as its head a leader who understands the human side of life, who has the force of character and the keenness of brain to take, instinctively, the right course. . . ."[18]

Mr. Roosevelt insisted that the election of Mr. Smith would be the "greatest possible step forward in our relations with the other nations of the world." He described Mr. Smith as "one who believes that nations are not very different from individuals and who believes that more can be accomplished by sitting down around the table and talking matters over than fighting it out with their fists." To this he added that if we want to end war "let us take up with the other nations the elimination of the cause of war."[19]

At Manchester, Georgia, on October 2, 1928, Mr. Roosevelt discussed foreign affairs at some length and, without mentioning the League of Nations, except as "a plan" advanced by President Wilson, contented himself with refer-

17. In an article in *Foreign Affairs* for July, 1928, Mr. Roosevelt joined issue with Ogden Mills on the subject of "Our Foreign Policy," and stated "A Democratic View" of it. In this article Mr. Roosevelt said that even without our participation the League of Nations had become "for the rest of the world the principal agency for the settlement of international controversy," but he did not advocate the entrance of the United States into the League; he defended occupation of Santo Domingo and Haiti during President Wilson's Administration as excellent pieces of "constructive work," and yet declared that as a net result of these instances and recently of the far less justified intervention in Nicaragua the United States had fewer friends in the Western hemisphere (pp. 573 ff.). Although it was favorable to internationalism, at least for Europe, Mr. Roosevelt's article gave no consolation to Democrats who advocated joining the League of Nations. At all events, since *Foreign Affairs* had only a small circulation among "intellectuals," his exposition of foreign policy had little if any influence in the campaign.

18. *New York Times,* June 28, 1928.

19. *Ibid.,* September 9, 1928.

ences to the resumption of moral leadership under the auspices of the Democratic party. The principal passages of the Manchester address follow:

There has been a change in the attitude of the rest of the world toward this country. Ten years ago we held a position of leadership among all the nations of the world. This was because we were seeking an ideal, the ideal of bringing about such an organization among the peoples of the world that there never again would be another war such as the one which had just been concluded.

Once in 1919 I was talking with Premier Clemenceau of France on the subject of disarmament.

"Mr. Roosevelt," he said to me, "do you realize that in a thousand years there has never been a generation of Frenchmen who went through life without seeing their nation involved in war?"

We can't say much better for ourselves, can we? The Revolution, the so-called war with France in 1800, the War of 1812, the Mexican War in 1846, the war between the States in the Sixties, the Spanish-American War in 1898 and the World War in 1917. Yes, we are a very peace-loving people, aren't we?

But in those days we were looked to for leadership and we were liked by the nations of the world, and the President of the United States advanced a plan which was accepted by all the nations except Mexico, Soviet Russia and the United States. That plan is in effect today. It has its faults, but it has brought about improvements in a great many things.

In these ten years the position of the United States in its relations to the rest of the world has changed. Now the United States is not loved anywhere outside of its own borders. This is no exaggeration, it is a fact.

The people of Europe speak of us as money-grabbers and self-seekers, and think we are concerned only with our own pocketbooks.

The nineteen or twenty republics to the south of us in Latin-America do not scorn us, they hate us. They have seen us in Haiti, Nicaragua and San Domingo. They have seen what they call our *imperialism.*

I could talk to you for hours about how the United States has hurt itself with the rest of the world. We are asked in the election to choose between a continuance of the present American policy toward other nations and a change in this policy. . . .

In voting for the Republican ticket we are voting to retain the complete lack of ideals in our dealings with other people of the world.

It is a clearly announced Democratic policy, announced both in the nominee's speech of acceptance and the party platform, to undertake to resume our friendship with the other nations and to assume again the position of moral leadership.

It is an announced Democratic doctrine not to interfere in the internal affairs of our neighboring sister republics.[20]

In two campaign addresses, one at Bridgeport and the other at Boston, Mr. Roosevelt sought to assure the public that the Democratic platform and Mr. Smith were sound on the protective tariff—the policy generally regarded as incompatible with internationalism. In accordance with their wont, Republicans had charged the Democrats with intending to break down the trade barriers that protected industrial capitalists and industrial workers against the influx of cheap goods made by cheap labor abroad. It is true that neither the Democratic platform of 1928 nor the speeches of Mr. Smith had lent any countenance to free-trade doctrines; on the contrary both were decidedly protectionist in letter and spirit. But Republicans persisted in raising the specter of "pauper labor," and at the manufacturing city of Bridgeport Mr. Roosevelt squarely faced it: "Does any man with any common-sense think if the Democratic Party is returned to power it is going to commit political suicide by putting in free trade or anything like it? . . . The Democratic Party will do nothing that will take one dollar away from any American wage earner."[21]

At Boston, on October 12, Mr. Roosevelt was even more emphatic: "I am here to tell the people of New England that if we have a Democratic President and a Democratic

20. *Ibid.*, October 3, 1928.
21. *Ibid.*, September 9, 1928.

Congress during the next four years they need not fear that a Democratic tariff will do them the slightest conceivable harm. I will go further and say that if there is any conceivable way of changing the tariff laws of the United States so that the great industries of the New England States can be revived, we Democrats are in favor of that change." [22]

Other Democratic speakers in the campaign conformed to the framework of foreign policy set by Mr. Smith and Mr. Roosevelt. Newton D. Baker, who had fought the great battle for the League of Nations in the Democratic convention of 1924, heartily supported the party ticket in 1928. An examination of the *New York Times* reports of Mr. Baker's campaign speeches discloses no reference to any party obligations in respect of entering the League of Nations. President Wilson's biographer, Ray Stannard Baker, former leader in the propaganda for the League of Nations, came out for Mr. Smith with an avowal that Woodrow Wilson would have supported the Democratic candidate on account of his "stand on prohibition." [23]

In a radio address on October 12, 1928, Walter Lippmann said: "So far as I can see from reading the two platforms and what little the two candidates have had to say in their acceptance speeches with regard to foreign policy, there is no clear-cut dispute between the two parties." At the same time Mr. Lippmann assured his auditors that it would be infinitely safer for those who favored an idealistic program of international cooperation, as Woodrow Wilson did, to vote for Mr. Smith, the Democratic candidate for President.[24]

On the other side of the line in 1928 the Republicans repeated the pledge of 1924 to reject membership in the League of Nations, while favoring cooperation in humanitarian and technical services undertaken by the League. The Republican candidate, Herbert C. Hoover, took his stand on this platform and expressed a willingness to work with the

22. *Ibid.*, October 13, 1928.
23. *Ibid.*, October 21, 1928.
24. *Ibid.*, October 13, 1928,

League "in its endeavors to further scientific, economic, and social welfare, and to secure limitation of armaments."

Owing to Republican references to cooperation with the League and to the fact that Mr. Hoover had once been known, in 1920, as a supporter of the League, critics of Alfred E. Smith could allege that the Republicans were more internationalist than the Democrats. But a respect for the meaning of words and for the history of Republican operations in foreign affairs after 1898 gave little warrant for this allegation unless imperialism was by definition to be identified with internationalism. For, as an eminent expert in internationalism, Arthur Sweetser, remarked, "The Republicans [in 1928] began to return to the policy which had led to America's most active foreign development, as shown in the expansion of foreign trade, the Spanish war and first overseas development, and leadership in the Hague Peace Conference." [25]

Whatever love of peace could be ascribed to Republicans in 1928,[26] one thing was certain at the close of the campaign: Democratic leadership had abandoned internationalism as represented by the League of Nations and had returned to the independence which they had followed for many years prior to President Wilson's departures. During that period Democratic leaders had fiercely opposed Republican imperialism as an insidious betrayal of the American Republic, rejected "the white man's burden" as hypocritical cant, denounced "the greedy commercialism" of the Republican policy, and spurned the idea that the United States must resort to imperialism in order to demonstrate its "maturity," its

25. *American Year Book* (1928), p. 71. Since documents for the inside history of the Hague peace conferences are now available, any student of history willing to spend a few weeks examining them can readily discover how much "internationalism" there was in Republican "leadership" at the Hague "peace" conferences.

26. It seems unnecessary to lay much emphasis on the Kellogg–Briand Peace Pact of 1928. In that year a specialist in foreign affairs, John M. Mathews, noted: "It is possible to find so many legal loopholes in the Kellogg pact that, from a legal point of view, it may be considered a mere futile gesture." Its moral influence, to which Mr. Mathews then referred, was indicated by current and subsequent events. *American Year Book* (1928), p. 54.

"responsibility to the world," or its superior virtues as a nation. In the campaign of 1928 Democratic leaders had again denounced imperialism and they had deserted the League of Nations. But they had not openly and specifically repudiated the League as constituted. This climax in the trend of Democratic leadership was soon to come.

CHAPTER V

Franklin D. Roosevelt Repudiates the League of Nations in 1932

As the presidential campaign of 1932 approached, a number of circumstances conspired to direct the attention of political leaders and the people away from foreign affairs and concentrate it on domestic issues. Since the panic of 1929 the country had been floundering in the morass of a great depression and as the campaign drew near there seemed to be no letup in the economic distress that afflicted the country.

According to estimates presented at a congressional hearing by William Green, President of the American Federation of Labor, the total number of unemployed stood at 6,800,-000 in October, 1931, and at 10,900,000 in October, 1932. The plight of the farmers, if not worse, was certainly no better; besides being ridden by debts and bankruptcies, they were receiving for their produce prices ruinously low, when they could find any market at all. Millions of people were on relief and physical suffering was widespread. Banks by the hundreds had closed their doors. Stocks of thirty prime industries had fallen from 364.9 to 62.7 dollars a share. Bankruptcies among business concerns had risen to a staggering figure.[1] For the first time in American history, persons of first rank in the business world were wondering whether the capitalist system could weather the storm.

When this calamity fell upon the nation, Franklin D. Roosevelt was Governor of New York. Urged by Alfred E. Smith to lend his strength to the Democratic ticket, he had entered the lists in 1928 and had carried the state, despite the large plurality of votes cast in New York for the Republican candidate for President, Herbert C. Hoover; and in 1930

1. C. A. Beard and G. H. E. Smith, *The Future Comes* (The Macmillan Company, 1933), chap. I.

Governor Roosevelt was reelected by the largest plurality ever won by any candidate for the office of governor in the history of the state.[2] And New York was a pivotal state in the politics and economics of the country. In New York City was located the financial capital of the United States. New York had a large farming population and was at the same time a highly industrialized state. It was, therefore, badly shaken when the panic came in the autumn of 1929; and, during the period of mounting misery that followed, Governor Roosevelt had to wrestle with every kind of ordeal that tormented the people: unemployment, agricultural depression, financial dislocations, disorders among utilities, bankruptcies, and social insecurity in menacing forms. Moreover, by the very nature of his office, he was called upon to deal with domestic affairs, not the foreign relations of the United States.

From the autumn of 1929 to the autumn of 1931 Governor Roosevelt sponsored and secured the enactment of numerous measures designed to mitigate the effects of the economic depression in the State of New York; and he demonstrated to the country a resolve to employ the agencies of government in the interest of recovery from the domestic calamity. This fact in itself illustrated a new stage in the history of governmental action with reference to panics and depressions. In former times it had been the fashion for Democrats to lay the blame for economic disasters on Republican tariff policies, if Republicans were in power at the moment; and the process had been reversed if misfortune had befallen the country while Democrats were in power. Under Governor Roosevelt a new pattern was set: other government measures must be employed to overcome the domestic crisis.

By his public addresses and actions in respect of unemployment, economic disturbances, and poverty, Governor Roosevelt attracted the attention of progressive leaders in all parts of the country, then eagerly searching for ways and means of overcoming the depression. He also captured the loyalty

2. *American Year Book* (1932), p. 2.

and confidence of men and women from the younger generation who regarded agitations over the tariff and foreign affairs as little more than subterfuges for avoiding an effective
attack on the economic crisis.

In his capacity as Governor and at length as a candidate for
the Democratic nomination for President, Mr. Roosevelt
gathered around him a small group popularly styled "the
brain trust," which included such men as Raymond Moley,
Rexford Tugwell, and Adolf Berle, three professors from
Columbia University. He did not neglect the methods of
politics; on the contrary, he caught the affection of practical
politicians within his party, notably James A. Farley, who
knew how to win friends and keep them. But for ideas,
policies, and plans, the Governor relied heavily on the advice
and labors of a few young men, most of them Democrats,
who firmly believed that economic recovery and the maintenance of a high standard of life for the American people
were to be achieved, first and foremost, by domestic measures
of reform. Although these young counselors by no means
left foreign affairs out of account, their emphasis was on
domestic measures of recovery and reform, and Mr. Roosevelt was in accord with them on this crucial matter of policy.

It is true that many "old-line" Democrats, particularly
Cordell Hull, clung to the idea that America could and
should recover from the depression and reach a high level of
prosperity by lowering at once the tariff rates on imported
goods. This meant no government interference with the
historic processes of capitalism, the introduction of no
"novel" and "dangerous" ideas into politics and economics.
As the Republicans had once wrung victories from "the
bloody shirt" of the Civil War, many Democrats in 1932
hoped to wring a victory out of a tariff debate in the traditional style. Yet, while this hope was cherished by older
Democrats during the years of the great depression, it had
little appeal to the younger generation and none whatever to
Governor Roosevelt's most intimate associates in "the brain
trust."

Such was the general state of facts and opinions when in 1931 preparations for the presidential campaign got under way. Progressives—Democratic and Republican alike—"planners," men and women in economic distress, and *novi homines* of various kinds were turning to Governor Roosevelt. If the country on the whole was in no radical mood, the dissenters and experimenters were numerous enough to make a substantial diversion in politics. They were aware that victory would not be easy for them and that allies had to be sought in many directions, as they cast about for the necessary quota of delegates to nominate Mr. Roosevelt at the Democratic convention.

But at the opening of 1932, the chances for the nomination of Governor Roosevelt as the Democratic candidate for President were at best highly speculative. Other influential candidates were in the field. Despite his defeat in 1928, Alfred E. Smith was a powerful contender and felt himself entitled to the honor now that a Democratic triumph seemed definitely at hand. In the Southwest friends of John Nance Garner put him forward for the presidency, if not with the hope of being able to nominate a Southern man, at least with a view of winning for him the second place on the Democratic ticket. The name of Owen D. Young was frequently mentioned, although his associations with great capitalism in the East cast a shadow on his availability. In the Middle West, Newton D. Baker commanded a following strong enough to organize an effective drive for him, particularly in case there was a deadlock between the major aspirants, Alfred E. Smith and Governor Roosevelt. More than once in history a man with only a few votes on the first ballot at a convention had overcome two or more mighty foes in the final showdown.

On January 1, 1932, no seeker after the Democratic nomination could be sure of winning it and all who entered the race had to reckon with the most powerful journalist in their party, William Randolph Hearst, the ruthless publisher whose chain of newspapers stretched from coast to coast. Mr. Hearst had started his journalistic career as a radical and had once been regarded as a red terror by Republicans of Mark Hanna's school; but in 1932 he was entrenched in the camp of conservative Democrats. In respect of foreign affairs, he was an intransigent isolationist, hostile to the League of Nations, an inveterate enemy of everything that savored of internationalism. His influence was enhanced by the fact that many conservative politicians of Democratic leanings had shared his sentiments on foreign affairs even during the second Administration of President Wilson. The general disillusionment that followed the first World War added to Mr. Hearst's strength as a doughty foe of internationalism; and in any case, owing to the immense circulation of his journals in strategic centers, he was a force to be reckoned with by all candidates for the Democratic nomination in 1932.

In a radio broadcast to the nation on New Year's Day, Mr. Hearst "cracked his whip" by serving due and sufficient notice to all and sundry aspirants for the Democratic nomination that they must repudiate internationalism if they wanted his support. With characteristic vehemence, he denounced Woodrow Wilson and his foreign policies as dangerous to the United States. President Wilson, he declared, was "a theorist, a visionary, with no deep-seated convictions, certainly none that interfered with his personal ambition and advancement; a brilliant speaker, an unstable thinker and an unreliable performer; an advocate at some time or other in his career of both sides of almost every public question; an opportunist in his support of any principle at any time." Wilson, he continued, led the nation into "the morass of complication and catastrophe." His successors in leadership, Cox, Davis, and Smith, as Democratic candidates for President, had encountered "disastrous defeats," for the reason that "Mr. Wilson led his party up a political blind alley, and everyone who has followed in his footsteps has crashed against a stone wall of defeat at the end of that blind alley."

Besides condemning Mr. Wilson as a visionary whose

nomination was "the greatest misfortune" that had befallen the country, Mr. Hearst turned his battery on President Hoover. He attacked Mr. Hoover as "a Wilsonite," who had led the Republican party up Mr. Wilson's blind alley into the Democratic wreckage at the end of the alley. Lest the aspirants for the Democratic nomination overlook his notice, Mr. Hearst named them. He said that Governor Roosevelt, Newton D. Baker, Alfred E. Smith, and Owen D. Young were "all good men in their way," but were "all, like Mr. Hoover, disciples of Woodrow Wilson"—men who had "fatuously followed Wilson's visionary policies of intermeddling in European conflicts and complications." After warning these four men by name, Mr. Hearst proposed the nomination of John Nance Garner.

Doubtless aware that the nomination of Mr. Garner was a forlorn hope, Mr. Hearst confessed that he did not know who would be the next President; but he appealed to his national audience for the nomination of a man committed to "America first": "Do not allow the international bankers and the other big influences that have gambled with your prosperity to gamble with your politics. Unless we American citizens are willing to go on laboring indefinitely merely to provide loot for Europe, we should personally see to it that a man is elected to the Presidency this year whose guiding motto is 'America first.' " [3] Such was Mr. Hearst's warning to the Democratic aspirants then preparing for the nomination campaign.

Although in messages to the annual convention of the League of Nations Association in mid-January, 1932, Newton D. Baker had reiterated his contention that the national interests of the United States demanded full participation in the affairs of the League, and had called for sympathetic cooperation with the League,[4] later in the month he definitely read the question of the League out of practical poli-

3. *New York Times*, January 3, 1932.
4. *Ibid.*, January 15 and 16, 1932.

tics. In a release to the press on January 26, 1932, Mr. Baker reversed the position he had taken in 1924.

Any opinion that I entertain on the subject of America's relationship to the League of Nations must be such as any private citizen is entitled to entertain. I have stated publicly several times within the past two or three years that the question of America's joining the League is at present not a matter in the field of practical political discussion.

I repeat what I frequently stated previously. I would not take the United States into the League if I had the power to do so until there is an informed and convinced majority sentiment in favor of that action by the United States. I am not in favor of a plank in the Democratic national platform urging our joining the League. I think it would be a great mistake to make a partisan issue of the matter.

I think that we will go into the League some day, and I think we ought to, but I don't think we should take that action until the people of the United States have had a chance to see the League in action, and to study its action enough to be fully satisfied as to the wisdom of such a course.

I do not think that the Democratic party should advocate our entrance into the League just because Woodrow Wilson favored it. On the other hand, I do not think that the Republican party ought to be for or against the League for any like reason. Republican membership or Democratic membership in the League based on a sharp division of partisan sentiment in this country would be a feeble thing, and would not give the United States the opportunity to exercise whatever power for good our membership there might be hoped to produce.

In the meantime, I feel that it is wise for the United States to cooperate with the League with the utmost sympathy in its efforts to preserve peace, and for the American people to study the League and so overcome some of our unwarranted prejudices against it.[5]

In the issue which contained Mr. Baker's press release excluding the League from "the field of practical political dis-

5. *Ibid.*, January 27, 1932.

cussion," the *New York Times* commented editorially on his statement as a bid for the nomination: ". . . his friends have undoubtedly told him that, since he may be nominated, it is best that his League position be exactly defined to remove any handicaps which misinterpretation might bring. That yesterday's statement has made Mr. Baker much more available as a candidate with the practical Democratic politicians is, of course, a significant result of having made it. Henceforth, whatever his personal preferences, Mr. Baker will be regarded as at least a receptive candidate." [6]

Prominent Democrats such as Colonel House, Frank Polk, and John W. Davis endorsed Mr. Baker's manifesto excluding the issue of the League from the coming campaign. And the chorus of endorsers was joined by eminent Democratic leaders in Congress. According to the report of their opinions in the *New York Times:*

Senator Thomas Walsh of Montana declared: "I know of no one who is attempting to raise the League issue at this time. In fact, it has been pretty generally ignored since the 1920 campaign."

Senator Clarence Dill thought it "extremely encouraging that such extraneous issues as the League are to be taken out of the political situation at this time so that we may concentrate on the hard-times issue. It is gratifying that the leading proponent of the League is willing to submerge that issue in the interest of harmony. The economic issue greatly affects the great mass of our people who are out of work and it should not be beclouded by any other issue."

Senator Walter George expressed the opinion that Mr. Baker "is entirely correct in saying that the League is not and ought not to be a vital question in this campaign."

Senator William King gave his approval: "It is a wise statement. I always have been a supporter of the League, but it should not be made an issue until a majority of the people have a larger understanding of it. It would be futile to project it into political discussions now."

6. *Ibid.*

The Democratic floor leader of the House, W. R. Rainey, said he had heard of no agitation for a League of Nations plank in the national platform.[7]

While, in his release to the press on January 26, Mr. Baker publicly abandoned the position he had so stoutly maintained at the Democratic convention in 1924[8] and declared the League issue to be out of practical politics, he also expressed the private conviction that the United States ought to go into the League "some day." This was sufficient to warrant his followers in believing that Mr. Baker was still the best hope for the ultimate success of the internationalist cause in the United States. For example, Wendell Willkie, of Ohio, then a regular Democrat and ardent advocate of President Wilson's internationalism, who had supported Mr. Baker at the Democratic convention in 1924, now plunged into the campaign with a resolve to win the nomination for his hero at the Democratic convention of 1932, if possible. In a statement made public in the late summer of 1944, Mr. Willkie described himself as one of the enthusiastic "Baker Boys" of 1924, and told how hard they had worked to secure the victory of Mr. Baker at Chicago in 1932.[9]

Whatever the merits of Mr. Baker's statesmanship or strategy, his pronouncement on January 26, 1932, was unsatisfactory to William Randolph Hearst, who demanded a candidate prepared to cast off all allegiance to the League of Nations idea and adopt unequivocally the motto of "America first." And while Mr. Baker's statement on the League was under discussion, Mr. Hearst's representative was in communication with another aspirant for the Democratic nomination at the coming convention of the party—Governor Franklin D. Roosevelt of New York.

Few men were better acquainted with the range of Mr.

7. *Ibid.*, January 28, 1932.
8. Above, pp. 48 ff.
9. First printed in the Birmingham *Age-Herald* and reprinted a week later in *The United States News*, September 8, 1944. For a fuller account see below, pp. 100 f.

Hearst's power than Governor Roosevelt and his immediate associates. It was in New York City that Mr. Hearst had started his journalistic career on the national stage, after an experiment in California, and, although he had suffered reverses, he still wielded telling influence in the State of New York as well as in its great metropolis. At some time, not yet fixed on the basis of documentary records, a representative of Governor Roosevelt approached a representative of Mr. Hearst with a view to winning the journalist's support for the Governor's nomination at the Democratic convention. Immediately there arose the question of the Governor's stand on foreign affairs: Was Mr. Roosevelt in fact an internationalist and did he really believe that the United States should join the League of Nations? Or was he prepared to renounce his former position in favor of "America first"?

Such was the tenor of the inquiries directed to Governor Roosevelt's agent. From the document printed below, only one inference is permissible: either at the time these inquiries were made or later, Mr. Hearst was privately assured that Mr. Roosevelt was not an internationalist and was not in favor of American participation in the League of Nations. But Mr. Hearst was not satisfied with this assurance as to the Governor's views, conveyed privately. He insisted on a public statement from Governor Roosevelt to that effect, and he published an ultimatum.

Mr. Hearst's demand that Governor Roosevelt take a public stand against the League of Nations and internationalism came in the form of an open letter to Mr. E. D. Coblentz, dated San Simeon, California, January 21, 1932. It was printed in the *New York American* ten days later, January 31, 1932. The portion of the letter that contained the personal challenge to Mr. Roosevelt follows:

Dear Cobbie:
Please give my compliments to Mr. Farley, but tell him I beg leave to say that if Mr. Roosevelt has any statement to make about his not now being an internationalist, he should make it to the public publicly and not to me privately.

He made his numerous declarations publicly when he said that he WAS an internationalist and WAS in favor of our country joining the League of Nations even at the sacrifice of some portion of our nation's sovereignty.

He should make his declaration publicly that he has changed his mind and that he is NOW in favor of keeping the national independence which our forefathers won for us; that he is NOW in favor of NOT joining the League or the League Court.

I must say frankly that if Mr. Roosevelt is not willing to make public declaration of his change of heart, and wants only to make his statement to me privately, I would not believe him.

My experience has proved that a man who is running for office and is not willing to make his honest opinions known to the public, either has no honest opinions or is not honest about them.

If a man is hiding his opinions from the public, and only expressing them privately to people whose support he wants, I would consider him either not courageous or not trustworthy.

If he does not want to express his opinions publicly, because he thinks they would hurt his candidacy, then he is certainly not courageous, while if he is privately playing Peter to one and Paul to another, or rather Peter to one and Judas to another, then he is certainly not worthy of public or private trust.

I do not think any man has a right to ASK to be elected to public office unless he is willing to let the public know exactly what kind of man they are electing.

Otherwise politics merely becomes a shell game in which the public is made to pick out the shell which the pea is NOT UNDER—a gold brick game where the brick which is sold the public is not gold but merely gilded; or as the Bible more exaltedly expresses it, "Like unto whited sepulchres, which indeed appear beautiful outward, but are within full of dead men's bones, and of all uncleanness."

I do not see why politics cannot be open and honest, and clean inside and out.

I am for Mr. Garner in this campaign . . .

I am for him because he is plain and direct and sincere and HONEST—morally and mentally honest.

His record is an open book. His convictions are in the record, without compromise, without contradiction. . . .

WILLIAM RANDOLPH HEARST.

In an address to the New York State Grange, on February 2, 1932, two days after Mr. Hearst's open call upon him for a public repudiation of internationalism and the League of Nations, Governor Roosevelt squarely met the challenge. About two thirds of the speech was devoted to a discussion of farmers' problems, ending in an emphasis on the desirability of securing additional outlets for agricultural produce. This enlargement of the market, the Governor argued, could be achieved by reciprocal bargaining with other nations for mutually advantageous exchange of commodities. Although such an economic operation obviously did not in itself involve any political entanglements with European countries or with the League of Nations, Mr. Roosevelt went on to assure his auditors that he was definitely opposed to such entanglements in any form.

That part of the Grange address which dealt with this subject is here given in full. The passage printed in italics appears in the portion of the address reprinted in *The Public Papers and Addresses of Franklin D. Roosevelt*, I, 157; and the passages in roman are the supplementary passages omitted by President Roosevelt and Samuel I. Rosenman, his associate in compiling the *Papers*.[10]

Let me at the same time make it clear [Governor Roosevelt declared in his address to the Grange on February 2, 1932] *that a trade conference with the other nations of the world does not and should not, by any stretch of the imagination, involve the United States in any participation in political controversies in Europe or elsewhere. Nor does it involve the renewal in any way of the problem of twelve years ago of American participation as a member of the League of Nations.*

In common with millions of my fellow countrymen, I worked and spoke, in 1920, in behalf of American participation in a League of Nations, conceived in the highest spirit of world

---

10. The co-editor, Mr. Rosenman, explains that owing to the large number of the Governor's addresses a selection had to be made and that "those were chosen which most clearly show his general policies and objectives in so far as they forecast what was to come later in the Presidency." Foreword to Vol. I.

friendship for the great object of preventing a return of world war. For that course I have no apology to make.

If today I believed that the same or even similar factors entered into the argument, I would still favor America's entry into the League; and I would go so far as to seek to win over the overwhelming opposition which exists in this country today.

But the League of Nations today is not the League conceived by Woodrow Wilson. It might have been, had the United States joined. Too often through these years its major function has been not the broad overwhelming purpose of world peace, but rather a mere meeting place for the political discussion of strictly European political national difficulties. In these the United States should have no part.

The fact remains that we did not join the League. The League has not developed through these years along the course contemplated by its founder, nor have the principal members shown a disposition to divert the huge sums spent on armament into the channels of legitimate trade, balanced budgets, and the payment of obligations. American participation in the League would not serve the highest purpose of the prevention of war and a settlement of international difficulties in accordance with fundamental American ideals. Because of these facts, therefore, I do not favor American participation.

What the world needs most today is a national policy which will make us an example of national honor to other nations. The first lesson for all the world is recognition that a treaty is a nation's word of honor to another nation and that all just national debts are "debts of honor"; that, therefore, no honorable nation may break a treaty in spirit any more than they may break it in letter; nor, when it is a debtor, may repudiate or cancel a national debt of honor. On the other side it should be remembered also that the creditor on his part should use every honorable means to help the debtor set his house in order.

Europe owes us. We do not owe her. Therefore, we should call a meeting of our debtors here and not in Europe and demand an understanding. If it were considered advisable in the present condition of world finance to postpone the payment of debts for a while, we should nevertheless insist upon an accord as to when payments should begin and in what amount.

Europe has indulged herself in an orgy of spending and finds herself at the moment in a crippled financial position. She should look at the facts of her spending and bring about a change of policy to restore her financial equilibrium and enable her to meet her just obligations. She should cease to blame us for all the ills which have followed this reckless course of spending and try to remember the aid we gave her in time of need; aid for which she was once grateful but which she has forgotten.

The world ship of state cannot regain its safe course to port by reckless spending and by reckless vituperation, but it can steer safely home by unity of action and a determination eventually to meet its just obligations.

By economic cooperation this Nation can revive the trade of the world as well as trade within our own borders. In so doing we can extend a helping hand to our debtors as well as to ourselves. The highest ideals of America demand that, with strict adherence to the principles of Washington, we maintain our international freedom and at the same time offer leadership to a sorely tried humanity.[11]

In contrast to Newton D. Baker's public statement on the League of Nations, January 26, 1932, Governor Roosevelt's announcement of February 2, 1932, constituted a categorical denunciation as a matter of personal opinion and national policy. Mr. Baker had made it clear to the American people that he still entertained his private opinion in favor of the League, that he believed "we will go into the League some day," that it was wise to cooperate with the League in its efforts to preserve peace, that the American people should study the League and so overcome some of their "unwarranted prejudices against it." Governor Roosevelt, on the other hand, while justifying his former position on the

11. This text appears in the *Public Papers of Franklin D. Roosevelt, Forty-eighth Governor of the State of New York, Second Term, 1932*, pp. 551 f. This volume was published by the State of New York in 1939, with a Foreword by President Roosevelt dated September 13, 1939. The passage italicized, as published in President Roosevelt's *Public Papers*, I, 157 (Random House, 1938), ends with ". . . ." to indicate an omission.

League, declared that the League was not the League conceived by Woodrow Wilson; that it too often served as a meeting place for the discussion of strictly European national political difficulties; that "American participation would not serve the highest purpose of the prevention of war"; that he did "not favor American participation in the League"; and that Europe had not been dealing honorably in respect of her debts to the United States.

The repercussions of Governor Roosevelt's address to the Grange were swift and resounding. It was taken to mean just what Mr. Hearst had demanded of the Governor's agent: unconditional rejection of membership in the League of Nations and of internationalism as represented by that form of world organization; a call for the collection of the debts owed to the Government of the United States by former associates in the first World War; an endorsement of non-entanglement in the political controversies of foreign countries; and a firm adherence to the principles of George Washington[12] respecting foreign relations—in short an acceptance of the isolationist program, except perhaps a high protective tariff. Judging by the comments of public men and the newspapers and by protests from internationalists, the Grange address was a political "bombshell."

A dispatch from Albany to the *New York Times*, dated February 3, the day after the Grange address was delivered, reported: "Governor Roosevelt said tonight that he had received many messages from different parts of the country commending his stand in opposition to American entry into the League of Nations and the remission of war debts . . . He would not authorize publication of the missives."

To this paragraph quoting Governor Roosevelt directly, the *Times* reporter added a long story in the customary political style, as if on the record and yet off the record, in the manner of "it is said":

12. Washington's foreign policy, particularly his Farewell Address, was regarded in 1932 as the very foundation of the isolationist philosophy.

Moreover, the Governor, who was and is an ardent Wilson Democrat, *is said* to have received assurances prior to the writing of his speech that his attitude was shared by a large number of prominent Democrats who were and continue to be enthusiastic admirers of the ideals and program for world peace of which Woodrow Wilson was the exponent.

The Governor *was said* to have communicated with some of these Democrats before delivering his address, is well aware of their support in his stand and would not be surprised if there were, before long, public expression to make this clear.

When the challenge was issued to Mr. Roosevelt to speak out in open meeting, and set at rest speculation with regard to his attitude on what some have termed "internationalism," he, *according to a close friend*, was greatly surprised that there should be any doubt as to his views.

He was so firmly convinced that he had defined his opinion in a public address that he had a search made of newspaper files for the last half-dozen years, expecting they would reveal material that would constitute a complete reply to the challenge. Much to his disappointment and chagrin, *it is said*, the search was fruitless.

Today, however, *it was recalled by a person at the Capitol who was closely identified with the 1928 campaign* that while it was in progress Mr. Roosevelt had expressed his views on the League of Nations and American membership in it much along the lines that he spoke last night.

The occasion *was said to have been* a conference held behind closed doors at which many prominent Democrats identified with the Smith campaign spoke without fear of publicity. Mr. Roosevelt, with a group of four or five others whose names were not disclosed, contended vigorously against an "internationalism" slant in Democratic campaign speeches, especially those of Governor Smith. Thus, *it was stated here tonight*, how Mr. Roosevelt stood on membership of the United States in the League could hardly have been a secret or a matter of doubt to former Governor Smith.[13]

The subject under discussion at the conference, *it was stated*, was not as to participation of the United States in the League's work, but the stand the Democratic party should take in the

13. Above, pp. 53 ff.

national campaign regarding the entry of the United States into the World Court.

Mr. Roosevelt, holding the League had been diverted from the idealistic purposes advocated by President Wilson, opposed Democratic advocacy of entry into the World Court, because of the popular conception, right or wrong, that once a member, the United States might become entangled in European politics to an extent where, by force of circumstances, entry into the League itself would become the corollary.[14]

Conforming to immemorial party custom, Republican newspapers greeted Governor Roosevelt's renunciation of the League of Nations as a bid for the Democratic nomination for the presidency and grew ironical over his performance. In an editorial under the heading "Lovers Once," the *New York Sun*, February 3, 1932, commented:

In the campaign of the "great and solemn referendum" of 1920 no voice was raised more earnestly or frequently for American entrance into the League of Nations than the voice of Franklin D. Roosevelt. He was running for Vice-President of the United States. He and Mr. Cox made the League the big issue of the day. Mr. Roosevelt, then only 38 years old and imbued with the idealism of President Wilson, traveled the country trumpeting the glories of the League and challenging every opponent of Mr. Wilson's internationalistic program. Nor did Mr. Roosevelt's enthusiasm for the League die with the passing of Mr. Wilson. He became, and we believe still is, a trustee of the Woodrow Wilson Foundation, which so recently as 1929 awarded its peace prize to the League in recognition of its ten years' work in behalf of peace. Indeed, he served as the Foundation's national chairman for one term.

Last night Franklin D. Roosevelt, now fifty and the leading candidate for the Democratic nomination for President, laid the League ideal on the ash heap of the past, where it keeps company with the recent renunciation of another Presidential candidate, Newton D. Baker. If Governor Roosevelt's rejection of his old ideal looms larger than that of Mr. Baker it is because he made it

14. *New York Times*, February 4, 1932. (Italics supplied.)

more complete, less tied with strings. The League, he says, is not the League conceived by WILSON. It has not developed along the lines laid down by its founder. . . . We remember no murmur of dissent from Trustee Roosevelt when the Wilson Foundation laid its laurels at the League's foot two years ago. But let that go; the acolyte of other days finds that the League is not what it used to be. We may add, with due reverence to *Punch*, that it never was.[15]

The following day the *New York Herald Tribune* treated the Grange address under the caption, "Not an Eggshell Broken":

For treading a devious course among the political eggs of the hour, Governor Roosevelt's first major effort in the national field deserves the highest praise. At a dozen points he might have said something that would alienate votes. Not once did he so much as graze a risky topic. His score was perfect.

In two cases he achieved this end by the simple expedient of resolutely turning his back on the danger spots. He ignored both prohibition and Tammany Hall. In another case his acrobatics might be criticized as almost too nimble. No one asks a public man, or any one else, never to change his mind. But for Franklin D. Roosevelt, ardent Wilsonian advocate of the League of Nations, to come out as a complete enemy of the League, damning it for all time as a dangerous European contraption, seems a little bit thick. Mr. Baker certainly showed more sincerity and we suspect lost less by his realism than has the Governor by his recantation.

All the passages relating to Europe, to debts and to reparations, suggest a similar resolve to join the procession and never mind the haste. We regret to say that they suggest *little more* either in the way of study, understanding or candor. . . ." [16]

Republican politicians, like the editors of the party press, hailed Governor Roosevelt's "recantation" with ill-concealed derision. Senator William E. Borah, the irreconcilable of

15. *New York Sun*, February 3, 1932.
16. *New York Herald Tribune*, February 4, 1932.

1920, seemed to be especially pleased and inquired about the next step:

"Repent ye, for the kingdom of heaven is at hand." I presume the Governor is seeking the kingdom of heaven in the Presidency. When these gentlemen get through explaining their positions on the League I would like them to say where they stand on the World Court.[17]

Senator George Moses, whose claim to historical eminence lay partly in his characterization of Western radicals as "sons of the wild jackass," jeered at the Democratic leaders who appeared to be denying their principles:

The Reno-like celerity with which Democratic leaders—and especially Democratic candidates—are seeking to divorce themselves from the League of Nations is interesting and amusing. It has apparently dawned upon their consciousness that the 7,000,-000 majority by which the American people repudiated this issue in both 1920 and 1924 has a validity as applied to the election of 1932.

Death-bed conversions, however, smack of the theatrical, and are generally as unreal as most theatrical performances. As further evidence of the genuineness of the Democratic views which are now coming so belatedly to light, I suggest that there should be added to their renunciation of the League of Nations an equally emphatic renunciation of the League's pet baby—the so-called World Court.[18]

Governor Roosevelt could afford to ignore the Republicans who ridiculed his conversion, for many powerful members of his own party, after learning about his speech to the New York Grange, rallied to his support. From an influential Democrat of Montana, Burton K. Wheeler, came high commendation and, what was more, aid in marshaling sympathetic delegates for the coming Democratic convention.

17. *Ibid.*
18. *New York Times*, February 4, 1932.

In later years Senator Wheeler, the isolationist of 1932, was to draw down upon his head severe denunciations from his party brother on account of his own resolute adherence to the doctrine of non-entanglement in Europe's wars; but in February, 1932, things were different.

At that moment the two men saw eye to eye, for Senator Wheeler thoroughly approved the Governor's declaration of independence for the United States: "I am glad Governor Roosevelt has taken this position on the League of Nations. I am opposed to American entry into the League myself, but I was one of those who once favored the League and have changed my mind after seeing it in operation. The attitude of Japan and the fumbling manner in which the League has handled the Far Eastern situation should be enough to convince anyone that the United States should have nothing to do with the League." [19]

Senator Wheeler's position on the League was upheld by Senator Kenneth McKellar, of Tennessee, in almost the same language: "I was also strong for the League when it was being formed, but in view of its recent performances, then in the Japanese–Chinese controversy, I do not see how anyone could uphold it. I commend Governor Roosevelt for speaking out plainly about it." [20]

Thomas Walsh of Montana, colleague of Mr. Wheeler in the United States Senate, agreed with Governor Roosevelt that adherence to the League was no issue in 1932, but he evidently felt that the less said about it the better: "I see no occasion for the statements by either Governor Roosevelt or Mr. Baker. No one, so far as I know, is at present urging membership by the United States in the League. I see no prospect of it developing into an issue in 1932." [21]

Advocates of American membership in the League of Nations, to whom the labors and prophecies of Woodrow Wilson remained a precious heritage, were apparently as much

19. *New York Herald Tribune,* February 4, 1932.
20. *Ibid.*
21. *New York Times,* February 4, 1932.

shocked by Governor Roosevelt's act of renunciation as William Randolph Hearst was pleased with it. The editors of the *New York Times*, in a long "leader" on February 4, 1932, treated the "public recantation" as a political maneuver and assailed the logic of the argument made in support of it:

Plato reasoned well, but it can't be said that Governor Roosevelt does in explaining why he has given up his former ardent advocacy of the League of Nations. A public man is entitled to change his mind. He may announce that he has done so, and let it go at that. But if he attempts to argue the case, his reasoning ought to hold water. Mr. Roosevelt's is all aleak. He asserts that the League of Nations has not developed along the lines of President Wilson's hope that it would prevent war, and has been merely an organization to discuss "strictly European national difficulties." With a straight face the Governor adds: "In these the United States should have no part."

Was not the outbreak of war in 1914 a strictly European difficulty? How can we be sure that another one like that might not as inevitably as the first draw the United States into the conflict? The fact is that every peaceful settlement made in Europe by the League of Nations—and it has made several important ones—has contributed to the welfare of the United States. And what can Governor Roosevelt have in mind when he declares that the members of the League have not "shown a disposition to divert the huge sums spent on armament into the channels of legitimate trade . . ." If there is any one thing which the League has steadily sought to do it is to bring about limitation of military expenditures. . . . If Mr. Roosevelt had said that the League had given too much time and energy to efforts to bring about disarmament, without having achieved large results, there might have been some force in this particular complaint of his.

It will be generally regretted, we think, that Governor Roosevelt should have been so plainly swayed by political motives in this public recantation. He frankly admits that in 1920 he worked and spoke and was a candidate for the Vice Presidency with entire commitment to the policy of America joining the League. Now he has suffered a sea-change, but his account of it is not at all convincing. People will see in him merely an inclination to be ever strong upon the stronger side. They will even express the suspicion that he is resentful of the way in which Newton D. Baker got ahead of him in reaching the conclusion that it would be inexpedient to have a League of Nations plank in the Democratic platform this year. There is, however, a difference in the cases of these two men. Mr. Baker has not abandoned his early faith. He still believes in the League of Nations, and hopes that the time will come when the American people will be convinced of the need of casting in their lot with it. Before that can happen, time will have to pass and the work of education be done. For the present, therefore, Mr. Baker holds that it would be futile to promise to do what cannot now be done. This is an intelligible position, if not very inspiring. But Governor Roosevelt was content to renounce the whole project of the League, and to defend his course by arguments which could easily be shown to be fallacious. It would have been better for him if he had merely announced his decision without giving any reasons for it, and had stood solely on the ground of his personal political advantage as a candidate for the Presidency.[22]

Three days later, February 7, 1932, the editors of the *Times* came back to the "recantation" and warned Governor Roosevelt that he had embarked on a "dangerous adventure." Under the heading of "A Perilous Passage," they made another classical reference and reminded the Governor and Newton D. Baker of the passionate devotion to President Wilson's memory that still existed in many parts of the country, as if suggesting that they were tacking carefully between the whirlpool and the rock:

Because this is the year when Presidential candidates will be nominated, two distinguished Democrats, who have been more than "mentioned" as their party's possible choice, explained their present views concerning the League of Nations. They selected their words with extreme care because the requirement was just that. For a Republican it is a simple political thesis; for a Democrat, and particularly a Democrat who was associated with Woodrow Wilson in an official capacity, it is a complex and

22. "The Governor and the League," *ibid.*

dangerous adventure. There are whole States in this country where the name of the War President is still revered . . .

. . . The War President's Assistant Secretary of the Navy, Governor Roosevelt, steered his course more carefully [than Baker] between the Charybdis of the League's unpopularity and the Scylla of passionate devotion to Wilson's memory existing in many parts of the country . . .

Neither could possibly have mentioned the League without naming its founder. . . . Wilson has been dead for nearly a decade . . . But, even though Democratic conventions dodge or forswear the League, the late President is a living issue within his party.[23]

The views expressed in the columns of the *New York Times* were shared by the editors of the *Christian Science Monitor*. They too compared the pronouncements of Mr. Baker and Mr. Roosevelt on the League question and likewise attacked the logic and validity of the latter's argument:

Both Mr. Newton D. Baker of Ohio and Governor Roosevelt of New York are possible candidates for the Presidency on the Democratic ticket this year. Perhaps they are the two leading candidates, although the figure of former Governor Smith steadily grows more and more prominent in the struggle for this honor. But Mr. Baker and Mr. Roosevelt alone have been making formal proclamation of their positions on certain issues likely to be prominent in the campaign.

It is rather significant that each of them is very desirous of leaving out of controversy the question of the United States' participation in the League of Nations. For a time advocacy of such action seemed likely to crystallize into a standard plank in the Democratic platform. But as the great figure of Woodrow Wilson recedes farther into the background and perhaps as American impatience with the complications attending any relationship with Europe increases, there is a growing tendency on the part of politicians to thrust this issue out of consideration.

Mr. Baker, not very long ago, reaffirmed his personal fealty to the League, but declared he did not think the time was propitious

23. *New York Times*, February 7, 1932, Sec. III, p. 1.

for making a political issue of it. He indicated, by implication at least, that if he should be the nominee of his party, he would do nothing to thrust the League forward as a campaign issue, but, on the contrary, would take the ground that it must yield place to more pressing matters of domestic concern.

Governor Roosevelt assumes a different attitude. He frankly abandons the League altogether as a matter of personal advocacy, declaring that it is no longer the League which Woodrow Wilson founded. One might discern in this attitude a desire to hold that very large Democratic support which still insists upon loyalty to the last of the Democratic Presidents while at the same time getting rid of an issue which may be embarrassing.

How can Governor Roosevelt support his contention that there has been any material change in the League? Wherein has there been any change? He complains that it has done nothing but discuss "the political difficulties of Europe in which the United States should have no part." It could not very well discuss the political difficulties of the United States, although perhaps had America been a member some of its more embarrassing problems might have been clarified by League discussion.

Nor for that matter has the United States itself escaped discussion of political difficulties in Europe by not being a member of the League. . . .

Both of these eminent Democrats may be, and probably are, exceedingly sagacious in attempting to keep the League issue out of the campaign. While there are an immense number of believers in the League in the United States, it cannot be held to be so popular an organization that advocacy of it would tend to increase a candidate's strength. But it is observed that Mr. Roosevelt also would keep the concrete tariff issue out of the campaign by advocating an international conference. . . . One begins to wonder what the Democratic Party is going to present to the people as its issue? . . .[24]

With alacrity and anger, President Wilson's former Secretary, Joseph Tumulty, shortly after Governor Roosevelt's address to the New York Grange, sprang to the defense of the internationalist cause against Democratic leaders who

24. "The League in American Politics," *Christian Science Monitor*, Boston, February 5, 1932.

pursued the course of "expediency." Commanding first-hand knowledge of Democratic politics, James Kerney had said: "Of all the insiders, no other ever reached the point of intimacy held by [Colonel] House and [Joseph] Tumulty, and of course no other so long had such close association with Wilson." [25] At all events, in 1932, it is highly probable that no Democrat was more loyal to President Wilson's internationalist ideals than Mr. Tumulty or more passionately attached to his memory. Stirred to wrath by the renunciations made publicly by Mr. Baker and Mr. Roosevelt, Mr. Tumulty told these candidates for the Democratic nomination just what he thought of them and their tactics:

When the only agency for peace now available is working to prevent a world catastrophe in the Orient, it is a sad commentary upon American politics that some Democratic leaders, lured on by circumstances, find it expedient, by an artful kind of indirection, to run away from the peace ideals of Woodrow Wilson.

As I consider the matter, I am picturing the plight and distress of these leaders should the League of Nations, after all, bring peace to the world. Should that great thing happen, what a picture these leaders would present, standing in sackcloth and ashes before the shrine of Woodrow Wilson, saying: "You are again the captain of my soul!"

Surely these leaders have chosen a most inopportune time to throw sticks and stones at the League of Nations. While I agree that the League of Nations should not be made an issue in 1932, and that handsome compromises are sometimes necessary to bring great reforms, I am wondering if the time selected for this act of surrender, in giving aid and comfort to the enemies of Woodrow Wilson, does not proclaim the act one of expediency. Surely, a leadership like this, that is afraid to fight, that is afraid to stand firm against the crowd, does not captivate one like myself who had the privilege of being associated with President Woodrow Wilson, who, to use his own words, would rather "lose in a cause that some day would triumph than triumph in a cause that must inevitably lose."

25. *The Political Education of Woodrow Wilson* (The Century Company, 1926), p. 485.

The Democratic leadership of 1932, I beg leave to say, must be made of finer stuff. That leadership must have in it the blend of courage and fortitude, and the vision of a new world.

Fortunately, the tides of peace running in the hearts of men, women and children throughout the world cannot be held in check by leadership like this—so foolish, so inept, so impotent. Behind the League of Nations lies deeper still the cause of peace, a cause that has been greatly embarrassed by statements that have recently appeared by men high in the councils of the Democratic party.

How mighty and majestic appears the figure of Woodrow Wilson in the present situation. The leadership of 1932 must not have in it the base metal of expediency, that kind of expediency that has brought the world to its present plight of unhappiness and misery. If we are to be successful in 1932, we must shake off the sterile curse of expediency. . . .

These leaders have surrendered the cause of peace to the mob. There is not one who will say that there is anything fine, handsome or courageous in that kind of surrender. Time, and time alone, will decide these things and vindicate the far-flung vision of Woodrow Wilson.[26]

The day after Mr. Tumulty's blast—for such it was— Governor Roosevelt replied brusquely to the "denunciation," saying: "Does he [Mr. Tumulty] want to go into the League? That is the main idea." Having dismissed Mr. Tumulty in a few words, the Governor added that he had received several thousand letters and telegrams from all over the country expressing a favorable reaction to his statement opposing United States membership in the League.[27]

Thus brushed aside curtly, Mr. Tumulty, several days later, took advantage of a public occasion again to characterize Governor Roosevelt and his renunciation in harsh language. In an address before the Democratic Women's Luncheon Club of New Jersey, February 17, 1932, which was broadcast, Mr. Tumulty, while declaring that he had no

26. *New York Times*, February 5, 1932.
27. *Ibid.*, February 6, 1932.

wish to project the League issue into the campaign, expressed his sentiments in this fashion:

With the first shot from the gun of the arch-enemy of the League, Mr. William Randolph Hearst, with whom I have no quarrel because he has hated the League in the past, a former devotee of the League cried "Kamerad, Kamerad!" and weakly surrendered. With the world on fire, with tinder lying about that might quickly ignite into a world conflagration, a real lover of peace would have refrained from attacking the League when, by the merest chance, it might have checked a world conflagration in the Orient.

With a critical situation confronting us; with the administration at Washington, to its everlasting credit be it said, attempting to reach a solution through the League that would prevent a war, what a melancholy hour was selected for this most disastrous retreat . . .

And what a time for personal ambition to thrust its ugly head into a critical world situation. At the very moment when this attack came sixty nations were meeting at Geneva to attempt to bring about a reduction of armaments, a commission containing an American was under way to investigate conditions in Shanghai; Senator Swanson, that sturdy Democrat from Virginia, a member of the Disarmament Conference, stated that the whole atmosphere at Geneva was saturated with the ideals of Woodrow Wilson.

After remarking that the average voter was disturbed by the "double-dealing, pretense, and hypocrisy" in our politics, Mr. Tumulty came down to cases: "Always with some candidates in these days, when great decisions have to be made affecting the peace and prosperity of the world, the main question seems to be, How easily can I win an election? How easily can I gain power and office without risking anything? . . . All things to all men, Mr. Facing-Both-Ways on the great issues of the day, he is unmindful of the virtue of lasting principle."

Continuing in this vein, Mr. Tumulty charged "an expediency-serving candidate" with appeasing certain journalistic leaders and currying favor with nationalists instead of thinking about service to the nation. He wondered how this candidate could shake hands with "bitter-enders," the foes of Woodrow Wilson, and "at the same time stand in reverence" before the shrine of the late President. Then taking up one of the main points in Governor Roosevelt's Grange address, Mr. Tumulty retorted: "The League of Nations as it exists today, which at this time is trying to settle questions in the Orient that may sweep into a great conflagration, is exactly the League of Nations as conceived by Woodrow Wilson." [28]

In the weekly journals of "opinion," the comments on Governor Roosevelt's address before the New York Grange were scarcely less caustic than those made by Republicans and the opposition newspapers. The New York *Nation*, then under the management of Oswald Garrison Villard, charged the Governor with trying to catch votes for himself and with a lack of realism in his thinking:

Franklin D. Roosevelt, who stood with Wilson in 1920 for the League of Nations and the new internationalism, has now gone over to the nationalists and isolationists. He has turned against the League of Nations, and he insists that Europe must pay its debts. He seems to realize that the trend in American sentiment today is away from Europe, and if we may take his speech before the New York State Grange at its face value, he apparently means to cater to this growing nationalist sentiment in the hope of catching votes for himself as a Presidential candidate. The League today "is not the League conceived by Woodrow Wilson," he said. "It might have been had the United States joined." But as we did not join, "the League has not developed through these years along the course contemplated by its founder." Therefore, "I do not favor American participation." Just what does this mean? Clearly nothing except that Governor Roosevelt has not the courage to stand out bravely for the internationalism he once sponsored. His attitude on the war debts is equally unrealistic. He would grant the European nations a respite "if it were considered advisable in the present condition of world finance," but he would "insist upon an accord as to when payments should begin

28. *Ibid.*, February 18, 1932, p. 2.

and in what amount." The high spot of his address was his denunciation of the Smoot–Hawley tariff, which he correctly pointed out was adding to the cost of living in this country. But instead of urging that the American tariff be reduced, or pledging himself to work to that end when and if he becomes President, he vaguely recommended that an international tariff conference be called.[29]

Later in the year 1932 Henry F. Pringle, in an article entitled "Franklin D. Roosevelt—Perched on the Bandwagon," published in the *Nation*, spoke of compromises and of the relation between William Randolph Hearst's demand and Governor Roosevelt's reply in his address before the Grange:

The habit of compromise grows. The intelligent politician gives in, at first, only when the probable result justifies it. After a time he bends his head when there is very little real need for it. Soon he is doing it constantly. Franklin Roosevelt, for example, has not for years been identified with the League of Nations. Newton Baker was carrying the onus of that troublesome issue and he was, in all probability, justified in his public statement that he would not force the United States to join. But on the night of February 1 of this year a letter lay on the Governor's desk at Albany, a letter in which William Randolph Hearst demanded an expression on the League. It is true that Hearst had published the letter in all his newspapers. It is also true, however, that his political influence is waning. If Roosevelt had declined to make a statement, the matter would have been forgotten in short order. On the night after receiving Hearst's letter, however, Roosevelt announced that he did not favor American participation in the League.

The truth is that Franklin Roosevelt hauls down banners under which he has marched in the past and unfurls no new ones to the skies. . . .[30]

Under the heading "Democratic Light Horses," the *New Republic*, commenting on steps recently taken by Democratic aspirants for the presidency, treated Mr. Baker and

29. *The Nation*, Vol. 134, February 17, 1932, p. 182.
30. *Ibid.*, April 27, 1932, p. 489.

Governor Roosevelt as playing the well-known trick of politicians:

Three men, all of whom have been discussed as possible Democratic nominees for President, have lately taken steps in furtherance of their various candidacies. Newton D. Baker, who has been fulfilling what is supposed to have been a personal pledge to President Wilson by recommending the League of Nations in season and out, has suddenly come down to earth and announced that the League, of course, is not an issue in this year's campaign. Thereupon Governor Franklin Roosevelt, presumably alarmed by the impetus thus accorded Mr. Baker's cause, has given the League an even more vigorous repudiation, and one which, considered purely as fact and not as political propaganda, has much to commend it. It is not, he explains, the League Mr. Wilson envisioned; if it were, he would still be for it. It is dominated now by selfish European Powers and America must keep clear of it. And as though to clinch his position as a Little American, Governor Roosevelt adds that the war debts must be paid in full—something which he, as an intelligent realist, must know cannot and will not happen, not even though, as he suggests, the tariff should be lowered to make it possible. . . .

. . . The statements of Messrs. Roosevelt and Baker give good examples of the old trick of the politicians—trying to be all things to all men, to seem isolationist to those who want isolation and internationalist and cooperative for the other school. . . .[31]

Among thoughtful and earnest advocates of internationalism, Governor Roosevelt's renunciation of the League on February 2, 1932, dropped with a crash. And, while they were deeply concerned with the political aspects of the Governor's declaration of faith, they sought especially to refute the argument he had made in support of his new position. A fairly representative illustration of their case against his contentions was supplied by Manley O. Hudson, elected Judge of the World Court in 1936, and a defender of the League and international cooperation, in a letter to the *New York Times*, dated February 10, 1932:

31. *New Republic*, February 17, 1932, p. 5.

Governor Roosevelt's address to the New York State Grange must be a profound disappointment to many Americans interested in our foreign policy. As a program, it contains no constructive suggestions. Instead, it expresses a negative attitude which would turn the clock back on advances already made by the United States in international cooperation.

To explain the reversal of his own attitude, Governor Roosevelt said that "the League of Nations today is not the League conceived by Woodrow Wilson," that it "has not developed through these years along the course contemplated by the founder." Even if that were true, it would not be a justification for his position. Only if Mr. Wilson had been omniscient could he have foreseen all of the post-war developments.

"Too often, through these years," said Governor Roosevelt, "the League's major function has been not the broad, overwhelming purpose of world peace . . ." The major function of the League has never been anything else than safeguarding the world's peace. For ten years it has been engaged in an effort to complete our law concerning pacific settlement. It has functioned in numerous disputes, not all of which have been between European States. For months the Council has been earnestly seeking ways of securing peace in the Far East. Surely Governor Roosevelt does not disapprove the Council's making such an effort. Does he approve the hot-and-cold attitude of our government? Does he really believe that at Shanghai, for instance, our government should play a lone hand? Or that if we cooperate with other powers, as we are doing, such cooperation is more effective outside the League?

"American participation," Governor Roosevelt said, "would not serve the highest purpose of the prevention of war . . ." He does not mention the World Court, created by the League of Nations. Nor does he mention the General Act for Pacific Settlement, adopted by the Assembly of the League of Nations in 1928. Are these accomplishments not "in accordance with fundamental American ideals"?

Governor Roosevelt shows no appreciation of the extent to which the government of the United States is now participating in various activities of the League of Nations. Our government has gradually and laboriously, over a period of ten years, worked out methods by which the United States is taking a large part in the activities at Geneva.

Nor does Governor Roosevelt offer any positive policy. He says that "what the world needs most today is a national policy which will make us an example of national honor to other nations." Suppose his policy were adopted by all of the fifty-five members of the League of Nations. Logically it would mean that they should abandon the League. How can the United States better make herself an "example" than by pushing forward organized international cooperation to meet the day-to-day needs of the world?

Governor Roosevelt envisages a "trade conference with the other nations of the world" at which other nations "will meet us half-way and put all their cards on the table." He seems to be unaware of the fact that many such conferences have been held in Geneva during the past few years, and that the United States has participated in some of them, and has even signed and ratified some of the treaties drawn up at such conferences.

He wants us to "call a meeting of our debtors here, and not in Europe, and demand an understanding." He reminds the farmers that they are "dwellers in a world in which economic and political conditions that affect one nation affect many nations." Yet he repudiates the possibility of our joining with other nations to deal with such conditions by sharing a common international responsibility.

Governor Roosevelt states that "the world ship of state . . . can steer safely home by unity of action." He thinks it possible that "by economic cooperation this nation can revive the trade of the world as well as trade within our own borders." Yet he states that "the highest ideals of America demand that, with strict adherence to the principles of Washington, we maintain our international freedom." Apparently, our cooperation to meet the needs of the twentieth century must be chained by eighteenth-century ideas.[32]

During the turmoil over internationalism in January, 1932, Mr. Hearst's New York papers continued to discuss the theme with reference to the fortunes of the Democratic party. In the issue of the *New York Evening Journal* for January 28, 1932, Claude Bowers, the distinguished political

32. *New York Times*, February 18, 1932.

writer from Indiana, declared with reference to the League of Nations that "as a party issue it is as dead as Pharaoh," and then laid stress on the central problem, as he saw it, namely, the crisis in domestic economy: "If the Democrats are wise in their generation they will not inject into the platform any controversial topic having no relation to the solution of the economic problems of these days. The politicians cannot make issues after all. They can put planks in a platform that no one thinks about, cares about, or talks about; and that is one of the vices of modern platforms . . . When millions are anxious about their ability to buy bread and prevent the eviction of their families for non-payment of rent, it is sheer nonsense to try to turn their attention to any academic questions. The next Democratic platform should be brief, positive, and confined to economic questions and only such political questions as are fundamental. . . ." [33]

While the controversy over the action of Governor Roosevelt in repudiating the League was raging, the *New York American* added fuel to the fire by chiding the Democrats for not having decided "which or what kind of man they will offer for President," and expressed wonder that a "Wilsonite" was still being considered: "The extraordinary thing is that, with the country now paying the gigantic bills incurred through the folly of the Wilson Administration, many Democrats actually advocate the choice of some League of Nations Wilsonite. The most conspicuous men mentioned are men that have committed themselves to the theory that this country is not able to take care of itself, that it should join the League of Nations and be governed by the decisions of other countries. It is inconceivable, but that is the fact." [34]

Under the caption, "Baker's Japanese Boycott a 'Sure Way to War,'" the *New York American*, on February 25, 1932, devoted an editorial to attacking Mr. Baker as an internation-

---

33. "The League Is Out" by Claude G. Bowers. *New York Evening Journal,* January 28, 1932.
34. *New York American,* February 7, 1932.

alist bent on pursuing internationalist doctrines despite his recent rejection of the League of Nations as a political issue. That was not enough for Mr. Hearst: he demanded nothing less than a whole-hearted renunciation of internationalism as a creed, and a commitment to the basic tenets of isolationism. Mr. Baker had recently approved the idea of an attempt to bring Japan to book by a resort to the boycott, and of this excursion into foreign affairs the *American* editorial declared:

Newton D. Baker's new pair of "spring heel" League of Nations gum shoes, that he now wears for 1932 campaign purposes, do not conceal the cloven hoofs of his internationalism.

In joining the demand upon Congress for a boycott of Japan he reveals himself in his true light.

He, like all the other internationalists who have half-heartedly abandoned the League of Nations for reasons of expediency, is still dominated by the passion for foreign entanglements.

They are too completely saturated in Wilsonian doctrines to wring themselves out on a mere political wringer.

Wherefore Mr. Baker, availing himself of the first opportunity for meddling in foreign affairs that has been presented since his recent back-tracking on the League of Nations issue, promptly proposes that the United States Government pursue a course of action which, in the opinion of the soundest thinkers in the Senate, WOULD BE TANTAMOUNT TO A DECLARATION OF WAR.

The ink scarcely dry upon his announcement that he would not seek to put the United States into the League of Nations until American public opinion favored the adherence of this Government to the League, the petition which he has now signed, and which has been presented to the President in favor of a war-making boycott against Japan, reveals Mr. Baker as deliberately seeking to influence that American public opinion upon which, according to his own statement, he was willing to wait until it should, of its own accord, become favorable to membership in the League. . . .

Even as late as April 24, 1932, Mr. Hearst, in a signed editorial, "A Plague o' Both Your Houses," paid his respects to both Alfred E. Smith and Governor Roosevelt. He assailed Mr. Smith for attacking Mr. Roosevelt in a recent speech, charged him with having been an internationalist himself in 1920, when the latter was a candidate for Vice-President on an internationalist platform, and with having supported Mr. Roosevelt in 1928 when he was a candidate for Governor of New York. Mr. Hearst also accused Mr. Smith of favoring "the international bankers' policy of European debt cancellation."

Having disposed of Mr. Smith as a candidate for the Democratic nomination at the coming party convention, Mr. Hearst gave an additional warning to Governor Roosevelt:

Mr. Roosevelt, on the other hand, repudiated the League of Nations this year, but not the League Court.

The Hearst papers accepted his repudiation as sincere, or at least opportune, but most of the press found it difficult to conceive how a gentleman who had been a fanatical friend of foreign nations all his political career could suddenly adopt the principles of George Washington and genuinely become imbued with loyal American spirit just on the eve of a Presidential election.

The fact, therefore, that Mr. Smith is still an adherent of the international bankers' policy of debt cancellation, while Mr. Roosevelt adheres merely to the devious policy of projecting the United States into foreign entanglements by the back door of the League Court, is probably not the real reason for the quarrel between Mr. Smith and Mr. Roosevelt. . . .

Mr. Roosevelt is concerned about the unknown American man.

He might well be concerned also about the American spirit, which seems to be equally unknown to him.

And he might become interested in the elemental principles of political economy, which seem to be likewise unknown to him.

The unknown American man is not going to be benefited by Mr. Roosevelt's plan to put this country into foreign complications by the trap door of the League Court.

He is not going to be benefited by Mr. Smith's plan to cancel foreign debts while the American man, known or unknown, makes up the amount cancelled in added taxes.

But the whole country will be benefited by putting eight million men to work and so starting prosperity on its way back to us . . .

In the meantime the days are passing, and Democratic opportunity is passing with them, while these Broadway and Bowery politicians quarrel over their own small policies and their own petty ambitions.

A plague on both their houses.

The Democratic Party needs a genuine leader—and also some genuine Democracy.[35]

About two weeks after this challenging editorial appeared in the *New York American,* it became known that one of Governor Roosevelt's leading sponsors, Joseph P. Kennedy, was in touch with Mr. Hearst in California. By that time it had been made evident that the Hearst–Garner–McAdoo combination had control of ninety delegates to the convention—forty-six from Texas and forty-four from California. Nominally assigned to Mr. Garner, who had no chance whatever to win the nomination, they probably could make or break Mr. Roosevelt at Chicago, by swinging one way or another.

In a dispatch from Warm Springs, Georgia, dated May 8, 1932, the *New York Times* stated that Mr. Kennedy was a guest of Governor Roosevelt there over the week end, and then reported on their negotiations in the following terms:

The visit of Mr. Kennedy excited some attention here [Warm Springs], as he had just come from California on a business trip, in which he paid a call on William Randolph Hearst. Mr. Hearst was one of the original figures behind the boom to swing the California delegation for Speaker Garner. After the Speaker won, the question of what his managers planned to do with his votes became vital.

The Roosevelt forces have expressed the opinion that the Garner votes will not be allied with the group backing former Governor Smith in a "stop-Roosevelt" drive and that they will be handled independently. Whether this subject was brought up in

35. *Ibid.,* April 24, 1932.

the conversations between Governor Roosevelt and Mr. Kennedy was not learned, although considerable curiosity on the point was manifested.[36]

The extent to which Governor Roosevelt's repudiation of the League of Nations, after Mr. Hearst's open demand upon him, influenced the results at the Democratic convention in Chicago is and must remain a matter of conjecture. Nor can its effects in the election be measured. Undoubtedly the action fell with shocking impact upon the faithful band of men and women who still believed in the League, in the advocacy of American membership, and in the ideals expounded by President Wilson; but the Governor's party men in that group could minimize its importance. One of them, for example, Professor James Hart, of the University of Virginia, referring to that subject, remarked: "He [Mr. Roosevelt] had little to say about foreign relations in the campaign, though before his nomination he had apparently won the favor of Hearst by a weak statement opposing the League of Nations. To some Wilson Democrats his addresses had the flavor of Woodrow Wilson diluted with water." [37] This at least put the case in its mildest and most favorable terms.

What purported to be an inside account of Governor Roosevelt's triumph at Chicago was given to the public in 1944 by Wendell Willkie in a brief but significant article headed, "Democratic Party's Share in Isolationism." [38] Mr. Willkie said that he and other "Baker Boys" worked at the Chicago convention in 1932 for a deadlock between Governor Roosevelt and Alfred E. Smith in the hope of winning the nomination for Mr. Baker, "the leader who almost alone

36. *New York Times*, May 9, 1932. In *After Seven Years* (Harper & Brothers, 1939), pp. 30 ff., Raymond Moley describes the dramatic scene at Chicago when the votes of the ninety delegates from Texas and California were cast for Governor Roosevelt. Mr. Moley leaves Mr. Hearst out of account in dealing with the negotiations which preceded the nomination of Mr. Roosevelt.

37. *American Year Book* (1932), p. 12.

38. *The United States News*, September 8, 1944; see above, p. 72.

through the dark isolationist twenties had fought consistently for world cooperation." But their labors, Mr. Willkie explained, were in vain: "Again we lost. For Garner and McAdoo and Hearst and Joe Kennedy and Jim Farley got together and no subject interested them less than the cause of world cooperation." At all events, although Governor Roosevelt's supporters were far from sure of victory when the Democratic convention assembled in 1932, they managed, with the aid of "Garner and McAdoo and Hearst and Joe Kennedy and Jim Farley," to nominate the Governor after a brief season of "agonizing" uncertainty.

In planning the strategy of his campaign for President, Mr. Roosevelt decided to say no more about the League of Nations. He had squarely met Mr. Hearst's terms and that was deemed sufficient. For this resolve to avoid foreign affairs, we have the testimony of Raymond Moley, a member of the Governor's inner circle, who told an intimate story of the campaign in *After Seven Years*. Speaking of plans for the campaign, Mr. Moley said: "After further consideration Roosevelt decided to sidetrack the idea of a speech on foreign relations. The Republicans had scrupulously avoided the issue. Public interest in it, during the fall, was at a low point. It seemed needless to raise the question. A declaration of what I understood to be Roosevelt's views on the subject was likely to cost him more undecided votes than it would make for him. He was already sure of the West and Middle West, where his views on foreign affairs would be immensely popular. There was no advantage in alienating those Eastern elements which would shy at his policies" (p. 62).

An examination of Mr. Roosevelt's campaign speeches printed in the first volume of his *Public Papers and Addresses* confirms Mr. Moley's version of the strategy. The League of Nations is not cited in the index of that volume (although a reference to it appears on page 157 of the text where a partial report of the February 2 speech of repudiation is given); and apparently it was not mentioned by Mr. Roosevelt during the campaign. He delivered no campaign address devoted to the League or to any phase of foreign affairs involving an attitude to the League or to the principle of collective security. A line-by-line scrutiny of the speeches contained in Volume I of the *Public Papers* reveals no words that could offend the stoutest isolationist in the West or anywhere in the country and no words that could give aid and comfort to any citizen who still believed that the United States should be associated with the League. Nor is reference to the World Court to be found in the index.

During his quest for the nomination and election, Mr. Roosevelt, in the fashion consecrated by party custom, paid tribute to the great leader, Woodrow Wilson; but not to Woodrow Wilson as the advocate of the League of Nations. Speaking at Richmond, Virginia, in April, 1932, he quoted a passage from Mr. Wilson's writings on George Washington (pp. 592–593). In an address at Saint Paul, Minnesota, during the same month he cited a comment by Mr. Wilson on the Federalists as "a group 'possessed of unity and informed by a conscious solidarity of interest' " (p. 628). At Chicago, in his speech of acceptance, Mr. Roosevelt declared: "Let us feel that in everything we do there still lives with us, if not the body, the great indomitable, unquenchable, progressive soul of our Commander-in-Chief, Woodrow Wilson" (p. 648). In an address to the Commonwealth Club at San Francisco, September 23, 1932, he appealed to the authority of Mr. Wilson on the issue of great combinations in industry and added that "had Mr. Wilson been able to devote eight years to domestic instead of to international affairs—we might have had a wholly different situation at the present time" in respect of concentrated financial power (pp. 749–751). At Baltimore, October 25, 1932, Mr. Roosevelt referred to "the nomination of our great leader, Woodrow Wilson" (p. 831). But in none of his appeals to the electorate did Mr. Roosevelt manifest the slightest sympathy for internationalism or the League of Nations which President Wilson had espoused with singleness of devotion.

It was especially with regard to the protective tariff that

Mr. Roosevelt touched upon matters related to foreign affairs during his campaign for election. The Democratic platform of 1932 had condemned the "protectionism" approved by the party platform in 1928 and advocated by Alfred E. Smith, the party's candidate. By terms quite explicit the tariff planks of 1932 gave the country the right to expect a rather drastic downward revision of the Republican tariff then in effect. In his campaign speeches Mr. Roosevelt, however, took another line, much to the chagrin of those Democrats who firmly expected an immediate reduction in the rates of duty levied on imports. He did, it is true, pour scorn on the Smoot–Hawley Tariff Act. But he proposed no immediate scaling of the rates by congressional action. On the contrary he advocated a resort to bargaining with other nations under the principle of reciprocal interest. He rebuffed the efforts of men such as Cordell Hull to force upon him a commitment to a direct and immediate lowering of trade barriers—a cutting of all rates by at least a flat 10 per cent.[39]

As the campaign grew hotter and his attacks on the tariff in force were widely publicized, Mr. Roosevelt was called upon to name the specific rates which he proposed to cut by reciprocal arrangements. After one speech in the Middle West in which he had characterized the Republican tariff rates as "outrageously excessive," hundreds of telegrams from farmers and processors descended upon him, asking for particulars, especially as to agricultural products. From the industrial East and Northeast came a number of inquiries about his suggested reductions in the rates on manufactured goods.

Late in the campaign, at Baltimore, October 25, Mr. Roosevelt replied to the clamor from the West: "Of course, it is absurd to talk of lowering tariff duties on farm products. . . . I promised to endeavor to restore the purchasing power of the farm dollars by making the tariff effective for agriculture, and raising the price of the farmers' products. I know

39. Moley, *op. cit.*, pp. 47 ff., for an account of the rebuff administered to free traders and tariff-for-revenue Democrats, including Mr. Hull.

of no effective excessively high tariff duties on farm products. I do not intend that such duties shall be lowered." At Boston a few days later he reassured farmers and added some assurance for manufacturers: "I favor—and do not let the false statements of my opponents deceive you—continued protection for American agriculture as well as American industry. I favor more than that. I advocate, and will continue to advocate, measures to give the farmer an added benefit, called a tariff benefit, to make the tariff effective on his products." [40]

A careful reading of Governor Roosevelt's speeches on the one phase of foreign affairs which he discussed at length —reduction of the tariff in the interest of prosperity for Americans and better relations with foreign countries— could give no satisfaction to internationalists of the Wilson school. The third of President Wilson's Fourteen Points read: "The removal, so far as possible, of all economic barriers and the establishment of an equality of trade conditions among all the nations consenting to the peace and associating themselves for its maintenance." Nationalistic commercial rivalry was, in Mr. Wilson's opinion, among the potent "causes" of war, and equal trade conditions were among the prime objectives and guarantees of peace offered by the League of Nations. But by the close of Mr. Roosevelt's campaign in 1932, this kind of economic internationalism had gone into the discard, along with talk about the League itself. The Cobden–Bright–Hull program of world peace through world free trade, Mr. Roosevelt had made clearly evident, formed no part of his policy and would receive no support in case of his triumph at the polls in November.

As Mr. Roosevelt's campaign for election proceeded according to the strategy just described, William Randolph Hearst's papers waxed more and more enthusiastic, and

---

40. *Public Papers,* I, 836, 853–854; and Moley, *op. cit.,* pp. 51 f. Mr. Moley remarks: "For the student of statesmanship the process [of reverse action] was instructive."

wound up on the eve of the election with an unqualified paean. Immediately after the nomination of Governor Roosevelt and Speaker Garner at Chicago, Mr. Hearst, in a signed editorial, gave this whole-hearted endorsement of the two men:

Franklin D. Roosevelt will make a great President of the United States, and John N. Garner will make a splendid Vice-President and presiding officer of the Senate.

Both men are eminently qualified for these positions by long years of skillful public work and faithful public service.

It will be an enormous benefit to this nation of ours to have two such men in commanding public positions,—men who not only have the democratic spirit to desire to serve the public interest, but who have also the experience and the proven competence to be able to do it. . . .

Governor Roosevelt and Speaker Garner will bring to bear upon the present situation and upon every situation which may arise not only distinguished ability, but a lifelong experience in legislative and executive means and methods. . . .

Governor Roosevelt and Speaker Garner are both competent public mechanics and it probably will not take them long after they are ensconced in authoritative office to fix our stalled national engine and set it going smoothly again.

Surely we need not be niggardly in the only compensation they will require, which is public approval.

As practical evidence of his executive competence, Governor Roosevelt can point to the most notable record which has been made as Governor of New York State since the days of Grover Cleveland. . . .

Governor Roosevelt has much of the calm and conscientious attention to the business in hand, no matter what office he occupies, as had President Coolidge, and he has also, like his distinguished cousin and namesake, Theodore Roosevelt, what has been described as Theodore Roosevelt's distinguishing characteristic,—the faculty of being unerringly right on questions affecting the popular welfare.

Franklin D. Roosevelt, like Theodore Roosevelt, is not only "right" in his desire to do the right thing, but "right" in his intuition and in his experienced knowledge of what is the right thing. . . .

"Words are good when backed by deeds and only so," said Theodore Roosevelt.

The patriotic words of Franklin D. Roosevelt and John N. Garner are backed by their record of patriotic deeds.[41]

Two days later, July 5, 1932, the *New York American* hailed Mr. Roosevelt as the man qualified to deal with the economic crisis, as safe for "honest, conscientious business men and financiers," and as safe for "the people of the United States":

Is Roosevelt a safe candidate?

This question echoes a similar inquiry which used to reverberate through Wall Street concerning the Democratic nominee's illustrious cousin.

Before the query can be satisfactorily answered one might counter, "Safe" for Whom?

If Governor Franklin D. Roosevelt's conduct as President, if elected, squares with his past acts and expressions he will not be altogether safe for heartless, heedless speculators and pyramiders and blue sky operators or for the greedy gangsters in the power industry who seek to appropriate to themselves public facilities.

Governor Roosevelt's "Forgotten Man" radio speech indicates that he will not be complacently safe for and in smug harmony with those who, like President Hoover, preach the doctrine of "rugged individualism" to needy persons who are without employment, while practicing tender paternalism in the direction of financing the financiers.

But everything in Governor Roosevelt's record and program indicates clearly that he will be constructively and comfortingly safe for honest, conscientious business men and financiers. . . .

As the Presidential election looms, economic and labor problems are the dominant issues of the campaign. If voters want to use intelligent discrimination they will examine the record to test how Messrs. Roosevelt and Hoover reacted to the economic catastrophe. . . .

41. *New York American*, July 3, 1932, p. 1.

Now that time gives an opportunity to check up on the prognostications of the two men, the record plainly shows that Mr. Roosevelt has been far nearer right than Mr. Hoover.

In time of crisis, it is prudent to rely on men of proven worth, not on bunglers.

Franklin D. Roosevelt is safe for the people of the United States.[42]

As the campaign advanced, Mr. Hearst's *New York American* commended Governor Roosevelt's stand on the three issues of the conflict which had a bearing on foreign affairs: the cancellation of the debts owed to the Government of the United States by its former associates in World War I; tariff revision; and the expansion of the American Navy. The first of these issues—debt cancellation—would inevitably confront Mr. Roosevelt if successful at the polls in November, and Mr. Hearst rejoiced that in this case cancellation would be opposed: "The Democratic national platform declares against such debt cancellation. The Democratic Presidential candidate, Franklin D. Roosevelt, declares against such debt cancellation." [43]

On August 4, 1932, before Governor Roosevelt had toned down the language of his assault on the high protective tariff then in force, Mr. Hearst's *New York American* rejoiced in the Governor's suggestion for a "thoroughgoing revision of tariff policies," and connected it approvingly with the collection of the debts owed to the United States by foreign governments:

Franklin D. Roosevelt has given an American interpretation of the progress toward sound economics in international affairs which was attained at the Lausanne Conference.

Though suggesting a formula for resumption of more friendly economic intercourse, Governor Roosevelt unequivocally turns his back on the suggestion that Uncle Sam assume all of the unliquidated cost of the great war.

42. *Ibid.,* July 5, 1932, p. 1.
43. *Ibid.,* July 23, 1932. See below, Chap. VI.

Instead of giving aid and comfort to the renewed propaganda in favor of debt repudiation by great nations, Governor Roosevelt proposed a realistic course which would enable debtor countries to meet their obligations and retain their credit.

The Governor's remarks on this subject are heartening, and, if they prevail, they should start a renaissance of confidence throughout the world.

Recognizing the difficulties attendant on international transfers of funds under prevailing worldwide depression, the Democratic standard bearer suggests a thoroughgoing revision of tariff policies which will give a rebirth to trade among nations. . . .

Mr. Roosevelt has spoken with prophetic wisdom, and the country should follow him on this issue.[44]

When Governor Roosevelt couched tariff revision in terms of reciprocal bargaining with foreign powers, the *New York American* applauded that formula without reservations:

The two major candidates for the Presidency differ vitally on the issue of the tariff.

Franklin D. Roosevelt, in his address at Seattle, Washington, threw down the gauntlet to the Administration. . . .

Thus Mr. Roosevelt stands four square for the principle of reciprocity, which the Hearst newspapers have advocated for decades. He injects Yankee shrewdness and the principle of sales promotion into tariff making, whereas the Grundy tariff has tended to destroy the export trade and to antagonize our foreign customers.

The Hearst papers do not advocate indiscriminate tariff reduction, but rather reductions of the American tariff in response to trade concessions and advantages by other countries. . . .

Mr. Roosevelt urges that the United States take the initiative and leadership in revising tariff schedules to make profitable reciprocal foreign trade feasible.

On the other hand, Mr. Hoover, in the face of the current stagnation, insists on standing pat.

44. "Roosevelt Tariff Policy Will Make Collection of War Debt Feasible," *New York American*, August 4, 1932.

The policy of standing pat was a plausible one when conditions were satisfactory. It is an unsatisfactory policy when aggressive action is necessary to insure business recovery.[45]

Long an uncompromising opponent of Republican efforts to block the naval race among the great powers and an ardent advocate of a "big navy," with an eye to a possible war against Japan, Mr. Hearst's *New York American* attacked the Hoover Administration for "the destruction" of the American people's navy; and, under the heading "Democratic Victory Will Save American Navy and Give Shipworkers Jobs," made a plea for the election of the Democratic ticket: "Roosevelt and Garner will be inaugurated none too soon to save what is left of the American Navy and put thousands of jobless American wage earners to work replacing the ships that have become obsolete, and restoring to strength the strong right arm of America's national defense." [46]

Taking up this theme again two weeks later, the *New York American* assured the country that "Roosevelt Leadership Will Restore America's Historic Naval Policies":

Today's observance of Theodore Roosevelt's birthday as Navy Day has a new meaning for the American people.

Theodore Roosevelt was not a "Little Navy" man. His policy was at all times a powerful Navy. Out of his policy developed our historic policy of a Navy at all times "equal to the strongest."

That policy was established by Congress, reaffirmed by treaties and repeatedly endorsed by the American people at the polls. But under the Hoover Administration, our sound and patriotic policy has been scrapped in favor of a fatuous pacifism. . . .

This disgraceful chapter of neglect and naval deterioration will be ended next March, when the American people will have put another Roosevelt in the White House.

Ever since he entered public life as a young man, Franklin D. Roosevelt has emulated the example of his illustrious kinsman by

45. *New York American*, September 28, 1932.
46. *Ibid.*, October 12, 1932.

urging upon his countrymen the imperative duty of maintaining a strong Navy as "the surest guarantee of peace. . . ."

Navy Day finds our people this year fully resolved to end the steady decline of the American Navy in both men and ships, and to begin its restoration to complete equality with the strongest foreign power in every class of combatant ships.

And during the next four years, in fulfillment of this high purpose, the American people will observe the birthday of Theodore Roosevelt as Navy Day with a new spirit and a new patriotism, under the quickening leadership of Franklin D. Roosevelt as President and Commander-in-Chief.[47]

On November 6, 1932, after Governor Roosevelt had closed his campaign and the election was at hand, Mr. Hearst, in a signed editorial, commended the Governor to the American people in terms personal and unequivocal:

. . . Franklin D. Roosevelt was good enough to be Assistant Secretary of the Navy under Wilson.

He was good enough to be nominated by the Democrats for Vice-President in 1920.

He was good enough to nominate the Democratic candidate for President in 1928.

He was good enough to carry New York for Governor that year, although the National ticket lost it.

He was good enough to be renominated for Governor of New York State in 1930 and to carry the State by over seven hundred thousand plurality.

He was good enough to have the Democratic delegates of a vast majority of the States of the Union nominate him at Chicago in 1932 for President of the United States.

He has always been honest and frank and sincere with the public.

He has always been true to his principles and faithful to his pledges.

He has always been constructive and always conservative in the way which would best conserve the public interest.

What has he done in all his years of public service which is not constructive and conservative? . . .

47. *Ibid.*, October 27, 1932.

If you want to select a President to lead us out of the depression and to protect your interests now and hereafter, do not pick the man whom Wall Street wants, but vote for Franklin D. Roosevelt—capable, conscientious and conservative—and ever faithful to his public trust.[48]

By a curious shift in events, President Hoover, the Republican candidate in 1932, was widely represented, especially by the Hearst press, as an internationalist, while Governor Roosevelt was made to appear a simon-pure American. It is true that, in the campaign of 1932, the Republican party and Mr. Hoover stood fast by the platform promise to refuse membership in the League of Nations; while offering to cooperate with it in scientific, humanitarian, and economic undertakings, including the reduction of armaments. But before the campaign opened and while it was in progress, President Hoover's Administration or, at all events, his Secretary of State, Henry L. Stimson, was skirting around the edges of political cooperation with the League; and advocates of internationalism were insisting that the incorrigible isolationists of 1920 were more internationalist in 1932 than the Democrats.[49]

This turn in Republican foreign policy during President Hoover's Administration was due to special circumstances. Republicans had been the chief abettors of imperialism in the Far East since the war with Spain in 1898. They had employed that form of American intervention in China known as "the Open Door." Despite vehement protests from Democrats against this imperialism as foreboding tragedy for the American Republic,[50] Republican Administrations had forged

48. *Ibid.*, November 6, 1932, pp. 1–2.
49. The literature of this apparent shift in Republican tactics is large; but brief reviews of it by competent authorities are to be found in the *American Year Book* for the years 1931 and 1932, especially in the sections dealing with the United States and the League and World Affairs.
50. Under the leadership of William Jennings Bryan the Democrats made imperialism the paramount issue in 1900. In their platform they declared: "we warn the American people that imperialism abroad will lead quickly and inevitably to despotism at home"; they condemned "the greedy commercialism" which dictated the Philippine policy of the Republican Administration;

ahead, encouraging and lending diplomatic support to capitalistic struggles for markets, investment opportunities, and commercial advantages in the Far East. With increasing zest, they pursued this course as the United States became more and more industrialized and as Japan, having adopted machine processes of manufacturing, pressed harder and harder for commodity outlets on the mainland of Asia in competition with American business enterprise.

The growing friction between the United States and Japan, augmented by the manner in which Congress in 1924 passed legislation excluding Japanese immigrants from the United States, moved swiftly toward an explosion as time passed. In 1931 Japanese militarists, after a clash with Chinese forces in Manchuria, seized that province and, the following year, they transformed it into a puppet state, Manchukuo, headed by a puppet dictator, Henry Pu Yi, formerly the boy Emperor of China. These "incidents," for many reasons, immediately excited the Hoover Administration.

Both President Hoover and Secretary Stimson had acquired special knowledge of Oriental affairs. From 1895 to 1913 Mr. Hoover had been engaged in promoting business enterprises in China, India, and other parts of the world. As Secretary of Commerce under Presidents Harding and Coolidge, he had expanded the agencies for pushing foreign commerce and, while issuing warnings against unsound financing, had supported what were regarded as the "legitimate" drives of American capitalists for commercial and investment opportunities in foreign countries. His Secretary of State, Mr. Stimson, had been Secretary of War under President Taft in the age of "dollar diplomacy," and Governor General of the Philippines.

Owing to his long absences from the country, during the

they referred to the use of American armed forces to put down the Philippine insurrection, as "the war of 'criminal aggression.'" The Democrats also prophesied that Republican imperialism, if not checked, would lead to militarism, a vast military establishment, "a sure forerunner of compulsory military service and conscription." E. Stanwood, *A History of the Presidency* (1897–1916), chap. 1, "'Imperialism' the 'Paramount Issue.'"

years from 1895 to 1913, Mr. Hoover, whatever his political sympathies, had not been involved at first hand in the imperialist politics of the Republicans and had taken no public part in it. At all events, his personal opinions on the subject in 1932 remained undisclosed. Secretary Stimson, on the other hand, though well advertised as an advocate of international peace, was, in fact, an imperialist of the Theodore Roosevelt–Lodge–Mahan–Beveridge school.[51] He advocated a "strong" policy in the Far East and was vehemently hostile to independence for the Philippine Islands.

At a hearing on a Philippine independence bill held in 1930 by the Senate Committee on Territories and Insular Affairs, Mr. Stimson gave the classical reasons of imperialism for blocking Philippine independence: "First, I am opposed to it, because I believe it would be disastrous to the Philippine people; second, I am opposed to it, because I believe it would be disastrous to the interests of the United States both on the islands and in the Far East; and, third, I am opposed to it, because I believe it would inevitably create a general unsettlement of affairs in the Far East, in connection with the present conditions in the different countries having interests in and exercising sovereignty there," including, of course, the imperialist powers, Great Britain, France, and Holland.[52]

President Hoover likewise opposed independence for the Philippines as projected in the bill which was finally passed by Congress in December, 1932; but on different grounds. As far as the public record stood, he had been in times past no advocate of imperialism backed by the engines of government, with war as the *ultima ratio*. The bill in question had been designed and pressed largely under the drive of Democrats, who then had a majority in the House of Representa-

51. *Imperialism* is used in this volume as meaning: employment of the engines of government and diplomacy to acquire territories, protectorates, and/or spheres of influence occupied usually by other races or peoples, and to promote industrial, trade, and investment opportunities in competition with other imperialist powers or on occasion in collaboration with them where there is mutuality of interests or perils.

52. *Hearings*, Pt. 7, for May 22, 1930, pp. 658 ff.

tives and, in combination with insurgent Republicans, controlled the Senate. Although accompanied by noble professions made in the name of liberty, the measure had been especially supported by agricultural and labor interests as a bar to Philippine competition.

As finally formulated, the independence bill was, in any case, debatable. It was no clear-cut proposal for liquidating the imperialist interests of the United States in the Far East, once and for all. In respect of Philippine independence as provided for in the bill, President Hoover took the position maintained by the old school of "isolationists" who had condemned the imperialist adventure since 1900; namely, that independence should be granted to the Philippines, that the separation should be "complete and absolute," that the United States should hold no naval bases there and should henceforth assume no responsibility for the defense of the Islands.[53]

But whatever may have been President Hoover's attitude to American imperialism as policy, Mr. Stimson was his Secretary of State; and Mr. Stimson took the lead in dealing with the controversy over Manchuria in 1931–32. With an invincible persistence he eagerly sought support for his program of checkmating Japan from all favorable quarters, including the League of Nations and especially Great Britain and France as great powers with "vital interests" in the Far East and as members of the League. He entered into communications with the Governments of Great Britain and France; and, presumably as a representative of the Hoover Administration, he went to Geneva in April, 1932, to search for help. There he was greeted with enthusiasm by internationalists; and his appearance was treated as if foreshadowing a turn of the United States in the direction of political cooperation with the League.

53. W. S. Myers, *The Foreign Policies of Herbert Hoover, 1929–1933* (Charles Scribner's Sons, 1940), pp. 169 ff. By 1932 even Democrats had lost so much of their anti-imperialist zeal that they were not prepared to grant unconditional independence to the Philippines and withdraw definitely and completely from this imperialist adventure in the Far East.

In commenting on Secretary Stimson's visit to the League, Arthur Sweetser, then serving as an American member of the League Secretariat, reported: "A symbolic illustration of America's developing attitude occurred in April when for the first time in the history of the League a Secretary of State of the United States crossed the League's threshold and quietly and informally took his seat in a League meeting. Mr. Stimson was but following in the footsteps of Sir Austen Chamberlain, Aristide Briand, Gustav Stresemann and many others responsible for the foreign policies of their governments." [54] Indeed Secretary Stimson lent some countenance to this interpretation of his visit by announcing publicly: "Such personal contact is of the greatest assistance in promoting our best interests in the field of foreign affairs and contributes to a better understanding between the governments concerned and the individuals conducting those affairs." [55]

But Great Britain and France were cold to Secretary Stimson's advances, and politely steered a course of neutrality. The League of Nations, after sponsoring an investigation, finally declined to risk belligerent action in line with Mr. Stimson's desires. The United States naval command, recognizing the inadequacy of the American fleet then in being, was unwilling at the moment to embark on war with Japan. Even so, American advocates of internationalism insisted on seeing in the maneuvers of Secretary Stimson a sign that the United States was about to become affiliated with the League of Nations; when as a matter of fact he was seeking, among other things, parallel support for American interests in the Orient, and seeking it through a "concert of nations" in the historic style set by John Hay, Secretary of State during the imperialist outburst at the beginning of the twentieth century.

About the only thing that came out of the Manchurian affair immediately was an official pronouncement on the part

54. *American Year Book* (1932), p. 86.
55. *Ibid.* (1932).

of the United States on January 7, 1932. This pronouncement was called "the Hoover doctrine" by some observers
and "the Stimson doctrine" by friends of the Secretary.[56]
Briefly, it was a declaration that the United States would not
admit the legality or accept the validity of any situation,
agreement, or treaty brought about in contravention of the
treaty rights of the United States or its citizens in China and
contrary to the Open Door policy, the Nine-Power Treaty
of 1923, or the Kellogg–Briand Pact of 1928 by which nearly
all nations renounced war as an instrument of national policy
(with significant reservations, especially by France and
Great Britain).[57] This action by the Department of State in
proclaiming a non-recognition doctrine was greeted by internationalists as a movement in their direction, as a new form
or phase of internationalism for the United States—mild, it is
true, but promising and to be encouraged.

Thus Secretary Stimson's pronouncements and diplomatic
maneuvers afforded some grounds for the charge or the claim
that the Republicans were more internationalist than the
Democrats in 1932. But to American citizens bogged down
in the slough of unemployment, poverty, and distress known
as "the Great Depression," Secretary Stimson's "new" internationalism offered few promises of relief. At all events, they
were at the moment in no mood for a war with Japan over
the Manchurian "incident." Nor did staunch internationalists
among the Democrats become so disgruntled over Governor
Roosevelt's repudiation of the League of Nations that they
were ready for a wholesale desertion of the party at the polls
in November, 1932. Such conclusions at least seem to be
warranted by the fact that on election day Governor Roosevelt carried forty-two of the forty-eight states in the Union.

56. Indeed there were, apparently, two doctrines: one conceived and followed by President Hoover, with moral implications only; and another by
Secretary Stimson, with imperialist and internationalist implications involving,
unless the doctrine was to be futile, the agency of sanctions, and war in case
sanctions failed. Myers, *op. cit.*, pp. 166, 167, 229 n., 253, and *passim*. See below,
pp. 134 ff.

57. *American Year Book* (1932), pp. 59 ff.

CHAPTER VI

President Roosevelt Adheres to an Isolationist Policy in 1933

As a candidate for President, Mr. Roosevelt was free to avoid saying anything about foreign policy during his campaign; but after his victory at the polls, and particularly after his inauguration on March 4, 1933, he confronted four inescapable issues of that nature. Three of the issues involved, or were made to involve, the tenets of isolation and internationalism. The fourth, though given an internationalist flavor, was mainly imperialist in origins and practical upshot. All of them had specific bearings on the program of national action which Mr. Roosevelt and his close advisers had formulated with a view to recovery and reform in the United States and hence brought to a test the quality of his political and social philosophy.

At the center of the controversy lay one thorny question: In order to bring about a rapid rise in production, widen the market for American goods, and overcome the cyclical disasters that had long beset American economy, shall the United States rely mainly on domestic measures of reform or shall it seek an enlargement of the foreign markets by some process of negotiation and agreement with foreign governments? There was the crux of the matter as Mr. Roosevelt and his immediate counselors saw it.

Leading Republicans had long insisted that the pot of gold —ever-expanding markets—lay under the rainbow of imperialism. Old-line Democrats had long offered free trade or tariff reductions as the way to never-failing prosperity. President Hoover had been maintaining that the latest of the great depressions originated largely in European disorders and that certain actions in the international sphere were necessary to recovery in the United States. Mr. Roosevelt and his "brain trust," on the other hand, regarded these expedients of prosperity as exploded by the experiences of history and were of the opinion that, whatever was done in the international sphere, the United States must depend mainly and emphatically on domestic measures in striving to conquer the economic depression and stabilize prosperity.

One of the imperatives in foreign relations that confronted Mr. Roosevelt was a decision as to the debts which the associates of the United States in the first World War owed to the Federal Government. Most of these debts had been formally recognized and funded after the conclusion of the war. Debtors had been making payments on them as written in the bond until late in December, 1931, when Congress, at the solicitation of President Hoover, had sought to ease the tension in European economy by granting a year's moratorium. In December, 1932, however, on the expiration of the moratorium, the whole question of payment was opened again; France defaulted on her payment then due; and a general default was in sight.

Although apparently a mere matter of finance and good faith, the debts were entangled, in fact or by design, in primary conceptions of foreign policy. By internationalists, American and European, it was claimed that the tariff laws of the United States rendered payment impossible and that a cancellation or material reduction of the debts, coupled with a lowering of customs duties, was a prerequisite to economic recovery in this country and abroad. It was further asserted by American friends of the Entente Allies that cancellation would be an act of justice to them—an overdue recognition of the blood and treasure they sacrificed in a common cause of democracy and liberty before the United States saw fit to take up its own defense of these matters. To isolationists and indeed to most Senators and Representatives in Congress, Democrats and Republicans alike, such opinions were anathema: above all, to those Americans who now deemed the late war and the Versailles settlement to be the sour fruits of a great imperialistic quarrel.[1]

Powerful economic interests, as well as internationalist sentiments, were behind the movement to cancel the war debts or at least scale them to negligible amounts. American bankers had floated foreign loans by the billions during the years of Republican supremacy, including loans to German governments, central and local, and to German industries; and American investors—private persons, banks, and institutions—were in peril of losing heavily, perhaps all they had risked. If the war debts owed to the Government of the United States could be scaled, if expenditures for armaments in Europe could be cut down, then the prospects of collecting interest and installments on the other debts, owed to American banks and investors, would be brighter. So, many bankers and investors, caught in the falling structure of European economy (if it deserved that name), were eager to cancel the governmental war debts and transfer the cost of carrying that burden to the taxpayers of the United States. Their agents and the press which reflected their interests were actively engaged, along with the internationalists, in creating an opinion that prosperity could be recovered only if Congress would settle the debt question by wiping out the debts or reducing them to nominal sums. In this way, it was argued, Europeans could begin to buy American goods in large quantities and set the wheels of American industries revolving at high speed.

With these positions on the issue of the foreign debts, Mr. Roosevelt and his counselors were thoroughly familiar. Mr. Roosevelt had rejected them, as well as the League of Nations, in his Grange address of February 2, 1932; and, while willing to be considerate in dealing with the debtors, he was opposed to a cancellation or drastic reduction of the debts. Moreover, during the campaign he had refused to adopt Cordell Hull's proposal to attack the protective tariff by the

1. For a definition of imperialism, see p. 113 n.

traditional method of radically reducing the high rates all along the line by one stroke.

A few days after his election to the presidency, the issue of the war debts was brought urgently to Governor Roosevelt's attention by a letter from President Hoover, dated at the White House November 12, 1932, inviting him to a personal conference in Washington on the subject. In his message to the Governor, President Hoover took a position on the question that was pleasing, if not wholly satisfactory, to internationalists. To be sure he stated that he did not favor cancellation. Whatever his private opinion may have been, his endorsement of cancellation would have been futile in view of the open hostility in both houses of Congress to any such project.

But President Hoover declared to Governor Roosevelt that "we should be receptive to proposals from our debtors of tangible compensation in other forms than direct [cash] payment in expansion of markets for the products of our labor and our farms." He also connected the debts with disarmament: "substantial reduction of world armament which will relieve our own and world burdens and dangers has a bearing upon this question." Mr. Hoover likewise informed the Governor that he had recommended to Congress the creation of a debt commission to make a study of the subject. This expedient was perhaps the only concession he could wring from Congress. At any rate President Hoover hoped that through it he might set in train the solution of the debt problem.[2]

Governor Roosevelt and his advisers had a very definite idea of what it was that President Hoover was contemplating: commitment of the new Administration to a policy that was internationalist in conception. Raymond Moley later wrote that Mr. Roosevelt and he talked over the problems raised by the Hoover proposal and that to them the situation seemed to be "something like this":

2. For the correspondence, see Roosevelt, *Public Papers*, I, 873 ff.

The World War had been financed in large part, both before and after 1917, by the billions of dollars of loans we had made and credits we had granted to the Allies. At the end of the war the Allies had proposed to draw from Germany, in the form of reparations, at least enough to pay back what they owed us. This fantastic burden of debt Germany could not discharge, even if she was permitted to export goods which competed with their own. At the same time we had found that our farmers and industrial producers could not continue to find expanding markets abroad as Europe's production reached and exceeded prewar levels. Hence we had *lent* Europe the money to buy our products, or, if you will, to pay us what she owed us.

This jerry-built structure had begun to crumble the instant we ceased to make foreign loans, and the aftermath of its disintegration was political and economic crisis in Europe and the collapse of the system of international economics which had, up to that time, prevailed.

Those who believed that such a collapse must mark the end of civilization, those to whom the gold-standard and free-trade ideals were the twin deities of an unshakable orthodoxy—the international bankers, the majority of our economists, and almost every graduate of every Eastern university who had dipped into the fields of foreign relations or economics—had undertaken to discover a remedy for it. By common consent they had settled upon the reparations and the war debts. If these were canceled (these particular debts among all debts—public and private) or traded for general European disarmament or British resumption of the gold standard or what not, we would root out the cause of our troubles, they had announced. And so ponderous were the arguments that buttressed this formula in the Atlantic states —in academic and presumably "intellectual" circles, at any rate —that it was actually unrespectable not to accept them. There and in Europe, the more vociferously they were championed the more passionately they were believed. Only their prospective dupes, the majority of American citizens, stubbornly refused to swallow them.[3]

Having made some such analysis of the situation, Governor Roosevelt and Mr. Moley went to the White House

3. *After Seven Years*, p. 69.

and conferred with President Hoover and his Secretary of the Treasury, Ogden Mills. At the conference and in a subsequent statement to the press, Mr. Roosevelt lent no countenance to President Hoover's idea of easing down the debts or appointing a commission to start actions which might be headed in that direction. He indicated to Mr. Hoover that any measures proposed by the debtors should be duly considered, but neither at the conference nor in his statement about it to the press did he give the slightest consolation to international bankers, the majority of American economists, or the advocates of internationalism.

Of Mr. Roosevelt's statement, his aide, Raymond Moley, afterward wrote: "Viewed wholly apart from the debt question, the statement was of profound importance because it was the first spectacular step Roosevelt took to differentiate his foreign policy from that of the internationalists. It served notice on the League advocates, the pro-sanctionists, and those who desired a revival of foreign lending that Roosevelt was likely to be no Herbert Hoover or Henry Stimson on foreign affairs. It was a warning that the New Deal rejected the point of view of those who would make us parties to a political and economic alliance with England and France —policing the world, maintaining the international *status quo*, and seeking to enforce peace through threats of war. . . . The kickback in the Eastern papers, after Roosevelt's statement of November 23 was sharp." [4]

Neither in his subsequent negotiations with President Hoover over the war debts and related subjects, nor after he was inaugurated, did Mr. Roosevelt reveal any modification of his hostility to the internationalist thesis that a cancellation of the debts was indispensable to national recovery. He demonstrated that, as he had promised, he would listen to proposals of the debtors for alterations in the bond and that he cherished hopes of friendly cooperation among the nations; but nothing came of the debt negotiations which ensued in the spring and summer of 1933. Congress remained obdurate

4. *Ibid.*, pp. 78 f.

in its refusal to cancel. President Roosevelt was able to drive his domestic measures for recovery through both houses of Congress with a rapidity that was breath-taking: in other words, his power of leadership was extraordinary; and yet, if he had any faith whatever in debt cancellation as a design for recovery, he made no evident effort to convert Congress to that faith.

The second item on the calendar of foreign affairs that Mr. Roosevelt encountered after his election to the presidency was the issue of the policy to be pursued by the United States at the Disarmament Conference then in session at Geneva. This international assembly had been convened in February, 1932, under the auspices of the League of Nations, in a tardy fulfilment of a pledge made in the Treaty of Versailles; and delegates from the United States, sent by President Hoover, were cooperating in the proceedings throughout that year.

From the outset this Conference had been snarled in political controversies over collective security; for several of the nations represented in it, France in particular, were unwilling to approve real reductions in armaments without having guarantees of protection against possible aggressors, especially against Germany. Hence the question had arisen at Geneva whether, in case disarmament could be agreed upon, the United States would join in a pact of nations binding all the signatories to employ sanctions and if need be armed force against any aggressor designated by a common council. For internationalists this seemed to be an opportunity, in the name of peace, to get the signature of the United States to a covenant akin to that of the League of Nations—a covenant for designating aggressors and suppressing them by force, economic, discriminatory, or military. Accordingly Americans opposed to political entanglements in European and Asiatic conflicts were suspicious of all the maneuvers connected with "disarmament."

In December, 1932, several weeks before his inauguration

as President of the United States, Mr. Roosevelt was asked to consider the matter of what was to be done at the Disarmament Conference. Norman Davis, an American delegate to that assembly, an internationalist of the Woodrow Wilson school, fresh from Europe, laid the problem squarely before Mr. Roosevelt late in that month, at more than one long session. What commitments, if any, the Governor then made to Mr. Davis do not seem to be a matter of record, but there are grounds for inferring that he privately encouraged him to hope for American participation of some kind in collective action to protect nations against possible aggressors in case they agreed to a substantial or general reduction of armaments.

For this inference certain fragments of evidence offer justification. On January 11, 1933, for instance, Mr. Roosevelt, without consulting the aides who had served him during the campaign, issued a statement endorsing President Hoover's message to Congress on January 10, 1933, asking for legislation empowering the President at his discretion to limit or forbid the shipment of arms for military purposes. Such a measure, President Hoover declared, "would at least enable the Executive in special cases to place the United States in line with other nations who are willing to make such sacrifices in the prevention of military conflicts." [5]

After his inauguration, however, President Roosevelt did not press upon Congress any measure binding the Executive to embargo the export of arms to an aggressor designated in Europe. But in March, 1933, he appointed Norman Davis ambassador-at-large in charge of the American delegation at the Disarmament Conference at Geneva. Early in May, 1933, subsequent to a long conference with President Roosevelt held at Washington in April, the British Prime Minister, Ramsay MacDonald, issued a statement in London intimating that the United States was willing to take its part

5. R. L. Wilbur and A. M. Hyde, *The Hoover Policies* (Charles Scribner's Sons, 1937), p. 604.

in consultative pacts against war, on certain conditions. Norman Davis followed this lead by making a similar announcement, as head of the American delegation to Geneva.

By such incidents American internationalists were led to believe that the peace sentiments of the United States, now running parallel to imperialist sentiments in respect of pressure on Japan, could be channeled, through "disarmament" negotiations, into a positive commitment for putting down aggressors by "collective" action. For the moment this was the type of endeavor most promising to internationalists. To be sure, in his speech of February 2, 1932, Mr. Roosevelt had openly and emphatically declared himself against joining the League and against entanglements in the power politics of Europe; and during his campaign for President he had ignored all pleas for even a gesture in the direction of internationalism. But leaders among American internationalists, aware that a frontal assault would be forlorn, took a new line: if the United States would enter a "consultative pact" with other nations in connection with disarmament, the principle of "collective security" could be realized and at the same time Germany and Japan could be held down. Furthermore, some general statements made by Mr. Roosevelt, or in his name, led new directionists to believe that he would support them.

The expectation that President Roosevelt would repudiate in May, 1933, his repudiation of February 2, 1932, and adopt a policy of "collective security" for the United States was, however, soon dispelled by specifications which admitted of no doubt. That he still adhered to his commitment of February 2 was forcefully illustrated at his press conference of May 10, 1933, on the subject of "Foreign consultative pacts —Disarmament—Foreign debts and the Economic Conference [at London].[6]

The press interview was opened by the question: "did you see the speech that Ramsay MacDonald made yesterday in

6. *Public Papers*, II, 169 ff.

which he said that an agreement had been reached that we should enter into a consultative pact?" The President replied: "Careful; don't misquote him, get it right."

After some word-play, President Roosevelt read Prime Minister MacDonald's statement as published in a morning newspaper in New York:

> . . . I am very happy to say that the United States Government is prepared to play a further part in tranquilizing Europe by agreeing, if the Disarmament Conference comes to anything like a satisfactory issue, to take its part in consultative pacts, the effect of which will be to increase the security of Europe and the safety of threatened Nations against war.
>
> This is a very considerable advance. Secretary of State Stimson began it in that courageous statement he made before he went out of office regarding the need to redefine neutrality and the present Government has expressed its intention of going further in making its obligations quite definite and authoritative. . . .[7]

In commenting on the Prime Minister's statement, President Roosevelt minimized the idea of "a very considerable advance" on the part of the United States in the direction of collective security and unmistakably declared himself against restricting the independence of the United States. He said that both parties, certainly the Democrats, had favored consultative pacts and that if some kind of machinery was set up for consultation the United States would be very glad to have somebody to consult. But, he warned the journalists, consultation "does not tie the hands of the United States in any shape . . . We in no way—in no way—are limiting our own right to determine our own action after the facts are brought out . . . there would be a report to Washington as to what the other Nations think and then we will be entirely free to do whatever we want to do. In other words, we would not be bound by the American who happened to be sitting in the consultative pact. He would report home."

At this point a journalist broke in and the following colloquy occurred:

7. For Mr. Stimson's outlook on foreign affairs, see below, pp. 133 ff.

Q. Mr. President, it seems to me that the consultative pact is almost identical to our relations with the League of Nations.

THE PRESIDENT: It is an entirely different thing. You cannot use comparisons in that connection.

Q. But we always took the stand that we would consult as things came up but do nothing obligatory—not be obliged to consult. With this new arrangement, would we be obliged to consult?

THE PRESIDENT: We would say quite frankly that we would sit in and consult. There is nothing particularly startling about that, when you come down to it.

Q. But we have that machinery now.

THE PRESIDENT: Sure. In other words, it sounds like a huge change in policy, but it is very little change in policy. It is an announcement that we are going to do something that we would do anyhow.

These comments on Prime Minister MacDonald's statement about what the United States was prepared to do were "off the record," that is, made for the information of journalists, who cannot quote a president without his consent. But the President was positive in asserting that he would not agree to any consultative pact that bound the United States to implement the Kellogg–Briand Pact for the outlawry of war, such as internationalists were then urging upon him and upon this nation. Nor did he in his public statements on American foreign policy in that or in any other connection give the slightest hint that he would support the Stimson doctrine or any kind of internationalism for enforcing "collective security."

President Roosevelt's unwillingness to assume for the United States the obligation of helping to coerce aggressors was also made abundantly clear in his direct relations to the ill-fated Disarmament Conference. On May 12, 1933, the Conference reached the verge of collapse when it learned that Chancellor Hitler had called the Reichstag to hear an address criticizing the Conference and threatening a revolt against it. The British, French, and American delegates at

Geneva, fearing disruption of the Conference, decided that nothing except a firm declaration by the President could act as a real check on the intransigence of the German Chancellor. But President Roosevelt's "Appeal to the Nations" on May 16 put an end to the hopes of internationalists that he would in this extremity make a positive pledge of American official cooperation in a system of collective guarantees. In France and England, as well as in the United States, his appeal was understood as involving no guarantees of that kind.

In his "Appeal to the Nations" President Roosevelt referred to excessive armaments as related to fear of aggression, declared that the United States was prepared to participate in an effective reduction of armaments, called for a definite pact of non-aggression, and made a plea for an agreement among nations that they "will send no armed force of whatever nature across their frontiers" against any other country. But in making this appeal and offer of cooperation in reducing the burden of armaments, he gave no sign of any intention to reverse or materially modify his pronouncement of February 2, 1932, against the League of Nations and entanglement in the political conflicts of Europe. On the contrary, he adhered to the policy of independence—freedom of judgment and action for the United States.

If the Appeal left the slightest uncertainty on this point, it was soon removed by the fate of another trial balloon sent up by Norman Davis, head of the American delegation to the Disarmament Conference. Six days after the Appeal was issued, Mr. Davis proposed that, *if* some kind of arms limitation could be agreed upon at Geneva, the United States would consult other nations in case of a threat of war and that, *if* it concurred in a judgment as to the guilty party, it would not interfere with a collective effort of other nations to restore peace.[8]

At that time there was hanging fire in the Senate a resolu-

8. There has never been any generally accepted definition, in spite of many efforts, of the term "aggressor." This is convenient to the powers who wish to suppress a disfavored nation.

tion allowing the President to impose an embargo on the export of munitions to any nation about to disturb or actually then disturbing the peace of the world. Internationalists now saw another chance to work the United States into a scheme of collective security. By a combination of the Davis proposal with the resolution permitting the President to embargo the export of munitions to peace breakers, the United States could be morally bound to cooperate with the League of Nations or a concert of powers in applying sanctions to a government designated as an aggressor. But this elaborate project came to naught.

Although Mr. Davis' proposal was watered down with qualifications, even in that form it received little support from President Roosevelt. Moreover the Senate expressed an adverse opinion on the issue by amending the proposed arms embargo resolution in such a way as to make any embargo apply not merely to "aggressors" but to all parties to an international dispute affected by it.

After Hitler took Germany out of the Disarmament Conference and international cooperation began to deteriorate rapidly, Mr. Davis announced that the United States was not aligned politically with any European power and would take no part in the political negotiations that were being carried on in Europe. In Washington, Secretary Hull reassured American isolationists by issuing an official statement to the effect that the United States would remain aloof from the Disarmament Conference until the question of arms reduction as distinguished from political understandings became again the subject of consideration. Thus internationalists in Europe and the United States were definitely warned that the Roosevelt Administration was hostile to foreign entanglements even remotely akin to those arising from membership in the League of Nations.

Whether a commitment of the United States to a program for the collective action of nations against Germany and Japan would have made the Disarmament Conference a success is a question purely speculative in nature. What nations, how many nations, including particularly Great Britain, would have joined such a combination in the final showdown—this too is a matter for speculation. History merely records that, in connection with the Geneva Conference on Disarmament, President Roosevelt did not endorse any scheme which would have bound the United States to join other nations in designating an aggressor by name and in taking effective action, by arms if necessary, against the designee. And the Disarmament Conference simply dragged on through 1933 and subsequent years to a death of inanition.

By events not of his own ordering, Mr. Roosevelt was brought face to face with a third challenge relative to foreign affairs: the necessity of passing upon the policy to be followed by the United States at the coming World Economic and Financial Conference, called under the sponsorship of the League of Nations and to be shortly convened in London. In inception and purpose the Conference, arrangements for which were far advanced by November, 1932, represented the faith of internationalists and promoters of collaboration among nations in the power of a world assembly of diplomats and experts to mitigate substantially, if not overcome, the economic depression that was tormenting the nations of the earth, as well as to advance the cause of peace. President Hoover had accepted the League's invitation and with an authorization from Congress had appointed American agents to participate in framing the Agenda for the Conference—a document that finally embodied the internationalist doctrine of economic salvation by an ever-larger foreign trade.

In respect of the World Economic Conference, Mr. Roosevelt displayed first a lack of sympathy with internationalist projects and finally open hostility to the designs of this particular undertaking. His interest was solicited in December, 1932, when President Hoover invited him to share in the business of planning for the Conference and to designate one or more of his party members to serve as delegates,

Owen D. Young or Colonel House, for instance. Mr. Roosevelt and his aides knew very well that the Agenda for the Conference constituted an obvious argument for an economic internationalism which based the hope for "recovery" in the United States and elsewhere on the traditional formulas: lower trade barriers, sound currency, monetary adjustments, stabilization, and so forth.[9]

But Mr. Roosevelt declined to assume any public responsibility for the proposed Conference prior to his installation in office. Referring to the internationalist thesis of the Agenda, Mr. Moley afterward wrote: "We simply did not believe that it was true. . . . If Franklin Roosevelt can be said to have had any philosophy at all, that philosophy rested on the fundamental belief that the success of concerted international action toward recovery presupposed the beginnings of recovery at home. He did not believe that our depression could be conquered by international measures. He certainly did not believe that reduction in the debts or even the partial opening of international trade channels would rout it."[10] Speaking on this general subject, Mr. Moley also declared: "We were agreed that the heart of the recovery program was and must be domestic. . . . Ralph Robey, Rex Tugwell, and Adolf Berle . . . agreed with me in opposition to traditional internationalism."[11]

If, after the inauguration on March 4, 1933, some American citizens thought that President Roosevelt had any lingering faith in internationalism and international conferences as offering a promise of recovery for the United States, they must have been thoroughly disillusioned by his public actions and statements in relation to the Economic Conference at London, which was scheduled to open at London in June of that year. It is true that he carried out the obligation to take part in it which had been assumed by the previous Adminis-

9. For digest of the Agenda, see Beard, *The Open Door at Home* (The Macmillan Company, 1934), pp. 113 ff.
10. *After Seven Years*, p. 88.
11. *Ibid.*, p. 70.

tration and that he chose as head of the American delegation the Secretary of State, Cordell Hull, a free trader of the Cobden–Bright variety and known as an internationalist of the Woodrow Wilson school; but he associated with Mr. Hull other delegates whose views were different if not antagonistic or nebulous. And his instructions to them, while allowing for diversities of interpretation, were certainly noncommittal as to promises; moreover, when the Conference showed signs of floundering, he made no real effort to help it on the way to success, whatever success might have meant.

On the contrary. While the Conference was tossing to and fro in a fever, the American delegation, importuned by representatives of other countries, formulated a message to the President in the hope of getting his approval for at least one simple proposition in international finance. This message was drafted at conferences attended by Mr. Moley, who had been sent to London after the opening of the sessions as the President's personal representative. The proposal transmitted to the President was cast in such language, as Mr. Moley later explained, that it could not have been objectionable to "the most fanatical isolationist." It was, he added, "completely harmless." Mr. Moley's own changes in the phraseology of the original document, he thought, merely devitalized it. He was thoroughly convinced that the President's approval of the project would come promptly and that it would "mark the end of two weeks of alarms and fears" in London.

After a long delay, the President replied in a message which for practical purposes disrupted the London Conference and put an end to all projects for any kind of international agreement even on the mildest financial actions. The tone of this message, no less than its contents, shocked the American delegation and all other members of the Conference—indeed internationalists everywhere.

Besides charging the Conference with neglecting its large purposes and with wasting time on a temporary expedient, President Roosevelt proclaimed a nationalist doctrine in the name of the United States: "The sound internal economic system of a nation is a greater factor in its well-being than the price of its currency in changing terms of the currencies of other nations." He informed the Conference that the United States rejected the "old fetishes of so-called international bankers" and was planning its national currency with reference to its own needs and interests. The only comfort offered in the stinging message was a brief passage on the importance of mitigating embargoes on trade between nations.[12]

Stunned by the blow, the London Conference soon adjourned; and the inflated dreams that had attended its inauguration dissolved amid a loud verbal uproar. Notice was thus served on internationalists that the United States would pursue a domestic course to recovery.

The fourth dilemma in foreign affairs faced by Mr. Roosevelt after his election to the presidency was the problem of American policy in the Far East, specifically in the form given to it by Henry L. Stimson, President Hoover's Secretary of State.[13] In origins, this issue had been related to the imperialist designs promoted under Republican auspices in the Far East since 1898; but American internationalists had seen in Secretary Stimson's operations a chance to "implement" the Kellogg–Briand Peace Pact by inducing the United States to join or use the League of Nations for the purpose of thwarting Japanese imperialism. Thus the United States might be tied up closely with the League or the Great Powers that were managing it.[14] Given the internationalist implications of the Stimson maneuver, the Far Eastern question presented a thorny problem to Mr. Roosevelt. He handled it ingeniously.

12. For an inside account of the affair, see Moley, *ibid.*, pp. 196–296.
13. See above, pp. 112 ff.
14. In respect of Great Britain, it should be said that the government of that country categorically refused to be a party to Secretary Stimson's scheme. On February 27, 1933, Sir John Simon declared: "Under no circumstances will the Government authorize this country to be a party to the conflict." *The Collected Papers of John Bassett Moore* (Yale University Press, 1945), VI, 453. For the origin of the so-called Stimson doctrine see Benjamin B. Wallace, "How the United States 'Led the League' in 1931," *American Political Science Review*, XXXIX (February, 1945), 101.

Mr. Roosevelt's decision on the Stimson doctrine as Far Eastern policy was not made at a conference with President Hoover. It was adopted at an informal and private meeting with Secretary Stimson himself. On January 9, 1933, Mr. Roosevelt had the Secretary at a luncheon with him at Hyde Park; and it is noteworthy that he did not ask to this meeting his intimate adviser, Raymond Moley, who had ideas of his own on the subject and had been active in the negotiations with President Hoover.

Mr. Moley regarded the Stimson doctrine as positively dangerous to the American Republic and was strongly opposed to the adoption of that doctrine as policy for the United States. In Mr. Moley's opinion, the acceptance of that program "implied approval of the theory of collective sanctions and the approval of the fallacy that, as 'neutrals' in a foreign war, we ought to discriminate against one side or the other by embargoes and similar measures." In Mr. Moley's opinion it also meant "acquiescence in the Hoover–Stimson rejection of the traditional American concept of neutrality, of disinterestedness, impartiality, and non-participation in foreign quarrels. . . . It endorsed a policy that invited a major war in the Far East—a war which the United States and England might have had to wage against Japan had England not refused to go along with Stimson." [15]

Inasmuch as President Hoover's name was commonly associated with the Stimson doctrine and particularly by Mr. Moley at that time, it is necessary, in an attempt to grasp the significance of the agreement reached by Mr. Roosevelt and Secretary Stimson on January 9, 1933, to bear in mind that President Hoover had no part in the Hyde Park conference and was opposed to the non-recognition doctrine as Mr. Stimson conceived it. In Secretary Stimson's conception, the formula included the imposition of economic sanctions[16] and close collaboration, if possible, with other nations in

15. Moley, *op. cit.*, pp. 93–94.
16. William S. Myers, *The Foreign Policies of Herbert Hoover, 1929–1933*, p. 166, 229 n.

enforcing sanctions, coupled with a willingness to accept the almost certain consequence—war, in case sanctions failed. In other words, the Stimson doctrine meant in 1933 precisely what it proved to be when tried out in 1941.

To President Hoover, Mr. Stimson's conception of the non-recognition doctrine was obnoxious. Although he and Secretary Stimson did not come to an open break over the issue, President Hoover was firmly opposed to economic sanctions and other coercive measures and he regarded non-recognition as limited for use to moral persuasion, to an appeal to the moral sense and judgment of mankind.[17] As Professor William Myers later declared in a comment on the passage quoted above from Mr. Moley's memoir: "It should be said in the most definite way, *and without reference to what may have been in the mind of Secretary Stimson*, that this statement on the part of Mr. Moley is *the exact opposite to the policies and ideas of President Hoover* as the record has abundantly shown." [18]

In a memorandum which he read at a meeting of his cabinet late in 1931, President Hoover had fully expounded his own program: "Our whole policy in connection with controversies is to exhaust the processes of peaceful negotiation. But in contemplating these we must make up our minds whether we consider war as the ultimate if these efforts fail. *Neither our obligations to China, nor our own interest, nor our dignity require us to go to war over these questions* [in connection with the Manchurian conflict]. These acts [on the part of Japan] *do not imperil the freedom of the American people, the economic or moral future of our people. I do not propose ever to sacrifice American life for anything short of this.* If that were not enough reason, to go to war means

17. Even as President Hoover conceived the non-recognition doctrine, it represented a departure from American foreign policy as maintained from the establishment of the government under the Constitution to the first Administration of President Woodrow Wilson. Charles A. Beard, *A Foreign Policy for America* (Alfred A. Knopf, 1940), pp. 3–35, pp. 134–154. For the significance of this departure, see note below, pp. 146–147 n.

18. Myers, *op. cit.*, p. 229 n. (Italics supplied.)

a long struggle at a time when civilization is already weak enough. To win such a war is not solely a naval operation. We must arm and train Chinese. We would find ourselves involved in China in a fashion that would excite the suspicions of the whole world. . . . We have a moral obligation to use every influence *short of war* to have the treaties upheld or terminated by mutual agreement." After speaking of limiting collaborations with other nations to moral pressures, negotiation, and conciliation, President Hoover closed: "But that is the limit. *We will not go along on war or any of the sanctions either economic or military for those are the roads to war.*" [19]

Without grossly violating these principles of American foreign policy, which he had so clearly and cogently presented to his cabinet, President Hoover, therefore, could not have followed Secretary Stimson's program of sanctions and coercion on the almost certain road to war with Japan. If he was tempted, amid the tightening coils of the depression, to free himself from their iron grip by resorting to a war and bringing on the inevitable economic boom that would have made brighter his prospects for a reelection, Mr. Hoover made not even an open gesture in that direction. On the contrary, he privately held in leash his Secretary of State who, he knew, was committed to sanctions and other measures which were called, in his communication to the cabinet, "roads to war." And he clung to that line until the close of his Administration.

It was with Secretary Stimson, not President Hoover, that Mr. Roosevelt held the conference respecting the Far Eastern situation on January 9, 1933. The arrangement for the conference was mediated by a prominent Democrat who was later appointed to a high post under the Constitution by Mr. Roosevelt after he became President.[20] That Secretary Stimson went to Hyde Park with the knowledge and approval of President Hoover is reasonably certain, for the President had

19. Wilbur and Hyde, *op. cit.*, p. 601. (Italics supplied.)
20. This statement is based on what I regard as unimpeachable authority.

been earnestly seeking, in vain, for some time to reach under-standings with Governor Roosevelt for the purpose of pre-serving continuity with regard to specific foreign policies. But no evidence is available to the effect that the Secretary presented to Mr. Roosevelt, at Hyde Park, President Hoover's non-recognition doctrine. In fact there is evidence to the contrary, namely, that he presented his own.

Secretary Stimson was then smarting from the rebuffs he had received at the hands of the British Government in respect of the Manchurian controversy, and also at the hands of the League of Nations which, besides refusing to apply economic sanctions to Japan, had buried the "incident" in a report by the Lytton Commission. There is no doubt, either, that the Secretary had all along chafed under President Hoover's insistence that the sanctions advocated by the Sec-retary meant setting out on the road to war and that the commercial interests of the United States in China would not justify the shedding of American blood in a Far Eastern war. If anything in history is certain, it is that Secretary Stimson had not given up before January 9, 1933, his longing to see Japan brought to book by sanctions or some other mode of action even if likely to result in war. That he and Mr. Roosevelt reviewed foreign affairs for five hours on that day and reached some kind of agreement without reference to the Stimson program of sanctions is so improbable as to be beyond credence.

Besides this reasonable inference, there is positive evidence of high credibility that it was the Stimson doctrine, not the Hoover doctrine, which Secretary Stimson brought up at Hyde Park on January 9, and Mr. Roosevelt considered and accepted. This evidence includes, first of all, the statements which Mr. Roosevelt made "off the record" to the press a few days later and were paraphrased in the *New York Times* report on Mr. Roosevelt's account of what had taken place at Hyde Park.[21]

In addition, by way of confirmation, there is available Mr.

21. Below, pp. 147 ff.

Moley's memorandum on the affair contained in his volume, *After Seven Years*. It is true that Mr. Moley was under the mistaken impression that President Hoover was at one with Secretary Stimson on the non-recognition doctrine as including sanctions and other devices of coercion. It is true also that Mr. Moley did not participate in the conference on January 9, although he had shared other negotiations with the Hoover Administration in respect of foreign policies. But Mr. Moley was at the time firmly of the opinion that the so-called Hoover–Stimson doctrine of non-recognition, if adopted and applied by Mr. Roosevelt "invited a major war in the Far East"; and, at a conference which he and Mr. Tugwell held with Mr. Roosevelt a few days after the Hyde Park luncheon on January 9, Mr. Moley became convinced that Mr. Roosevelt had on that occasion actually committed himself to Secretary Stimson's version of the non-recognition doctrine.[22]

When, at the conclusion of his meeting with Mr. Roosevelt on that day, Secretary Stimson was greeted by representatives of the press seeking information for the public, he evaded questions by remarking that he had enjoyed "a delightful lunch." But according to a dispatch from Washington, dated January 16, 1933, couched in the cautious language of diplomacy, Secretary Stimson in effect declared that he and Mr. Roosevelt had actually made a great decision at their conference, on January 9, 1933. The dispatch of January 16, 1933, informed the public that, on instruction of Secretary Stimson, the non-recognition policy enunciated by the United States in the Far Eastern emergency had been restated to European foreign offices and to the League of Nations through American diplomatic officers abroad; and that similar information had been given orally to foreign envoys who had called at the State Department in recent days. So far, this seemed to represent action on the part of the Hoover Administration.[23]

Secretary Stimson's statement, however, did more than

22. Below, p. 142.
23. *New York Times*, January 17, 1933.

express his own views; the dispatch which reported it went on to intimate in ambagious terms that Mr. Roosevelt had definitely committed himself to the Stimson policy—a policy which, if effectuated, would in all probability lead to war in the Far East.[24] The following passages of the *Times* dispatch from Washington on January 16 bear on the nature of the obligations assumed by Mr. Roosevelt at the Hyde Park conference with Secretary Stimson on January 9:

It is understood here [Washington] that *there is no disposition on the part of President-elect Roosevelt to alter the administration's policy* with respect to Manchuria, and *a well-informed assumption is that the Secretary of State assured himself of this before re-enunciating the doctrine* that the United States would not recognize any treaty or situation brought about by means contrary to the Pact of Paris.

It is apparent that repeated rumors abroad that the Roosevelt administration intended to drop the Hoover–Stimson Far Eastern policy were causing uncertainty concerning the future attitude of the United States, thus tending to weaken the position of this country over the Manchurian problem. *The administration wished to offset this impression. . . .*

Notification that this policy stood was sent recently to Ambassador Mellon in London, Ambassador Edge in Paris and chiefs of mission in other European capitals, as well as to Prentiss Gilbert, consular representative at Geneva. Those officials were instructed to explain, "if asked," that the United States position remained unchanged.

The State Department explained today that this was done because of reports that the United States was relaxing its attitude. *In diplomatic circles the opinion was general that Secretary*

24. Every student of Oriental affairs acquainted with the posture of affairs in Japan and China knew very well that the Stimson doctrine was a *brutum fulmen* unless backed up immediately by an increase in United States naval forces and an inflexible will to war in case Japan refused to accept Mr. Stimson's doctrine, which was regarded by Japanese imperialists as a mere cloak for American imperialism. Mr. Stimson was warned to this effect by Dr. Stanley Hornbeck, his own expert on the Far East (Pearson and Brown, *The American Diplomatic Game*, a book dedicated to "the pawns in the game," pp. 301 ff.). Informed American naval officers knew this very well also and there is good reason for believing that, as Mr. Stimson plunged ahead on the road toward war, some of them warned him that "the Navy is *not* ready."

Stimson felt the Committee of Nineteen, as it was about to meet on *the thorny Manchurian problem,* should have a fresh reminder of *the American position.* . . .

The State Department denied emphatically a London press report today that President Hoover had instructed Mr. Mellon to inform the British Foreign Office that the United States believed the League had wasted too much time in dealing with the Chino–Japanese situation and that, since all conciliatory measures had failed, the League should act in accordance with its covenant.[25]

On January 17, 1933, the day following Secretary Stimson's announcement, Mr. Roosevelt, questioned by the press, gave publicity to his attitude respecting the Stimson doctrine. Did he in fact take over that doctrine as his own?

The *New York Times* news "story" of the interview with Mr. Roosevelt on the Stimson statement was divided into two parts. One part, as if off the record and yet inspired, seemed to represent him as concurring with the Far Eastern policy hitherto pursued, in one form or another, by imperialist secretaries of state from John Hay to Henry L. Stimson. This part was broken into two sections.

Between the sections was sandwiched a direct and brief quotation from Mr. Roosevelt in which he declined to endorse explicitly and at the moment the Stimson policy for the Far East and then indulged in a generality which could be interpreted as approving that policy obliquely and yet, standing alone, signified little or nothing in relation to it.

The second part of the *Times* dispatch went beyond the bare non-recognition doctrine and definitely indicated that Mr. Roosevelt had also endorsed Secretary Stimson's whole program for the Far East, including the possibility of modifications in the naval limitations treaty to which Japan was a party.

Both for its bearing on the immediate issue and as an illustration of Mr. Roosevelt's methods in dealing with the press and foreign affairs, the *New York Times* account of the interview on January 17, 1933, deserves close attention:

25. *New York Times,* January 17, 1933, p. 1. (Italics supplied.)

Franklin D. Roosevelt, President-elect, *indicated* yesterday that there would be no change *in the Far Eastern policy* of the United States after he became President.

This *indication* that he would continue the Far Eastern policy of the Hoover administration came when Mr. Roosevelt was questioned by reporters about newspaper reports from Washington that Secretary of State Stimson had notified the interested European governments that the United States would continue its policy of non-recognition in the Chino–Japanese dispute.

Seated in the study of his city home at 49 East Sixty-fifth Street, Mr. Roosevelt borrowed a pencil from a reporter and *wrote out a statement in reply to the question as to whether he had agreed to support the Far Eastern policy of the present administration in his talk with Secretary Stimson a week ago.* The statement follows:

"*Any statement* relating to *any particular foreign situation must, of course,* come from the Secretary of State of the United States.

"I am, however, wholly willing to make it clear that *American foreign policies must uphold the sanctity of international treaties.* That is the cornerstone on which all relations between nations must rest."

Mr. Roosevelt refused to amplify this statement, *construed as a declaration for continuation of the "open-door" policy for China,* either to disclose details of his conversation with Secretary Stimson or to make it apply to war debts. The President-elect said that this was all he had to say. . . .

It now appears that Mr. Roosevelt has endorsed not only the stand of President Hoover against recognizing gains won by Japan by means contrary to the Kellogg–Briand anti-war pact, but also *the insistence upon observance of the Nine-Power Treaty* with its *guarantee*[26] of the open-door policy and the integrity of China.

In addition *it is understood* Mr. Roosevelt has accepted the view Secretary Stimson set forth in his letter to Senator Borah on Feb. 24, 1932, that all the treaties of the Washington Conference were interdependent from the circumstance of their simul-

26. In the Nine-Power Treaty, the signatories, including the United States, *did not guarantee* the integrity of China. They merely agreed to *respect* it. This distinction has a vital bearing on American obligations in the premises.

taneous negotiation, and that *the four-power Pacific pact and the naval treaty might be affected by any change* in the status of the Nine-Power Treaty.[27]

The day after the press interview on the Stimson agreement had appeared, Mr. Roosevelt was asked by his advisers, Mr. Moley and Mr. Tugwell, whom he had not consulted about this commitment prior to his action, why he had accepted the Stimson doctrine for the Far East. To their surprise Mr. Roosevelt merely recalled the fact that his ancestors had been in the China trade and added: "I have always had the deepest sympathy for the Chinese. How could you expect me not to go along with Stimson on Japan?"[28] Mr. Moley and Mr. Tugwell regarded this decision as a tragic mistake, but the step had been taken.

Mr. Roosevelt's own brief statement of January 17, 1933, on upholding the sanctity of treaties, contained not a word about the Stimson doctrine. Hence it could be viewed, on its face, as giving no approval to that doctrine as such; but, considered in relation to Secretary Stimson's previous statement, it implied a promise to uphold the doctrine in dealing with Japan and, as Mr. Moley and Mr. Tugwell anticipated, this engagement bore fruit in years to come—1941–45.

At all events, Mr. Roosevelt's own bare statement of January 17 seemed to be in the domain of morals and awakened no great alarms among isolationists. As Mr. Moley observed, it was "quite without significance in itself." Indeed, Secretary Stimson's policy of blocking Japan in Manchuria had suited imperialist interests in the United States, in spite of his open efforts to collaborate with the League of Nations and his quest for collective support.

Furthermore, Mr. Roosevelt was not unacquainted with imperialism and its works. He had been from 1913 to 1920

27. *New York Times,* January 18, 1933, pp. 1–11. (Italics supplied.) Vol. I, chap. xxv of Roosevelt's *Public Papers,* which contains a few papers for the period November, 1932–March 4, 1933, makes no reference to the important announcement of January 17, 1933.

28. *After Seven Years,* pp. 94–95. Perhaps Mr. Moley and Mr. Tugwell were not as deeply entrenched in Mr. Roosevelt's confidence as they had imagined.

Assistant Secretary of the Navy—in the department that had charge of naval operations against Mexico, Santo Domingo, and Haiti, in the classical imperialist style under President Wilson. Indeed during his campaign for Vice-President in 1920, Mr. Roosevelt had referred with pride to some of his own achievements in extending American power over the Caribbean.[29] Therefore, when on January 17, 1933, he referred to the "sanctity of treaties," he could have been understood as allowing for exceptions to the rule.[30] In any case, on January 9, 1933, Secretary Stimson had achieved the great purpose on which he had set his heart and in due time he was to cooperate with President Roosevelt in realizing his design.[31]

If to adepts in international affairs Mr. Roosevelt's statement of January 17, 1933, on the Stimson doctrine suggested that he might immediately take strong action, as President, against Japan, he gave to the public no hints later in 1933 that he had any such purpose in mind. Neither Manchuria nor Manchukuo is mentioned in the index of his *Public Papers* for the year; and Japan is mentioned only three times. The first reference to Japan touches upon a visit of a representative from Japan, as well as similar visits from agents of other governments, in the spring of 1933, to discuss "the world economic situation"; the second lists Japan among the nations to which the President's "Appeal for Peace by Dis-

29. In August, 1920, during his campaign for Vice-President, Mr. Roosevelt boasted that the United States would control the votes of Haiti, Santo Domingo, Panama, Cuba, enough Central-American countries to make up a total quota of twelve votes in the Assembly of the League of Nations. *New York Times*, August 19, 1920, p. 15.

30. For American violation of the "sanctity" of a treaty, pledging peace and arbitration, by the seizure and occupation of Vera Cruz in an undeclared war against Mexico in 1914, see Moore, *op. cit.*, VI, 444-445.

31. In an eloquent tribute to Mr. Stimson on his retirement from the office of Secretary of War in September, 1945, Senator Joseph Guffey called attention to the fact that well before his inauguration on March 4, 1933, Mr. Roosevelt "had specifically endorsed Stimson's policy in the Far East." Senator Guffey thought that the country was to be congratulated for the eminent services rendered by Mr. Stimson. *Congressional Record*, September 25, 1945. This was after Russia had taken over certain ports and the strategic position in Manchuria formerly occupied by Japan.

armament" was sent, May 16, 1933; and the third is to a conversation between the President and Viscount Ishii.

Only the third of these references—the conversation with Viscount Ishii—is more than formal in nature and the statement on this conversation conveyed an impression that relations between the United States and Japan were friendly. The President and the Viscount were "happy to note" that their views coincided on practical steps to solve outstanding economic problems of common interest to all nations; they hoped to see the countries of the Far East contribute substantially in the spirit of cooperation to laying the solid foundations for world peace and prosperity; they were "in close agreement" as to "many" measures necessary to economic and political health; they looked to the convening of the World Economic Conference and to the Disarmament Conference in the spirit of cooperation and expectancy.[32]

Although President Roosevelt continued the policy of non-recognition in respect of Japan and her puppet state, Manchukuo, he made no public statement during the year 1933 to the effect that he intended to "implement" it. A careful student of foreign affairs, John M. Mathews, after remarking that the use of sanctions to enforce it "would probably have involved us in war," reported that at the end of the year "the ultimate policy of the Roosevelt administration in the Far East has not yet been disclosed." [33] Japan, having given notice of her intention to withdraw from the League of Nations, showed no signs of a retreat in Manchuria; but neither the League of Nations nor any great European power was disposed to bring force to bear on her. And President Roosevelt made no sign that he contemplated drastic action against Japan, either alone or in cooperation with Great Britain or the League.

In dealing concretely with other phases of foreign policy during the year 1933—in addition to those connected with

32. *Public Papers*, II, 212 f.
33. *American Year Book* (1933), pp. 61 f.

the debts, the Disarmament Conference, the London Economic Conference, and the Stimson doctrine—President Roosevelt gave no encouragement to American internationalists. Early in his Administration he postponed action on the subject of American adherence to the World Court, subject to closely restrictive reservations. This proposition had been long pending. It had been endorsed by President Coolidge and President Hoover and only die-hard isolationists opposed it. To internationalists it seemed that this was the least possible gesture which the United States could make in the direction of world cooperation, and they looked to President Roosevelt for immediate help in expediting final action by the Senate of the United States. They looked in vain.

At a press conference on March 29, 1933, a journalist inquired of the President: "To get started on foreign affairs for a moment. I understand that the Senate Foreign Relations Committee has taken action on the American adherence to the World Court. Is it your desire, can you tell us whether you want the Senate to act at this session?" The President replied: "Not even off the record. You can make a guess. . . ." [34]

Also postponed until 1934 was action on the one measure of international implications which Mr. Roosevelt had so heavily underlined during his election campaign: modification of tariff barriers through the negotiation of reciprocal trade treaties. Not until June 12, 1934, did he sign the reciprocal tariff bill—that substitute for the flat cut in tariff rates which Mr. Hull had desired in 1932. By the middle of 1934 nearly all of President Roosevelt's great domestic measures directed toward recovery at home had been enacted

34. *Public Papers,* II, 98. The omission indicated in this official report was made by the editors in preparing Vol. I for publication. When in 1935 the Senate was on the verge of rejecting adherence to the World Court, President Roosevelt sent a message to the Senate urging favorable action, but, despite the fact that his party had an overwhelming majority in the Senate, he refrained from putting ratification on his program of "must" actions for that body. *American Year Book* (1935), pp. 67 f.

into law. First things had been put first and the time had come to deal with foreign trade. But as finally drawn the Trade Agreements Act of 1934 by no means conformed to the free and equal trade prescription of the third item in President Wilson's list of Fourteen Points.[35]

Nor in according recognition to Soviet Russia in November, 1933, did President Roosevelt follow the line, established by President Wilson, of outlawing governments whose political forms and economic institutions were not in accord with American conceptions of peace, morality, and propriety. Many practical considerations, no doubt, carried weight with President Roosevelt in restoring diplomatic relations with Russia. Even President Harding, President Coolidge, and President Hoover, in continuing the non-recognition policy pursued by President Wilson, had somewhat surreptitiously encouraged trade with Russia in the interest of American business enterprise; and in 1933 American industry, in the depths of the depression, was thought to need every crumb of commerce that could be found. Moreover, in view of his sympathy with the Stimson doctrine for the Far East, President Roosevelt could easily see in the recovery of Russia a great counterpoise to the growing strength of Japan.

In recognizing Russia, after about sixteen years of outlawry, President Roosevelt was returning to the policy that had been followed by the Government of the United States for more than a century after the foundation of the Republic; namely, the recognition of established governments without regard to their political forms and economic institutions. Hence his action in this respect was in harmony with the example set by George Washington, which had not been dubbed "isolationism" until after 1919. In any event, it was no contribution to internationalism as such.[36]

35. The Trade Agreements Act was partly offset by the Johnson Act which made unlawful in the United States the sale of the bonds and securities of foreign governments (and subdivisions thereof) that had defaulted on the payment of obligations to the Government of the United States.

36. The significance of the recognition or non-recognition accorded to foreign governments seems to be almost if not entirely lost to the generation of

In two other relations during the year 1933 President Roosevelt gave expression to his foreign policy for the United States. He declared in his Inaugural Address of March 4: "In the field of world policy I would dedicate this Nation to the policy of the good neighbor . . . the neighbor who respects his obligations and respects the sanctity of his agreements in and with a world of neighbors."

Near the end of the year 1933 President Roosevelt in effect renounced imperialism as a policy to be followed by the United States, at least in the Western hemisphere. Imperialism had been opposed by the Democratic party since the memorable campaign of 1900, despite certain divagations in Latin America during President Wilson's Administration. On several occasions, in 1928 and later, Mr. Roosevelt had condemned it either in name or in substance. In December, 1933, he declared: "the definite policy of the United States from now on is opposed to armed intervention" in the affairs of other American republics.[37]

Americans brought up in the school of "current affairs." Before 1913 the Government of the United States in deciding upon questions of recognition proceeded on the principle that it was under no obligation to reform the institutions, manners, and morals of any government seeking recognition or already recognized, as long as that government was willing to live at peace with the United States and fulfill the ordinary obligations of international intercourse. After 1913 President Wilson made a departure from the old rule, and it became popular in certain quarters to insist that the Government of the United States should break off relations with governments entertaining different conceptions of political and institutional forms; that it should only recognize governments that suited American conceptions of politics, economics, and morals. Communists in the United States and elsewhere now followed the one rule or the other according to "the Moscow line"; for example, they favored breaking off relations with "fascist" governments, except when Russia was bound to Hitler's Germany by a solemn pact (1939–41). They maintained in 1945 that the United States should automatically recognize any kind of government established in Eastern Europe under Russian tutelage and refrain from interfering with its internal affairs. For an examination of "recognition" in American policy, see Moore, *op. cit.*, especially IV, 355 ff. and VI, 470 ff. For Professor Moore's remarks on the "alarms" over relations with Communist Russia, see VI, 347 ff. Having served the country in the State Department for many years and devoted a long life to the study of international law and diplomatic history, Professor Moore could speak out of full knowledge. For the doctrine of non-recognition see article by Edwin Borchard and Phoebe Morrison in *Legal Problems in the Far Eastern Conflict* (Institute of Pacific Relations), 1941, pp. 157–178.

37. *On Our Way* (The John Day Company, 1934), p. 133.

Furthermore, President Roosevelt seemed ready to make good his words on imperialism by encouraging the movement for Philippine independence, which his good friend, Henry L. Stimson, had so actively opposed in the days of President Hoover's Administration. After the Philippine legislature had declined in October, 1933, to accept the terms of the Hawes–Cutting Independence Act of January, 1933, President Roosevelt reviewed the problem thus posed; and in March, 1934, he sent a message to Congress recommending that new legislation be passed for the purpose of giving effect to Philippine independence. Thus an old pledge of the Democratic party appeared on the eve of fulfilment. If, as Mr. Stimson had stoutly maintained in 1931, this would mean disturbing the imperialist situation in the Far East, the disturbance at last loomed on the horizon.[38]

By his intense concentration on his domestic program for recovery in 1933, as well as by his various pronouncements on foreign policy, President Roosevelt indicated his break with internationalism. From the first day of his administration to the end of 1933 he devoted his energies primarily to framing measures in respect of national economy, pressing them through Congress, and putting them into effect. In other words, he labored hard at promoting the general welfare in the United States by independent action, as distinguished from lowering trade barriers, seeking outlets for "surpluses" through imperialist expedients, or relying upon designs adopted at international conferences of some kind.

Support for this statement is provided by the second volume of the President's *Public Papers*, entitled *The Year of Crisis, 1933*, published under his supervision. No person can read that work, document by document, line by line, without discovering how firmly he centered his interest on domestic measures for domestic recovery through all the trying

38. The matter of American naval bases in the Philippines was reserved, however, though the final decision was postponed.

months of the period. Additional evidence for this statement is supplied by the President's own report to the nation on his designs and labors of the year, entitled *On Our Way:* of the thirteen chapters in this volume, twelve deal with domestic affairs and only one with foreign affairs.

Except for a few items dealing with foreign affairs, to the major points of which references have been made in the preceding pages, all the documents in the *Public Papers* for 1933 reveal the President as a man whose heart and mind were concerned above everything else with the interests, resources, industries, and welfare of the United States. They reveal his persistent contention that the American people, with the aid of their Government, could raise themselves out of the unemployment, poverty, and degradation into which they had fallen and his confidence in their capacity to do this without the assistance of international conferences.[39]

President Roosevelt's Inaugural Address on March 4, 1933, opened with the ringing declaration: "This is a day of national consecration." [40] Not a sentence in it asked the American people to seek relief through international conferences, negotiations, and trade manipulations. From start to finish it was a call to the American people to make "a disciplined attack upon our common problems" and a promise of leadership in that national undertaking. The President recognized that "our international trade relations" are "vastly important," but he declared that "in point of time and necessity" they are "secondary to the establishment of a sound national economy. I favor as a practical policy the putting of

39. Anyone who desires to test the validity of this statement relative to the President's fundamental interests in 1933, and yet does not have the time and patience to read all the documents in this volume of the *Public Papers,* may at least check general impressions by studying the titles of the 195 items as given in the table of contents, pp. vii–xxi.

40. This sentence does not appear in the Inaugural Address as printed in the *Public Papers,* II, 11; but it appears in the address as printed in the President's volume entitled *On Our Way.* It seems that the address as given in the *Public Papers* was taken from the official copy issued by the Government Printing Office, which followed the original mimeographed copy released to the press, and that President Roosevelt, in a resolve to strengthen its appeal to the nation, added the sentence quoted above after the mimeograph had been made.

first things first. I shall spare no effort to restore world trade by international economic readjustment, but the emergency at home can not wait on that accomplishment."

As if aware that this statement would be attacked as isolationist in sentiment, the President immediately elaborated his views: "The basic thought that guides these specific means of national recovery is not narrowly nationalistic. It is the insistence, as a first consideration, upon the interdependence of the various elements in and parts of the United States of America—a recognition of the old and permanently important manifestation of the American spirit of the pioneer. It is the way to recovery. It is the immediate way. It is the strongest assurance that recovery will endure." [41]

Not only did President Roosevelt's domestic measures for recovery ignore cooperation with foreign powers. The most vital of them, dealing with industry, agriculture, employment, and currency, either provided for, or were predicated upon, national insulation against impacts, fluctuations, and manipulations of foreign trade and finance. In many cases this insulation was explicit in the new measures and subsidiary orders. In others it was afforded by laws already in existence, which remained unchanged. Taken collectively these measures presented a four-square contradiction to all the main features of economic theory and practice sponsored by the internationalists who had sought to divert President Roosevelt from the course upon which he had resolved.

Take as an example of the new "insulation" the Industrial Recovery Act of 1933. Section 3 of the Act provided that, on his own motion or on application of any labor, industrial, or trade organization which had complied with the terms of the Act, the President could direct the Tariff Commission to inquire whether imports of any foreign article or articles were cutting into the maintenance of hour-wage-price codes

41. This was a clear and definite warning to the internationalists who believed that American recovery could and should be effected by international agreements designed to "stabilize" the world exchange and "lower trade barriers."

created under the Act; and after a finding of facts he could prescribe such limitations on the import of such article or articles as he might deem necessary to uphold the domestic code, with its hour-wage-price schedules. Under this section of the Act President Roosevelt raised the duties imposed by the Tariff Act of 1930 on a number of commodities; that is, he imposed special fees on the import of such articles, in addition to the duties laid by the Tariff Act. Under the Recovery Act, also, quotas were fixed for sugar imported into the continental United States.[42]

Only once during the year 1933 did President Roosevelt speak generally on the League of Nations. That was on December 28, 1933, when he made an address before the Woodrow Wilson Foundation. Apart from references to this address, the index to his *Public Papers* for 1933 contains only two items relative to the League. The first refers to the so-called "Consultative Pact" and the League[43] and the second to the efforts made by the League of Nations in the interests of peace between Bolivia and Paraguay in the Chaco.[44] And in neither of these statements by the President is any sympathy exhibited for the idea that the United States should join in the suppression of aggressors by collective action or become a member of the League of Nations.

Nor in his address before the Woodrow Wilson Foundation did President Roosevelt in any way modify the opposition to American membership in the League expressed in his speech of February 2, 1932. On the contrary he reaffirmed that opposition. After dwelling in this address at some length on Woodrow Wilson's domestic policies and his contribution to better relations with other countries in this hemisphere, Roosevelt turned to foreign affairs in the large. "In the wider world field, however," he said, "a chain of events has led of late, we fear, away from, rather than toward, the ultimate objectives of Woodrow Wilson."

42. *American Year Book* (1934), pp. 485 ff.
43. This item is discussed above, pp. 125 ff.
44. *Public Papers*, II, 521 ff.

How had this reversal of tendencies come about? Dealing with this question, President Roosevelt made two points which had long been emphasized by American opponents of membership in the League.

First, he exonerated the people of the world from responsibility and laid the blame on politicians: "The superficial observer charges this failure to the growth of the spirit of nationalism. But, in so doing he suggests a nationalism in the wrong sense, a nationalism in its narrower, restrictive sense; he suggests a nationalism of that kind supported by the overwhelming masses of the people themselves in each Nation.

"I challenge that description of the world population today.

"The blame for the danger to world peace lies not in the world population but in the political leaders of that population."

Second, President Roosevelt scoffed at many of the politicians who had dominated the scene at Paris in 1919 and made the alleged settlement of that year; and he did it in language akin to that used by Senators who objected to the ratification of the Versailles Treaty in 1919–20. ". . . fifteen years ago," the President declared, "the imagination of the masses of world population was stirred, as never before, by President Wilson's gallant appeal to them—to those masses—to banish future war. His appeal meant much to them, but it meant little to the imagination or the hearts of a large number of the so-called statesmen who gathered in Paris to assemble a treaty of so-called peace in 1919. I saw that with my own eyes. I heard that with my own ears. Political profit, personal prestige, national aggrandizement attended the birth of the League of Nations, and handicapped it from its infancy."

Yet on this occasion President Roosevelt did not speak as bitterly about the League as he had in his speech of February 2, 1932. In that address he had said that "the League has not developed through these years along the course contemplated by its founder, nor have the principal members shown a disposition to divert the huge sums spent on armament into the channels of legitimate trade, balanced budgets, and the payment of obligations." On December 28, 1933, he paid some tribute to the League and differentiated between its political aspects and its activities relative to social and economic cooperation and welfare.

". . . through the League directly, or through its guiding motives indirectly," he now maintained, "the States of the world, in the years that have gone by, have groped forward to find something better than the old way of composing their differences.

"The League has provided a common meeting place; it has provided machinery which serves for international discussion; and in very many practical instances of which you and I know it has helped labor and health and commerce and education, and last but not least, the actual settlement of many disputes great and small between Nations great and small. . . . The League of Nations, encouraging as it does the extension of non-aggression pacts, of reduction of armament agreements, is a prop in the world peace structure, and it must remain."

What then should be the relation of the United States to the League in such circumstances? President Roosevelt answered that question squarely: "We are not members and we do not contemplate membership. We are giving cooperation to the League in every matter which is not primarily political and in every matter which obviously represents the views and the good of the peoples of the world as distinguished from the views and the good of political leaders, of privileged classes and of imperialistic aims."

Having made clear his own position on the League and power politics, President Roosevelt expounded his constructive program. He declared that about 90 per cent of the world's population were content with their territorial boundaries and willing to reduce armaments if the other 10 per cent would go along with them and abide by a policy of peace. On this ground he proposed that all nations pledge themselves to eliminate, in a short period of time, every weapon of offense and to refrain from allowing any of their armed forces to invade the territory of another nation. If an overwhelming majority of the nations would sign such an agreement, Mr. Roosevelt contended, the sheep would be separated from the goats.

But apart from making the suggestion that the nations so pledging themselves to peace should allow an international inspection of their armaments in the interest of preventing the production and maintenance of "offensive weapons," the President proposed no machinery for action after the goats had been separated from the sheep, the aggressors from the peace-loving nations. He hewed strictly to the line that he had followed during the previous months in dealing with the Disarmament Conference and the London Economic Conference: the United States would seek peace, agree to a reduction of armaments, and offer to consult in the interest of preserving peace; but he did not so much as intimate that he would recommend any participation of the United States in the political activities of the League or in any association of nations to designate aggressors and apply sanctions or force in suppressing them.

In short, on December 28, 1933, President Roosevelt gave no encouragement to those American citizens who were laboring then "to implement the Kellogg–Briand Pact" or to make the United States a member of the League of Nations.

In sum and substance, none of President Roosevelt's public pronouncements in 1933 indicated any break with the foreign policy he had proclaimed on February 2, 1932, after Mr. Hearst's demand for a repudiation of the League of Nations and political entanglements with Europe.

Of this internationalists were well aware. In a report for the year on "The United States and the League of Nations" for the *American Year Book*, "the Associates at the Geneva

Research Center" sought to make all the capital they could for their cause by emphasizing "American cooperation" with the League; but in the end they were compelled to concede defeat. Even in their highest pitch of enthusiasm, they could only resort to ambiguities: "It was not surprising that the President of the Assembly was able to say that American co-operation with the League had never been 'so important, so close, and so varied' as in 1933. There had been no change of principle or juridical relationship; there was, however, an accentuation and extension of normal and helpful coopera-tion. This was due, not so much to any conscious pro-gramme, as to a combination of factors: in part the frequency and gravity of the various crises, in part the wide sweep of League influence and the convenience of its methods, and in part also to the freer psychology in Washington." [45]

Having cited all the credits on their side of the ledger, the Associates took account of the countervailing items on the other side. They noted: "In view, however, of 'erroneous and misleading reports,' Secretary of State Hull declared on September 19, that the Government was 'not contemplating any change whatever in its political relations with the League.'" They also quoted President Roosevelt's reserva-tion set forth in his address of December 28 to the Woodrow Wilson Foundation: "We are not members [of the League], and we do not contemplate membership. We are giving cooperation to the League in every matter which is not pri-marily political, and in every matter which obviously repre-sents the views and good of the peoples of the world, as dis-tinguished from the views and good of political leaders, of privileged classes or of imperialistic aims." Such had been President Roosevelt's warning to internationalists in general and also to those of imperialist inclinations in particular.

So the year ended with the foreign policy of non-entangle-ment, neutrality, and peace for the United States reaffirmed and reinforced.

45. *American Year Book* (1933), p. 89.

Note to Chapter VI

IN SOURCES other than President Hoover's public papers there is supporting evidence for the proposition that Secretary Stimson believed strongly in the enforcement of the non-recognition doctrine by the application of sanctions, as distinguished from President Hoover's view of the doctrine. While Secretary Stimson was in Geneva in 1932 (above, p. 114), the Under-Secretary of State, William R. Castle, delivered an address before the American Conference on International Justice in Washington, May 4, 1932, in which he touched upon the subject of sanctions. The address was published by the American Peace Society in its journal, *World Affairs*, for June, 1932. In this paper Mr. Castle rejected, as out of keeping with the American tradition, a proposal for putting "teeth in the [Kellogg] Pact" by an amendment binding the signatories to make war on the nation that breaks the pledge to settle disputes by peaceful means. The idea of war to prevent war Mr. Castle regarded as a contradiction in terms. He likewise rejected the idea of using such sanctions as the embargo or official boycott as an instrument for bringing pledge-breakers to book. "This idea also," he said, "is opposed by the [Hoover] administration, primarily because an official boycott is an act which would almost surely lead to war."

In response to an inquiry which I directed to Mr. Castle in January, 1946, he replied that he had showed this address to President Hoover before it was delivered and that the President had approved it.

On May 5, 1932, Mr. Castle, also with the approval of President Hoover, delivered an address before the Methodist Convention at Atlantic City, in which he reiterated his objection to the use of sanctions, such as the boycott, in attempts to enforce the Kellogg Pact. After his return from Europe, Secretary Stimson informed Mr. Castle that he regarded the Atlantic City address as ill-advised and as cutting the ground from under his feet in respect of the embargo question.

CHAPTER VII

Hewing to the Isolationist Line in 1934, 1935, and 1936[1]

ALTHOUGH during the year 1934 the war clouds grew bigger and blacker on the world horizon, President Roosevelt adhered to the course of non-entanglement in foreign quarrels. In his annual message to Congress in January, he devoted nearly all his attention to the progress of the domestic recovery. To foreign affairs he granted only a few paragraphs.

The President confessed that he could not present to Congress "a picture of complete optimism regarding world affairs." Outside this hemisphere, he said, fear of immediate or future aggression, vast expenditures for armaments, and the continued building up of trade barriers prevented "any great progress in peace or trade agreements." As to the war debts, the President expressed the hope that he could report later on these obligations "owed the Government and people of this country by the Governments and peoples of other countries." He referred to small payments made by several nations during the previous year and noted that Finland had paid her obligation in full.

And what in these circumstances was the policy to be pursued by the United States? President Roosevelt announced that he was opposed to political entanglements with Europe, although ready to cooperate on certain terms: "I have made it clear that the United States cannot take part in political arrangements in Europe but that we stand ready to cooperate at any time in practicable measures on a world basis looking to immediate reduction of armaments and the lowering of the barriers against commerce." [2]

Few indeed are the references to international affairs in

1. For definition of isolationism, see above, p. 17 n.
2. *Public Papers and Addresses of Franklin Delano Roosevelt*, III, 12.

Volume III of President Roosevelt's *Public Papers* for the year 1934, correctly described in the subtitle: "The Advance of Recovery and Reform." Only one item on the League of Nations appears in the index: a note on the withdrawal of Paraguay from the League. In a special message in June the President reported to Congress on the subject of the payment of the war debts and gave no evidence of any disposition to recommend either cancellation or material reduction. He reminded the debtors that, if they did not pay, the people of the United States would have to shoulder the burden and that the people of this country were taking note of the use which debtor countries were making of their resources instead of paying their debts. He refused to accept any scheme for connecting these war debts with the treatment of reparations in Europe, informed the debtors that they were expected to make substantial sacrifices in efforts to meet their obligations, and invited them to regard these obligations as sacred.[3]

During the year 1934 President Roosevelt acted on his campaign promises with regard to measures for reciprocal tariff bargaining with foreign countries (above, p. 145). On March 2 he asked Congress to empower the Executive to make commercial agreements with foreign nations and to "modify existing duties and import restrictions in such a way *as will benefit American agriculture and industry*." While stating clearly that a full and permanent domestic recovery depended "in part" upon a revived and strengthened international trade, he appended a fundamental reservation: *"it is important that the country possess within its borders a necessary diversity and balance to maintain a rounded national life,* that it must sustain activities vital to national defense and that such interests cannot be sacrificed for passing advantage." As if remembering that under the National Industrial Recovery Act he was endeavoring to uphold domestic price, hour, and wage schedules, the President assured Congress

3. *Ibid.*, III, 275 ff.

that in any reciprocal tariff bargaining "due heed" would be paid to such requirements in reducing tariff rates.[4]

To internationalists who regarded a lowering of trade barriers as a step toward world unity, the President's message offered no consolation. Here was no flat proposal to cut tariff rates all along the line, as Cordell Hull had urged in 1932, on the theory that thereby American economy would prosper, standards of life be raised all over the earth, and the cause of peace advanced. Nor was there in the message anything more than a program for protecting and promoting American agriculture and/or industry by entering into cautious bargaining with commercial rivals abroad. Doubly assured by the message, Congress responded by passing the measure known as the Reciprocal Tariff Act or the Trade Agreements Act, signed on June 12, 1934.

In the administration of the law, President Roosevelt was careful. No revolutionary cuts were made in the tariff rates; indeed on the average few cuts that excited alarms among the well-protected interests.[5] When the President reported on progress under the law in 1938, he expressed the opinion that the trade agreements negotiated according to its terms "have substantially increased our foreign trade." Only then did he offer a crumb of comfort to peace advocates; after speaking of the tangible benefits, he said, "there have been even greater and more far-reaching intangible effects which are measured in terms of the spirit of peace and of more friendly relations between Nations." [6]

Although on its face the Trade Agreements Act looked like an economic document pure and simple, it became in time an instrument in the diplomatic skirmishing between the United States and Great Britain over political difficulties in Europe and Asia. In the Act both the President and Secre-

4. *Ibid.*, III, 113 ff. (Italics supplied.)
5. The per cent of imports for consumption which came in free of duty was actually lower on the average for 1936–40 than for 1931–35. *Statistical Abstract of the United States* (U. S. Government Printing Office, 1942), p. 536.
6. *Public Papers*, III, 117.

tary Hull found a wedge for breaching the wall of tariff preference around the British Empire and increasing American trade with the Empire, not forgetting the sale of raw cotton. On the other side Great Britain, while reluctant to offend the outlying members of the British Commonwealth of Nations, realized that a trade agreement with the United States would be useful as a sign to Germany and Japan that an Anglo-Saxon understanding had been effected. As time went on the political and diplomatic phases of "reciprocal trading" became more and more evident to observers in London and Washington.[6] But when the Act was passed in 1934 only adepts could foresee all the main political utilities inherent in reciprocal "trade negotiations."

Internationalists who scanned the record of American foreign policy for the year 1934 could find therein no sign of retreat on the part of President Roosevelt from the repudiation of the League of Nations publicly announced on February 2, 1932. They could, it is true, report a few "moral gains." A representative of the United States had taken part in another session of the Disarmament Conference (at which nothing visible was accomplished). The United States had joined the International Labor Office (but that meant little more than participation in endless discussions, the collection of statistics, research, and the publication of reports; certainly it involved no commitments whatever to internationalism or collective security).

Cooperation with the League in its technical and humanitarian work continued along lines well established under previous Republican administrations. Efforts were made to reach agreements with Great Britain and Japan for a continuation of naval arms limitations, but the result was a notice from the Japanese Government that the Washington Naval Pact would come to an end on December 31, 1936, with the expiration of the London Naval Pact of 1930. William T. Stone, of the Foreign Policy Association, tersely summed up

6. Frank C. Hanighen, "Will the U. S. Take Trade and Fight for the British?" *New York Post*, September 13, 1938; London date line.

the record: "The year, 1934, was marked by a continuation of the trend toward national self-sufficiency which had become apparent since the onset of the world depression in 1929." [7]

Nevertheless the Associates of the Geneva Research Center, as usual, unearthed vestiges of growing internationalism in the United States and announced their discoveries: "American relations with the League of Nations during 1934 were intensified as a result both of the growing strength and vitality of the League and of the slow evolution of American foreign policy out of the 1920 isolationist period." [8] They made much of American cooperation in the non-political activities of the League and in a section on "Intellectual Cooperation" they reported that Professor James T. Shotwell, of the Carnegie Endowment for International Peace, had taken an active part "unofficially" in the work of the League's committee on Teaching and Intellectual Cooperation.[9] Yet the Geneva Associates did not and could not cite a single statement or action by President Roosevelt that transgressed the doctrine of American neutrality and non-entanglement in the power politics of the League, which he had expounded on February 2, 1932.

The Roosevelt Administration, it is true, continued the policy of refusing to recognize Manchukuo,[10] but it announced no intention to work up a program of collective security or collaboration with other powers for the coercion of Japan. John M. Mathews correctly described the tactics of the year when he said that the Administration showed "no disposition to adopt the role of leadership in marshaling world opinion against Japan." [11] Secretary Hull made no journey to Geneva in 1934, after the manner of Secretary Stimson in 1932, seeking the aid of the League or its powerful members in attempts to oust Japan from Manchukuo.

7. *American Year Book* (1934), p. 70.
8. *Ibid.* (1934), pp. 76 ff.
9. *Ibid.*
10. See above, pp. 114 ff.
11. *American Year Book* (1934), p. 55.

Secretary Hull restricted himself to the delivery of speeches on transgressions of international morality, violations of "the sanctity of contracts," the flouting of "international treaty obligations," and warlike threats indulged in by other governments in various parts of the world.[12] Yet, whatever their implications in terms of ultimate actions, these speeches, even if taken in connection with the non-recognition doctrine, conveyed to the American public in general no intimations of departures from the Administration's official pronouncements against entanglement and participation in foreign wars.[13]

President Roosevelt's pronouncements in 1935 reconfirmed his dedication to peace for the United States, abstention from political entanglements abroad, and promotion of

12. For example, Secretary Hull's address before the American Society of International Law, April 29, 1933; address to the alumni of Cumberland University, May 5, 1934; address to the Graduating Class of the College of William and Mary, June 11, 1934; address before the National Foreign Trade Council, November 1, 1934.

13. Having before me a dossier of American and European materials on American imperialism in the Far East, many papers pertaining to Secretary Stimson's maneuvers in respect of that region, copies of Secretary Hull's addresses on international morality, and the little information which the State Department had seen fit to make public in 1934, I came to the conclusion that the Roosevelt Administration would eventually involve the United States in a war with Japan. If studies of diplomatic history and international law under Professor John Bassett Moore and on my own account had taught me anything, it was that the high officials of great States could not continue indefinitely to lay down moral rules for other governments to follow without being called upon to retract or to employ the historic instrument for enforcing them—war. My conclusion as to where insistence on the non-recognition policy, Secretary Hull's formulations of morality for the world, and the prolongation of the crisis in domestic economy would finally lead was presented in an article, "National Politics and War," published in *Scribner's Magazine* for February, 1935. In this article I said that President Roosevelt "will choose" this war or "stumble into" it, and closed with the following lines: "The Jeffersonian party gave the nation the War of 1812, the Mexican War, and its participation in the World War. The Pacific War awaits. Beyond that lies the Shadowy Shape of Things to Come." In passing, it may be noted that the Democratic platform of 1900, although it denounced Republican imperialism in unmeasured terms and favored independence for the Filipinos, also assured to the Philippines "protection from outside interference such as has been given for nearly a century to the republics of Central and South America." A short time before his death Theodore Roosevelt himself discovered that the Philippines were "the Achilles' heel" of the American Republic.

recovery at home by resort to domestic measures. Volume IV of his *Public Papers* carries a domestic subtitle, "The Court Disapproves." While it contains more references to peace and foreign affairs than Volume III, for the year 1934, it provides more emphatic evidence of the President's resolve to stay out of the League of Nations and similar commitments of an international character.

In his annual message of January 4, 1935, to Congress, he spoke of the old jealousies abroad, old passions, and "new strivings for armament and power" and he drew a contrast in the American spirit: "I believe, however, that our own peaceful and neighborly attitude toward other Nations is coming to be understood and appreciated. . . . There is no ground for apprehension that our relations with any Nation will be otherwise than peaceful." And turning to domestic affairs, he repeated a statement that he had made in 1934: "Among our objectives I place the security of the men, women, and children of the Nation first." [14]

On its own motion, in January, 1935, the Senate began a final debate on the last fragment of internationalism inherited from President Wilson's regime: resolutions providing for the membership of the United States in the World Court established under the general auspices of the League of Nations. The issue had been dragging along for years. By tortuous negotiations and by reservations on vital points, the resolutions had been diluted until they contained no words that could possibly impair the sovereignty of the United States. Supported by platform declarations of the Republican party, President Coolidge and President Hoover had approved the idea of joining the World Court, despite its Democratic origins. Organizations of many kinds, including the League of Women Voters, flooded the Senate with petitions demanding American adherence to the Court. On no grounds could the matter of adopting the resolutions be considered partisan in nature. Moreover, there were sixty-eight Democrats in the Senate—enough to carry the resolutions

14. *Public Papers*, IV, 15 ff.

without aid from the Republican side in case a party split occurred. Advocates of the Court expected victory.

By a vote of fourteen to seven the Foreign Relations Committee of the Senate, on January 9, recommended ratification, with an additional reservation. But a storm of opposition to the project was blowing. Father Charles E. Coughlin inveighed against it over the radio and William Randolph Hearst denounced it through the newspapers he controlled in strategic centers over the country. Accordingly the issue was "hot" when President Roosevelt decided to act. On January 16, 1935, he sent a special message to the Senate urging that body to pass resolutions of adherence to the World Court.

In this message the President brought into notice the non-partisan character of the proposal, spoke of it as representing an "obviously sound and thoroughly American policy," and said: "I hope that at an early date the Senate will advise and consent to the adherence by the United States" to the protocals in question. He recommended "that the Senate's consent be given in such form as not to defeat or to delay the objective of adherence." He expressly declared that "the sovereignty of the United States will be in no way diminished or jeopardized by such action." [15]

Despite the President's urging, the opposition in the Senate, including many Democratic Senators, was unshaken. Advocates of ratification, remembering how easily the President had brought recalcitrant party members in Congress into line during and since the famous "hundred days" of 1933, argued that he should now designate the resolutions of adherence to the World Court as a "must" measure and give the necessary orders to Democratic Senators.[16] But appar-

15. *Ibid.*, IV, 40 f.
16. At the time this contest was on, I was in Washington and in touch with advocates of entering the World Court. Several of them expressed to me great regret that President Roosevelt did not "instruct" recalcitrant Democratic Senators to vote for adherence to the Court. It was reported in the Senate lobby that he was in close negotiations with the Democratic managers in the Senate. If so, he did not or could not bring sufficient pressure on them to force ratification.

ently he did not do this; or, if he did, his orders were disobeyed; for on January 29, 1935, the Court project was defeated by a vote of fifty-two yeas and thirty-six nays—a few votes short of the two-thirds majority necessary for adoption.

After the dispute between Italy and Ethiopia had advanced far on the way toward war, President Roosevelt issued a statement, August 1, 1935, in which he referred to proceedings of the League Council with regard to the quarrel and said simply: "I wish to voice the hope of the people and the Government of the United States that an amicable solution will be found and that peace will be maintained." [17] When the Italo–Ethiopian War broke out, the President proclaimed an embargo on the shipment of arms, under the recent Neutrality Act; and several days later, October 30, 1935, he made a public statement warning war profiteers, in which he declared: "This Government is determined not to become involved in the controversy and is anxious for the restoration and maintenance of peace." [18]

Not only did President Roosevelt make various incidental references to his resolve against involving the nation in foreign quarrels and wars during the year 1935. On several occasions he expressed this resolve with special force. In approving the Neutrality Act, August 31, 1935, he commented adversely on the inflexible provisions of that measure; but he informed the public that "The policy of the Government is definitely committed to the maintenance of peace and the avoidance of any entanglements which would lead us into conflict." [19]

In his press release of August 31, 1935, President Roosevelt expressed no objection to the purpose of the arms embargo section, which was to preserve the neutrality of the

17. *Public Papers,* IV, 315.
18. *Ibid.,* IV, 440. Isolationists, however, charged the President with making personal efforts to assist the League of Nations by applying at least "moral" sanctions to Italy, but his announcement of a determination to avoid involvement was clear and positive.
19. *Ibid.,* IV, 346.

United States in foreign wars. On the contrary, he said, "the objective is wholly good." Moreover, in speaking critically of the inflexibility of the section, he did not argue for change on the ground that the President should have discretion to make a discrimination between belligerents and to use the export of munitions to aid one belligerent while applying sanctions against another, as internationalists and sanctionists were advocating. He accepted the major premise on which advocates of neutrality rested their case, for he declared: "It is the *policy* of this government to avoid being drawn into wars between other nations." He also maintained that, owing to the difficulty of foreseeing future contingencies, "It is conceivable that situations may arise in which the wholly inflexible provisions might drag us into war instead of keeping us out." When he spoke of his *policy* of cooperation with other similarly minded governments to promote peace, he attached to his policy the isolationist conditional clause: "*by every peaceable means and without entanglement.*" [20]

About a month later, on his own motion, in no connection with any particular foreign issue brought officially to his attention, President Roosevelt took special pains, it seems, to reaffirm his policy of abstention from "fierce foreign war." In an address at the San Diego Exposition, October 2, 1935, the President spoke of war perils abroad and then gave the country a solemn assurance: "In the face of this apprehension the American people can have but one concern—the American people can speak but one sentiment: despite what happens in continents overseas, the United States of America shall and must remain, as long ago the Father of our Country prayed that it might remain—unentangled and free. This country seeks no conquest. We have no imperial designs. From day to day and year to year, we are establishing a more perfect assurance of peace with our neighbors. . . . We not

20. (Italics supplied.) For the President's press release and a critical analysis of its meaning and implications, see E. M. Borchard and W. P. Lage, *Neutrality for the United States* (2d ed. Yale University Press, 1940), pp. 315–317.

only earnestly desire peace, but we are moved by a stern determination to avoid those perils that will endanger our peace
with the world." [21]

A determination to keep free from entanglements leading
in the direction of war was again expressed by President
Roosevelt, in a message to a women's conference on current
questions, October 17, 1935. "In facing the problems involved in a world in which international discord still stalks
abroad," he said, "the vivid interests of women in the preser-
vation of safe peace should be enlisted. Constant vigilance is
necessary in a Nation like ours, to see that forces that make
for discord are discovered and discouraged. I have pledged
myself to do my part in keeping America free of those entanglements that move us along the road to war. I want to
feel at all times that I have the sustaining influence of a
healthy, sound, and, above all, thoroughly American public
opinion on the subject." [22]

Speaking at the Arlington National Cemetery on Armi-
stice Day, November 11, 1935, President Roosevelt, after
referring to warlike events and ambitions abroad, said that
"we cannot and must not build walls around ourselves and
hide our heads in the sand." But from this truism he drew no
internationalist conclusions. Far from it. He dedicated the
country to peace, warned youth against the glamour of war,
and limited self-defense to self-defense. "The primary purpose of the United States of America," he said, "is to avoid
being drawn into war. . . . The children in our schools,
the young men and women passing through our colleges into
productive life have, unlike us [of the older generation], no
direct knowledge of the meaning of war. They are not im-
mune to the glamour of war, to the opportunities to escape
from the drabness and worry of hard times at home in the
glory and heroism of the arms factory and the battlefield.
Fortunately, there is evidence on every hand that the youth

21. *Public Papers*, IV, 410 f.
22. *Ibid.*, IV, 423.

of America, as a whole, is not trapped by that delusion. They know that elation and prosperity which may come from a new war must lead—for those who survive it—to economic and social collapse more sweeping than any we have experienced in the past."

After declaring that "we must go forward with all our strength to stress and strive for international peace," the President added: "In this effort America must and will protect herself. Under no circumstances will this policy of self-protection go to lengths beyond self-protection. Aggression on the part of the United States is an impossibility in so far as the present Administration of your Government is concerned. . . . If we as a Nation, by our good example, can contribute to the peaceful well-being of the fellowship of Nations, our course through the years will not have been in vain. . . . The past and the present unite in prayer that America will ever seek the ways of peace, and by her example at home and abroad speed the return of good-will among men." [23]

Among internationalists such Executive pronouncements against intervention in foreign disputes were often treated as unwise or unsound. According to their thesis the United States could not or should not stay out of any major conflict in Europe or Asia. Therefore, their arguments continued, American peace efforts should be directed to preventing such wars by close, official, and vigilant cooperation of the United States with the League of Nations or some other concert of nations. But President Roosevelt had been saying that the United States must consider the security of its own people first, must refrain from political entanglements, should and must keep out of war. At San Diego, on October 2, he had declared that the United States, in the presence of war perils, should and must remain unentangled and free. In so declaring he had arrayed himself specifically on the side of George Washington, whose Farewell Address was the prime

23. *Ibid.*, IV, 441 ff.

document of American foreign policy for isolationists—a dangerous document, in the eyes of internationalists.

Deeply moved by the President's repeated averments that he would avoid political entanglements with the League and shun the road to war, internationalists voiced objections in positive language. One of their leaders, Bishop G. Ashton Oldham of Albany, for example, took the President to task in October, 1935. The Bishop, born in England and educated in the United States, was a member of the English-speaking Union and a member of the Pilgrims of America and was especially concerned about ties with the mother country. He was active in the peace movement: member of the Council on Foreign Relations, the Foreign Policy Association, the World Alliance for International Peace, and the Churches and World Peace Association. In his letter to President Roosevelt Bishop Oldham stated that the effort of the fifty-two nations may come to naught if the United States stands aloof—the internationalist formula to the effect that the peace-loving nations of the world could not keep peace unless the United States became a member of the League or some kindred association of governments.

Bishop Oldham's letter posed a problem for President Roosevelt. The President agreed that the best insurance for American peace was to take steps to prevent "all fires." He informed the Bishop that on many occasions the United States had taken such steps, that the United States under his presidency was not standing aloof, and that in a number of respects he had gone beyond actions so far taken by other countries. He reminded Bishop Oldham, however, that it had become "incumbent on me to give first thought to the unquestioned mandate of our people, expressed in recent legislation and in numerous other ways, through the press, through public gatherings and through petitions and letters, that, above all, the United States should not be drawn into the conflict [between Italy and Ethiopia]." He closed this private communication by assuring Bishop Oldham that he would continue to play the dual role—of attempting to smother fires and of keeping out of war.[24]

On the basis of President Roosevelt's public and official statements on foreign policy, Francis Brown, Associate Editor of *Current History*, correctly reported, in a review of international affairs for the year 1935: "The American attitude toward Europe throughout 1935 was dominated by the desire to keep out of that continent's turbulent affairs. On this note the year began and ended." That attitude, Mr. Brown said, was not due to the advice of the Founding Fathers against "entangling alliances," nor to perverse unwillingness to cooperate with other nations, nor to intense preoccupation with domestic problems; it was based in part on disillusionment as to the recent World War; "but there was more than memory. Events of the post-war years convinced many Americans, leaders as well as led, that the League of Nations . . . was hardly more than a league of conquerors to enforce an unjust peace." [25]

By 1936 three of the particular issues in foreign relations thrust upon President Roosevelt in 1933 had, for practical purposes, faded away: the war debts, the Disarmament Conference, and the World Economic Conference. In the Far East, the Manchurian question remained open as a source of perplexity to the State Department. Secretary Hull in various public addresses on international morality adverted to it obliquely without indulging in specifications, but European governments manifested little interest in it and even less inclination to start a war over it. On the other hand, international relations in Europe had gone from bad to worse. Italy had waged a brutal war on Ethiopia. Hitler, having achieved dictatorial power, had gone far on his career of persecuting Jews, socialists, Communists, and liberals, had withdrawn from the League of Nations, and was rearming Germany in defiance of the Versailles Treaty. Great Britain, without the

24. *Ibid.*, IV, 452 f.
25. *American Year Book* (1935), p. 67.

advance consent of France, had made a naval compact with Hitler, also in defiance of the Versailles Treaty. The governments of Europe, great and small, had begun that frenzied scramble for power and safety described trenchantly and ironically in Frederick Schuman's *Europe on the Eve.*

As the months of 1936 passed, the dangers of a general European war grew more evident. Hitler's troops reoccupied the Rhineland in defiance of the Versailles Treaty. The Falangist revolt against the Republican Government in Spain flamed up and spread, sending alarms far and wide. Italy and Germany formed the Rome–Berlin Axis. Japan and Germany established the Anti-Comintern combination— which Italy joined the following year. Meanwhile the British Government, instead of uniting with France and Russia in a bold front against Hitler, was seeking to reach a *modus vivendi* with him, if not actually to encourage him in his designs against the Soviet Union. Nothing that President Roosevelt had done so far and was doing in the way of pacification by moral persuasion had produced any visible effect in easing the diplomatic tensions and conflicts of the Old World.

No informed American citizen could be oblivious to the roaring violence across the seas. More than once in the course of the year 1936 President Roosevelt spoke solemnly and extensively of grave disturbances in world affairs but he made no pronouncements which indicated a departure from his previous pledges to avoid political entanglements in Europe and Asia and involvement in the wars of those continents. All his public addresses on the subject in that year, despite numerous references to the perils of war in the world, conformed to the line of the non-entanglement policy he had followed since February 2, 1932.

In his message to Congress, January 3, 1936, the President devoted more than three pages to war dangers in Europe and Asia and expressed the fear that an era of mad scramble for power might return. "We hope," he said, "that we are not again at the threshold of such an era," and immediately declared: "But if face it we must, then the United States and the rest of the Americas can play but one role: through a well-ordered neutrality to do naught to encourage the contest, through adequate defense to save ourselves from embroilment and attack, and through example and all legitimate encouragement and assistance to persuade other Nations to return to the ways of peace and good will." [26]

Near the middle of the year, in an address at Dallas, Texas, on June 12, 1936, President Roosevelt took cognizance of the dangers that beset the world and reiterated the doctrine of non-intervention: "As I have said, we seem to understand very well what the problems of the world are. We have, perhaps, a kind of sympathy for their problems. We want to help them all that we can; but they have understood very well in these latter years that help is going to be confined to moral help, and that we are not going to get tangled up with their troubles in the days to come." [27]

In accepting the renomination for the presidency at Philadelphia, June 27, 1936, Mr. Roosevelt concentrated his attention entirely on domestic affairs, the recent domestic achievements of his Administration, and the tasks ahead. To foreign policy as such he gave no consideration; but he concluded his address with the lines: "In this world of ours in other lands, there are some people, who, in times past, have lived and fought for freedom, and seem to have grown too weary to carry on the fight. They have sold their heritage of freedom for the illusion of a living. They have yielded their democracy. I believe in my heart that only our success can stir their ancient hope. They begin to know that here in America we are waging a great and successful war. It is not alone a war against want and destitution and economic demoralization. It is more than that; it is a war for the survival

26. *Public Papers,* V, 12. For the nature and history of "the administration's or Senator Pittman's New Neutrality Bill," and for the Neutrality Resolution of 1936, signed by President Roosevelt, see Borchard and Lage, *op. cit.,* pp. 324 ff.

27. *Public Papers,* V, 217.

of democracy. We are fighting to save a great and precious form of government for ourselves and for the world." [28]

Only occasionally during his campaign for reelection did President Roosevelt dwell upon his foreign policy, and only once at length—in his address at Chautauqua on August 14, 1936. In all his other speeches he laid stress upon domestic issues and the necessity of carrying forward the work of domestic reform which he had thus far advanced. If his campaign addresses and other public papers for the year 1936 fully disclosed his hopes and purposes at that time, the building of civilization in America was first and last in his resolve of heart and mind. Furthermore he displayed a determination to refrain from political entanglements in European controversies and maintain peace for the United States.

In the address at Chautauqua, the President dealt broadly with the foreign situation and his own policy respecting it. He began by expressing his concern about the perils of "world conditions." He reviewed the actions taken under his Administration in giving effect to the good-neighbor policy in this hemisphere. He spoke at length about recent violations of solemn obligations beyond the seas. He laid stress on America's efforts to cooperate in the reduction of armaments, in the continuance of limitations on naval armaments, and in the "humanitarian" work of the League of Nations. He declared that nations which provoke war forfeit the sympathy of the American people. Then he solemnly warned the country against the thousands of Americans who would, in case a general war came overseas, seek to "break down or evade our neutrality," in a hunt for profits, "fools' gold," in a hope that "America once more would capture the trade of the world."

With regard to his own sentiments, policy, and measures

28. *Ibid.*, V, 235 f. The Democratic platform of 1936 reaffirmed opposition to war, favored the pacific settlement of disputes among nations, and declared: "We shall continue to observe a true neutrality in the disputes of others; to be prepared resolutely to resist aggression against ourselves; to work for peace and to take the profits out of war; . . ."

relative to foreign perils and foreign wars, President Roosevelt held fast to the line of neutrality and non-involvement:

We shun political commitments which might entangle us in foreign wars; we avoid connection with the political activities of the League of Nations; . . .

We are not isolationists except in so far as we seek to isolate ourselves completely from war. Yet we must remember that so long as war exists on earth there will be some danger that even the Nation which most ardently desires peace may be drawn into war.

I have seen war. I have seen war on land and sea. I have seen blood running from the wounded. I have seen men coughing out their gassed lungs. I have seen the dead in the mud. I have seen cities destroyed. I have seen two hundred limping, exhausted men come out of line—the survivors of a regiment of one thousand that went forward forty-eight hours before. I have seen children starving. I have seen the agony of mothers and wives. I hate war.

I have passed unnumbered hours, I shall pass unnumbered hours, thinking and planning how war may be kept from this nation. . . .

The Congress of the United States has given me certain authority to provide safeguards of American neutrality in case of war.

The President of the United States, who, under our Constitution, is vested with primary authority to conduct our international relations, thus has been given new weapons with which to maintain our neutrality.

Nevertheless—and I speak from a long experience—the effective maintenance of American neutrality depends today, as in the past, on the wisdom and determination of whoever at the moment occupy the offices of President and Secretary of State. . . .

No matter how well we are supported by neutrality legislation, we must remember that no laws can be provided to cover every contingency, for it is impossible to imagine how every future event may shape itself. In spite of every possible forethought, international relations involve of necessity a vast uncharted area. In that area safe sailing will depend on the knowledge and the experience and the wisdom of those who direct our foreign policy. Peace will depend on their day to day decisions.

At this late date, with the wisdom which is so easy after the event and so difficult before the event, we find it possible to trace the tragic series of small decisions which led Europe into the Great War in 1914 and eventually engulfed us and many other Nations.

We can keep out of war if those who watch and decide have a sufficiently detailed understanding of international affairs to make certain that the small decisions of each day do not lead toward war and if, at the same time, they possess the courage to say "no" to those who selfishly or unwisely would let us go to war. . . .[29]

At New York City President Roosevelt closed his campaign of 1936 for reelection on the clarion note of peace for America. After reviewing again the domestic aims of his Administration, he declared: "All this—all these objectives—spell peace at home. All our actions, all our ideals, spell also peace with other nations. Today there is war and rumor of war. We want none of it. . . . You know well that those who stand to profit by war are not on our side in this campaign. 'Peace on earth, good will toward men'—democracy must cling to that message. . . . That is the road to peace." [30]

Relying upon the evidence of the year's record, the Vice-President of the Foreign Policy Association, William T. Stone, reported in a review of American foreign policy for 1936: "The desire to avoid involvement in the turbulent affairs of Europe continued to dominate American policy throughout the year 1936. As the swift current of events carried Europe from the Italo–Ethiopian conflict to the Rhineland crisis of March and the civil war in Spain, the Roosevelt Administration struggled to maintain its course of strict neutrality. . . . American public opinion remained predominantly isolationist. . . . Another major crisis [in Europe] served to emphasize once more the extent of American isolation. On March 7, without previous warning,

29. *Ibid.*, V, 285 ff.
30. *Ibid.*, V, 572 f.

Chancellor Hitler announced the occupation by German troops of the Rhineland zone demilitarized by the Versailles Treaty. . . . Throughout the period of diplomatic tension which accompanied the meetings of the League Council in London and Geneva, the United States maintained an attitude of strict detachment, and there was no suggestion from Europe that this country should participate, even informally, in the meetings in London and Geneva." [31]

31. *American Year Book* (1936), pp. 77 f.

CHAPTER VIII

Turn and Return in 1937–1938

TUMULTUOUS events, domestic and foreign, marked the course of 1937. The high tension already evident in Washington at the close of 1936 continued to increase rather than abate, from month to month till the end of 1937. President Roosevelt's program for domestic reform, known as the New Deal, had been practically completed, at least as far as the recent decisions of the Supreme Court had permitted. On February 5, 1937, the President presented to Congress a plan for the reorganization of the judicial branch of the government and thereby precipitated a bitter conflict within his party as well as in the country at large. While that tempest raged other affairs, foreign and domestic, were partly submerged; and this state of turmoil continued until August, 1937, when Congress gave a mortal blow to the President's project for what was called "packing the Supreme Court."

The contest over the reorganization of the judiciary had scarcely come to a conclusion when the promise of recovery and stability tendered by the President's New Deal was confronted by a financial crash almost as swift and terrifying as the panic in the autumn of 1929. As the economic specialist, S. S. Huebner, correctly reported: "During the next three months, however, following August, the market experienced a decline which can only be described as a collapse. The decline in [stock] prices during September, October, and November was not only drastic but also general in its application to all groups of stocks. In fact there are few instances on record where a larger percentage decline has occurred within so short a period of time as three months. . . . Adverse news piled up so plentifully during the last three quarters of 1937 as to undermine the confidence of the investment and speculative community. Labor unrest of serious proportions confronted nearly all of the nation's basic industries, and resulted in widespread disorganization in production as well as huge financial loss to all concerned." [1]

In its range the shock of the economic collapse was startling to President Roosevelt and his advisers. Unemployment continued to be alarming in amount and effects. Labor agitation grew more turbulent. The hostility of the financial community was aggravated. To the Administration, an enlargement of federal spending seemed again necessary as a stimulus to business recovery, and that meant an extension of the "deficit financing" which had for a time been regarded, even by many New Dealers, as a temporary and deplorable expedient. Doubts came to the President and his counselors: perhaps they had been wrong in seeking recovery through the specific measures they had espoused and were at the end of their improvisation. At any rate, in the autumn of 1937 the outlook for the New Deal was discouraging and the discouragement affected all the Administration circles in Washington. The grand dream of 1933 no longer inspired unwavering optimism even among loyal Democrats.

Dark as was the domestic outlook, darker still was the state of affairs abroad. When the year 1937 opened the fury of the civil war in Spain was being accelerated: Germany and Italy were sending armed forces into Spain to aid the rebels; Russia was lending aid to the Loyalists; and volunteers from many countries, including the United States, were pouring into Spain to join in the fight against Spanish, German, and Italian Fascists. Indeed the struggle had the appearance of a frightful dress rehearsal for a coming war in Europe between Fascism and a "united front" of communists, liberals, socialists, and democrats. In July Japan began an undeclared war on China, setting the Orient aflame again, and threatening all the Occidental interests in that part of the world.

Meanwhile, with reference to the European convulsions

1. *American Year Book* (1937), p. 366.

and the new Sino-Japanese War, diplomatic maneuverings kept the chancelleries of the world in uproar and supplied the American press with sensational news of wars and war rumors. Mere observers commanding no "inside" information were reasonably certain that Hitler meant war and that despite efforts to "appease" him, he would spring the war when he was ready.[2]

As far as public pronouncements during the first nine months of 1937 were concerned, however, President Roosevelt indicated to the country no change in the policy of nonentanglement in the political maneuverings of the great foreign powers, whether in the League of Nations or outside, which he had reiterated so many times since February 2, 1932. Nor did he reverse the opinion, likewise often restated, that the United States could and should stay out of the war when it came.

His second Inaugural Address, in January, contained no passage on foreign affairs and the probability of American involvement in the war. On the contrary it displayed a resolve to grapple with domestic issues yet unsettled—issues presented in his own description: "one-third of a Nation ill-housed, ill-clad, ill-nourished." In his address at the Democratic victory dinner, March 4, 1937, the President expressed the desire to turn over to his successor on January 20, 1941, "a Nation intact, a Nation at peace, a Nation prosperous, a Nation clear in its knowledge of what powers it has to serve its own citizens, a Nation that is in a position to use those powers to the full in order to move forward steadily to meet the modern needs of humanity. . . ."[3]

2. For example, in an article in *Foreign Affairs* for April, 1936, on "Education under the Nazis," I wrote: "Turned in upon themselves, nourishing deep resentments, and lashed to fury by a militant system of education, the German people are conditioned for that day when Hitler, his technicians, and the army are ready and are reasonably sure of the prospects of success in a sudden and devastating attack, East or West. To cherish any other conception of Hitler's State or of the aims of German education is to cherish a delusion."

3. *Public Papers*, 1937 Vol. (The Macmillan Company, 1941), p. 115.

But while President Roosevelt publicly announced no reversal of his non-entanglement *policy* with regard to European political affairs, he took many *actions* which to members of Congress and private observers had the appearance of a resolve to abandon neutrality in favor of intervention in European and Asiatic conflicts. This is no place to review all those actions; nor until the diplomatic archives of all the Great Powers are opened, if ever, will it be possible to discover the various forms and ramifications of those actions. A few examples, however, will indicate reasons for the growing fear that the President's measures, as distinguished from his published statements of policy, were carrying the United States along "the road to war."

Early in the year certain steps taken by the Roosevelt Administration in respect of the Spanish Civil War offered a test of his policy. In some relations, it was known, the Administration was cooperating with the Non-Intervention Committee at London—a committee formed under British leadership for the general purpose of "localizing" the Spanish Civil War, keeping it from spreading to a general war. When the party conflicts in Spain had burst out in civil war, in the summer of 1936, the State Department had gone beyond the rule of strict neutrality and beyond the terms of the law; it had tried to discourage the sale of arms by American citizens to belligerents in Spain. Although the Department knew that the embargo provisions of the existing Neutrality Act did not apply to civil war, it continued to warn American citizens against shipping arms to the belligerents in Spain including the Spanish Republican Government then officially recognized by the Government of the United States. In January, 1937, President Roosevelt sought to make interference with arms shipments "legal," by asking Congress for a special act to authorize applying the embargo on "arms, munitions, and implements of war" to civil wars—in effect, to the Spanish Republican Government as well as to the Fascist rebels against the Spanish Republic. On January 9, 1937, this Act was signed and became law.

On its surface the new embargo law had the appearance of non-intervention. But in fact it was more than that. In the first place, it was a blow at the Republican Government of Spain, for Germany and Italy were notoriously supplying munitions to the Spanish Fascists in rebellion against the Republic and were aiding them with armed forces. In the second place the Act violated an established rule of international law that a neutral country should not change its legislation after a war had broken out, in such a way as to discriminate materially against a lawful belligerent. In the third place, it transgressed the terms of the Treaty of Madrid consumated in 1902 between the United States and Spain. In the fourth place, it played into the hands of Great Britain, then nominally neutral in the Spanish War but actually pursuing measures injurious to the recognized Government of Spain. In the fifth place, whether or not it materially aided in the destruction of the Republican Government in Spain, it was followed by the victory of the Falangist and Fascist rebels in that country and the installation as dictator of Francisco Franco, to whom President Roosevelt accorded official recognition with a celerity that was astounding in view of his professed attachment to democratic principles.[4]

Another illustration of President Roosevelt's apparent shift in the direction of intervention in foreign controversies occurred in connection with the Sino-Japanese War that began on July 7, 1937. The Neutrality Act of May 1, 1937, had made it mandatory on the President to embargo the shipment of arms and other materials *when he found* a state of war existing abroad. What appeared to be a war and was in fact a war continued to rage in China after July 7. It was expected in many quarters that he would *find* it to be a war, proclaim American neutrality, and embargo the sale of munitions and other articles of war use to belligerents in the Orient. But President Roosevelt refused to apply the em-

4. For the principle of "recognition" in the historic policy of the United States and for President Roosevelt's adherence to the non-recognition doctrine in the case of Japanese aggression in Manchukuo, see above, pp. 144 ff.

bargo; and in July, 1937, the State Department issued a manifesto to sixty governments of the world on the sanctity of treaties and international law. Thus the State Department suggested to citizens with long memories that the Administration was preparing to "implement" the Stimson doctrine to which the President had obliquely subscribed on January 9, 1933.[5]

More than one newspaper and magazine treated President Roosevelt's decisions in the case of the Spanish Civil War and the Sino-Japanese War as disclosing an intention to abandon his non-entanglement policy. Knowing the public concern over what had the semblance of a new line in American foreign policy, Spencer Brodney, editor of *Events*, a monthly review of world affairs, invited me to write an article for his journal on the subject "Will Roosevelt Keep Us Out of War?" In response I prepared the article, which was published in *Events* for July, 1937. I had been in Washington during the winter of 1936–37 and had followed as closely as I could the trends of opinion at the national capital. After a brief review of some recent tendencies which seemed to indicate a shift in the President's intentions, I concluded: "Taking these considerations together, the American people may well prepare themselves to see President Roosevelt plunge the country into the European war, when it comes, far more quickly than did President Wilson."

This article was followed by another prepared in July and published in the August issue of *Events*. In the second article, after referring to ominous events in Europe I said: "Beyond the Atlantic is the United States, also arming rapidly, with plans for landing a four-million army 'somewhere' off the American continent. On the whole President Roosevelt has made no open commitments. But his sympathies are so well known as to need no documentation. There is also a configuration of war sympathies in the United States. It ranges from professional peace advocates who support the Entente's League of Nations, through Conservatives who think that

5. Above, pp. 133 ff.

war would be a good thing for the country, to Stalinites who are bent on 'saving Russian democracy.' " [6]

On his own motion, without my knowledge, Mr. Brodney sent copies of my two articles to President Roosevelt, accompanied by a letter in which he suggested that the President would render a great public service if he "would make a statement to the American people that would set their minds at ease on a matter about which there is doubt and suspicion." In reply Stephen Early, the President's secretary, informed Mr. Brodney that "the President is grateful to you for writing as you did," and added: "For your information I am enclosing herewith copies of two addresses delivered by the President, one at Chautauqua, New York, and the other at San Diego, California." In the copies sent to Mr. Brodney the passages dealing with "our national determination to keep free from foreign wars and foreign entanglements" were marked. Mr. Early also assured Mr. Brodney that *"these formal and public pronouncements of the President still clearly and definitely set forth his views on the subject about which you write."* [7]

Thus in August, 1937, President Roosevelt, in response to a direct question, guaranteed his continued adherence to the non-intervention policy so often emphasized in his public addresses since February 2, 1932, never more positively and explicitly than in the Chautauqua and San Diego speeches.

6. At this time the Communist line was "a united front against Fascism." A representative of the Soviet Embassy in Washington called on me at my hotel in the winter of 1937–38 and argued at great length that a war of the United States against Japan would in no way partake of an imperialist character, would in fact serve the cause of "democracy" throughout the world. He was somewhat perturbed when I showed him a dossier of Communist writings from previous years, denouncing the operations of the United States in the Far East as "imperialistic" aggressions against exploited peoples, and contrasted them with writings of the new line—"The united front against Fascism."

7. (Italics supplied.) Mr. Brodney's letter to President Roosevelt, Mr. Early's reply, the pertinent extracts from the San Diego and Chautauqua addresses, and my rejoinder appear in *Events* for September, 1937. For these extracts, see above, pp. 166, 174.

A few weeks elapsed. Then suddenly at Chicago, on October 5, 1937, the President delivered, in a tone of decisive solemnity, an address on the world situation in which he discarded the doctrine of neutrality for the United States and espoused the idea of collective security—the cardinal principle of internationalism. He spoke with feeling about the "present reign of terror and international lawlessness," forecast more frightful scenes, declared that in such circumstances America could not expect mercy or escape from attack, and called for united action against aggressors on the part of the 90 per cent of the world's population that cherished peace, freedom, and security.

After reviewing recent destruction of life and property in wars raging abroad and quoting from an author's description of frightfulness impending, President Roosevelt said:

If those things come to pass in other parts of the world, let no one imagine that America will escape, that America may expect mercy, that this Western Hemisphere will not be attacked and that it will continue tranquilly and peacefully to carry on the ethics and the arts of civilization.

If those days come "there will be no safety by arms, no help from authority, no answer in science. The storm will rage till every flower of culture is trampled and all human beings are leveled in a vast chaos."

If those days are not to come to pass—if we are to have a world in which we can breathe freely and live in amity without fear— the peace-loving nations must make a concerted effort to uphold laws and principles on which alone peace can rest secure.

The peace-loving nations must make a concerted effort in opposition to those violations of treaties and those ignorings of humane instincts which today are creating a state of international anarchy and instability from which there is no escape through mere isolation or neutrality.

Those who cherish their freedom and recognize and respect the equal right of their neighbors to be free and live in peace, must work together for the triumph of law and moral principles in order that peace, justice, and confidence may prevail in the world.

There must be a return to a belief in the pledged word, in the value of a signed treaty. There must be recognition of the fact that national morality is as vital as private morality.

A bishop wrote me the other day:

> It seems to me that something greatly needs to be said in behalf of ordinary humanity against the present practice of carrying the horrors of war to helpless civilians, especially women and children.

> It may be that such a protest might be regarded by many, who claim to be realists, as futile, but may it not be that the heart of mankind is so filled with horror at the present needless suffering that that force could be mobilized in sufficient volume to lessen such cruelty in the days ahead?

> Even though it may take twenty years, which God forbid, for civilization to make effective its corporate protest against this barbarism, surely strong voices may hasten the day.

There is a solidarity and interdependence about the modern world, both technically and morally, which makes it impossible for any nation completely to isolate itself from economic and political upheavals in the rest of the world, especially when such upheavals appear to be spreading and not declining.

There can be no stability or peace either within nations or between nations except under laws and moral standards adhered to by all. International anarchy destroys every foundation for peace. It jeopardizes either the immediate or the future security of every nation, large or small.

It is, therefore, a matter of vital interest and concern to the people of the United States that the sanctity of international treaties and the maintenance of international morality be restored.

The overwhelming majority of the peoples and nations of the world today want to live in peace.

They seek the removal of barriers against trade.

They want to exert themselves in industry, in agriculture and in business, that they may increase their wealth through the production of wealth-producing goods rather than striving to produce military planes and bombs and machine guns and cannon for the destruction of human lives and useful property. . . .

The peace, the freedom and the security of ninety per cent of the population of the world is being jeopardized by the remaining ten per cent who are threatening a breakdown of all international order and law. Surely the ninety per cent who want to live in peace under law and in accordance with moral standards that have received almost universal acceptance through the centuries, can and must find some way to make their will prevail.

The situation is definitely of universal concern. The questions involved relate not merely to violations of specific provisions of particular treaties; they are questions of war and of peace, of international law and especially of principles of humanity. It is true that they involve definite violations of agreements, and especially of the Covenant of the League of Nations, the Briand–Kellogg Pact, and the Nine Power Treaty. But they also involve problems of world economy, world security and world humanity.

It is true that the moral consciousness of the world must recognize the importance of removing injustices and well-founded grievances; but at the same time it must be aroused to the cardinal necessity of honoring sanctity of treaties, of respecting the rights and liberties of others and of putting an end to acts of international aggression.

It seems to be unfortunately true that the epidemic of world lawlessness is spreading.

When an epidemic of physical disease starts to spread, the community approves and joins in a quarantine of the patients in order to protect the health of the community against the spread of the disease.

It is my determination to pursue a policy of peace. It is my determination to adopt every practicable measure to avoid involvement in war. It ought to be inconceivable that in this modern era, and in the face of experience, any nation could be so foolish and ruthless as to run the risk of plunging the whole world into war by invading and violating, in contravention of solemn treaties, the territory of other nations that have done them no real harm and are too weak to protect themselves adequately. Yet the peace of the world and the welfare and security of every nation, including our own is today being threatened by that very thing.

No nation which refuses to exercise forbearance and to respect the freedom and rights of others can long remain strong and retain the confidence and respect of other nations. No nation ever loses its dignity or its good standing by conciliating its differences, and by exercising great patience with, and consideration for, the rights of other nations.

War is a contagion, whether it be declared or undeclared. It can engulf states and peoples remote from the original scene of hostilities. We are determined to keep out of war, yet we cannot insure ourselves against the disastrous effects of war and the dangers of involvement. We are adopting such measures as will minimize our risk of involvement but we cannot have complete protection in a world of disorder in which confidence and security have broken down.

If civilization is to survive the principles of the Prince of Peace must be restored. Trust between nations must be revived.

Most important of all, the will for peace on the part of peace-loving nations must express itself to the end that nations that may be tempted to violate their agreements and the rights of others will desist from such a course. There must be positive endeavors to preserve peace. America hates war. America hopes for peace. Therefore, America actively engages in the search for peace.[8]

The "quarantine speech" at Chicago fell upon the country like a bolt from the blue. Internationalists greeted it with rejoicing as conclusive evidence that President Roosevelt had at last spurned, in the name of the United States, the principle of non-entanglement and non-intervention in the political and military operations of European and Asiatic powers, and had aligned himself on the side of full cooperation with "peace-loving" nations in designating and taking collective action against the aggressors—Germany, Italy, and Japan. With this interpretation of the speech isolationists agreed, but they criticized the President in blunt language. They accused him of having violated the pledges he had repeatedly made to the people and charged him with setting out on "the road to war." They alleged that he was trying to divert attention from his domestic "mistakes" by raising war scares. From the Atlantic to the Pacific a tumult of debate surged up

8. *Public Papers*, 1937 Vol., pp. 408 ff.

and demands for clarification were heard throughout the nation.

President Roosevelt was annoyed by the outcry which immediately followed his Chicago speech. Writing nearly four years afterward, on July 10, 1941, he said of his quarantine proposal: "Unfortunately, this suggestion fell upon deaf ears —even hostile and resentful ears. . . . It was hailed as war mongering; it was condemned as attempted intervention in foreign affairs; it was even ridiculed as a nervous search 'under the bed' for dangers of war which did not exist." [9] When the President met the journalists in a press conference on October 6, 1937, the day after the Chicago speech, he seemed bewildered by the outburst of discussion, approval, and disapproval that he had called forth.[10]

As soon as the subject of the quarantine speech was broached at the conference, President Roosevelt declined to say anything for publication and insisted that he could only speak "off the record," adding that he did not want to say anything "for background." He was asked to state what type of measure in respect of quarantining he had in mind and how he reconciled that proposal with the Neutrality Act. His reply was a citation of the last line in the Chicago speech: "Therefore America actively engages in the search for peace."

Bent on forcing the issue, a journalist inquired: "But you also said that the peace-loving nations can and must find a way to make their wills prevail." The President's comment was: "Yes?" The following exchange then took place:

Q. And you were speaking, as I interpreted it, you were speaking of something more than moral indignation. That is preparing the way for collaborative—

THE PRESIDENT. Yes?

Q. Is anything contemplated? Have you moved?

THE PRESIDENT. No; just the speech itself.

9. Introduction to *Public Papers*, 1939 Vol., p. xxviii.

10. For this description I am indebted to a distinguished journalist of New Deal sympathies, who was present and took part in questioning the President.

Q. Yes, but how do you reconcile that? Do you accept the fact that is a repudiation of the neutrality—

THE PRESIDENT. Not for a minute. It may be an expansion.

Q. Is that for use?

THE PRESIDENT. All off the record.

The President was then asked whether the quarantine doctrine did not mean "economic sanctions anyway." He turned the query aside, saying: "No, not necessarily. Look, 'sanctions' is a terrible word to use. They are all out of the window." [11] Unable to make any advance along that line, the questioner took another: "Right. Let's not call it that. Let's call it concert of action on the part of peace-loving nations. Is that going to be brought into play?" The President parried: ". . . We are looking for some way to peace . . ." The journalist thereupon wanted to know whether there was likely to be a conference of peace-loving nations, and was informed by the President: "No; conferences are out of the window. You never get anywhere with a conference. . . . We are looking for a program."

Determined if possible to discover what practical actions or measures the President had in mind as a means of giving effect to the quarantine doctrine, the questioner started the following discussion:

Q. Wouldn't it be almost inevitable, if any program is reached, that our present Neutrality Act will have to be overhauled?

THE PRESIDENT. Not necessarily. That is the interesting thing.

Q. That is very interesting.

Q. You say there isn't any conflict between what you outline and the Neutrality Act. They seem to be on opposite poles to me and your assertion does not enlighten me.

THE PRESIDENT. Put your thinking-cap on, Ernest [Lindley].

Q. I have been [thinking] for some years. They seem to be at opposite poles. How can you be neutral if you are going to align yourself with one group of nations?

11. This seemed to be a repudiation of sanctions such as Secretary Stimson had advocated. Above, pp. 134 ff.

THE PRESIDENT. What do you mean, 'aligning'? You mean a treaty?

Q. Not necessarily. I mean action on the part of peace-loving nations.

THE PRESIDENT. There are a lot of methods in the world that have never been tried yet.

Q. But, at any rate, that is not an indication of neutral attitude —'quarantine the aggressors' and 'other nations of the world.'

THE PRESIDENT. I can't give you any clue to it. You will have to invent one. I have got one.

After some side play a journalist asked the blunt question: "Is a 'quarantine' a sanction?" The President's reply was: "No." Then came another blunt question: "Are you excluding any coercive action? Sanction is coercive." The President answered: "That is exactly the difference." As if to drive the President into admitting that his quarantine doctrine belonged merely in the realm of moral appeal, a journalist immediately remarked: "Better, then, to keep it in a moral sphere?" [12] This the President refused to grant, for he replied: "No; it can be a very practical sphere." With these words the conference was brought to an end, leaving the journalists, as one of them remarked to the writer of these lines a short time afterward, "up in the air." [13]

If the upshot of the press conference seemed to be confusion, two remarks by the President gave an inkling that he had something definite in contemplation. The first was: "There are a lot of methods in the world that have never been tried yet." And the second was to the effect that he had some plan in mind: "I can't give you any clue to it. You will have to invent one. *I have got one.*" (Italics supplied.)

Was this the point in time at which President Roosevelt and Secretary Hull decided that it was necessary to turn the nation away from isolationism as expressed in the Neutrality

12. This was President Hoover's conception of the non-recognition policy to which Mr. Stimson attached sanctions and coercion. Above, pp. 134 ff.

13. For the stenographic account of this press conference, *Public Papers*, 1937 Vol., 414 ff.

Act and toward definite collaboration with the peace-loving nations as against the aggressors?[14] If it was, no information to that effect was given to the country in October, 1937; and furthermore, again and again after October 6, 1937, both the President and the Secretary proclaimed to the country their adherence to the doctrine of neutrality and non-entanglement for the United States.[15]

For many days after October 5, 1937, journalists studied the language of the quarantine speech and tried to work out its meaning in terms of some new policy—some principle of action that, in the nature of things, marked a departure from the policy of neutrality hitherto maintained. The *New York Times* reported on October 7, 1937, that the President "steadfastly refused to amplify" the Chicago address. The *New York Herald Tribune*, on the same day, was of the opinion that some passages in the quarantine speech "challenged the effectiveness of neutrality as a safeguard of peace and proposed a collective 'quarantine' of aggressor nations"; but it recorded that such information as had been gleaned from sources near to the President left "only a confused picture," although one of the President's "lieutenants" admitted "a marked deviation from the Congressional policy." At the same time the *Herald Tribune* attributed to another "source" the statement that the President had in mind a scheme for keeping the United States neutral while cooperating with the peace-loving nations in restraining aggressors—a scheme for applying effective restraints and at the same time avoiding entanglement in "economic or military sanctions."

On October 9, 1937, a reporter for the *Herald Tribune* suggested a possible key to the riddle of the President's meaning, plan, or "method." The article in question described the President as "playing his cards close to his chest and . . . deliberately leaving much to conjecture," and it interpreted some of his "hints" to indicate that he was planning to use the

14. See above, pp. 33 f.
15. See below, Chaps. IX and X.

Neutrality Act against Japan in conjunction with the application of economic sanctions to Japan by other important nations. Another conjecture, also based on "presidential hints," was that President Roosevelt might combine with certain foreign governments in applying the principles of the Neutrality Act to the whole war area wherever it might be. If this was indeed the "method" the President had in mind at his press conference on October 6, 1937, it came to nothing.

In the city of Washington rumor was rife. Administration officials were reticent. Suppositions relative to the long-range meaning of the Chicago speech were anxiously discussed. Hope that the President would soon clear up the confusion by an amplification of his quarantine proposal was freely expressed.[16] Among observers acquainted with the history of diplomacy and war, it was generally recognized that effective cooperation with other nations against an aggressor anywhere would lead the United States into political entanglements and very probably on the way to war.

October 9, 1937, the *New York Times*, in a front-page report, disclosed the fact that on the previous day President Roosevelt held "intensive discussions" with his cabinet and chief advisers in foreign affairs; and that they took under consideration the Far Eastern crisis "in the light of the new American policy of international collaboration for peace." But the White House and the State Department were unwilling to make "any announcement" about the next steps, if any, that had been devised. In such circumstances, the *Times* reported, the condemnation of Japan by the League of Nations and the United States left the "status of the problem" uncertain.

Contrary to expectations, President Roosevelt in his "fireside chat" of October 12, just after his proclamation calling Congress into a special session, offered no elucidation of his Chicago address in any concrete terms. He devoted nearly all the "chat" to domestic issues. Near the end of his broadcast he spoke of the coming conference of the parties to the

16. *New York Times*, October 8, 1937, p. 3.

Nine–Power Treaty of 1922, of American participation in it, and of "our purpose to cooperate with the other signatories to this Treaty, including China and Japan." Such cooperation, he explained, would be an example "of one of the possible paths to follow in our search for means toward peace throughout the whole world." To this he added a brief comment on decencies in the intercourse of nations.

In only one passage of his "chat" did the President attempt to satisfy public curiosity as to what he definitely proposed to do in the crisis, and even that passage was negative rather than informative. "Meanwhile," he remarked, "remember that from 1913 to 1921, I personally was fairly close to world events, and in that period, while I learned much of what to do, I also learned much of what not to do."

Since this statement referred to his service as Assistant Secretary of the Navy during President Wilson's Administration, it could be interpreted to mean that he did not propose to follow exactly in President Wilson's steps. But that was a negative inference. President Roosevelt's inner decision as to a positive program of action, if he had made one, remained hidden to the public.

As if to quiet his fellow citizens who might be worried lest his efforts to block the Japanese in China and his collaboration with European powers might lead to war after all, the President closed his "chat" by saying: "The common sense, the intelligence of Americans agree with my statement [at Chicago] that 'America hates war. America hopes for peace. Therefore, America actively engages in the search for peace.' " [17]

Instead of allaying speculations regarding his intentions and purposes in foreign affairs, the President's broadcast raised new doubts and questions. According to a report from Washington, "diplomatic circles" saw in the chat no retreat from the Chicago speech but they agreed that, "for several reasons, he had softened the tone." It was thought that "he wished to reassure the people in this country, who had been

17. *Public Papers*, 1937 Vol., pp. 437–438.

agitated over his Chicago speech," and also to reassure "other governments and particularly Japan. Therefore he purposely minimized reference to foreign questions. . . . His disposition appears to be to do nothing that would encourage Congressional action or agitation, especially as the nine-power treaty conference will probably be in session at about the time Congress convenes." [18]

Arthur Krock, experienced journalist, always in close contact with inside sources of information, like members of "diplomatic circles," found no clarification in the fireside chat. Commenting on the subject, Mr. Krock declared that in his Chicago speech "Mr. Roosevelt had mystified his own people and those abroad by referring to a 'quarantine' against treaty-breakers," and that there had been "some expectation that he would clarify his use of this disturbing word" in his broadcast of October 12. The expectation had not been met: "in his fireside chat he contented himself with announcing what the newspapers had already made known—that the United States stands ready to meet with other Powers signatory to the Nine-Power Treaty. And the rest of what he said about the march to peace, as directed by the United States, was a mere restatement, in far softer terms, of what he had already conveyed by radio at Chicago." [19]

Although journalists were no more eager than many of their fellow citizens to find out how the President could hope to "quarantine" powerful nations without resorting to strong measures likely to involve the country in war, they had opportunities to inquire, which were not vouchsafed to other persons, even Members of Congress. And they did inquire, again, during a press conference on October 15, 1937. [20]

At this conference the President was asked whether it was "fair" to infer from the fireside chat that the country would offer its services in mediation. He answered, "that was what

18. *New York Times*, October 14, 1937.
19. *Ibid.*, October 14, 1937.
20. The stenographic report of this conference does not appear in *Public Papers*, 1937 Vol., but press accounts give clues to the exchanges between Mr. Roosevelt and the correspondents.

he had said." But he did not amplify the remark; and "to all other questions as to the foreign situation Mr. Roosevelt saw fit to return completely uninformative replies. . . ." He was asked whether he would call upon Congress to revise the neutrality laws in line with the apparent reversal of previous policy embodied in his Chicago speech. His response was that "he could not discuss the matter." [21]

The remainder of the *New York Times* report on the press conference of October 15, 1937, gave no definite information on the foreign policy the country was supposed to be pursuing:

The President, speaking with some emphasis, then told the reporters that he hoped they would make it clear that any predictions of United States foreign policy must be pure guesswork, emphasizing that he did not know what it would be himself.

However, there are some indications that Mr. Roosevelt has some plan in mind that he thinks will be an effective "quarantine" against treaty-breakers and aggressor nations and at the same time not involve this country in political or economic sanctions, or in actual military demonstrations.

Just what his plan is Mr. Roosevelt has never demonstrated or even indicated but some of those close to him believe that he has a plan that he thinks will be effective.

That that plan does not involve any policies followed by the Administration of which he was a member during the last war is assumed by some who remember his remark in his radio address Tuesday night that as a member of the Wilson Administration he had learned what not to do.

There are also some indications that Mr. Roosevelt does not regard the policy of "quarantine" by "concerted action" as outlined in his Chicago speech as inconsistent with the neutrality policy of Congress as laid down in the present Neutrality Law and has even thought that action may be taken under the new policy without any change in the present law, which appears to most observers to enjoin complete impartiality as to the treatment of warring nations regardless of opinion as to the guilty party.

It has been the impression of some of those who have watched

21. *New York Times*, October 16, 1937.

the President since the Chicago speech that he feels he has some new way to meet the situation—a way that has never been tried before. But there has been no clue as to just what that way might be.[22]

The account of the same press conference given in the *New York Herald Tribune* added a few details to the *Times* report. The President was asked what he proposed to do if his efforts to "mediate" between China and Japan proved to be a failure. This was a searching question that sought to discover his next steps, in case peaceful negotiations came to nothing, and force—national or collective—appeared to be the only alternative to a confused retreat. The President "said this was an 'if' question and, besides, it was utter, sheer guesswork for anyone to try to say now what America's policy would be in the future." To this climax Mr. Roosevelt added a super-climax by saying to his questioners "that if he were a newspaper correspondent he would go out and play golf instead of trying to make news when there wasn't any." [23]

In the clashes of the discussion as reflected in the daily and weekly press all over the country immediately after the quarantine speech of October 5, 1937, certain divisions and confusions of opinion were manifest.

Internationalists greeted the speech as revealing a definite reversal of policy on the part of the President and applauded it; but they were cautious and uncertain in respect of suggesting to the President ways and means of "implementing" his new policy. In general they laid stress on the effectiveness of collective action if vigorously applied to the governments designated as aggressors; but they were diffident, and refrained from emphasizing the primary point of their doctrine: "moral" and "economic" sanctions are futile unless backed by adequate armed force and, if necessary, by war against the designated aggressors.

22. *Ibid.*
23. *New York Herald Tribune*, October 16, 1937.

Some internationalists, even so, maintained that the United States could apply moral and economic sanctions to "aggressors," on its own motion or in conjunction with other "peace-loving" nations, without incurring the risk of war, without assuming an obligation to go to war in case these measures failed to overcome the aggressors against whom they were directed. Those who took this position could therefore applaud the quarantine proposal on the theory that President Roosevelt might stop the Sino-Japanese War and prevent war in Europe by some hitherto untested expedient, while keeping the United States out of war in any pinch.

This conception of policy—coercion and discrimination without incurring a risk of war—was set forth later in a letter from Marguerite Wells, President of the League of Women Voters, addressed to President Roosevelt in connection with the Lend-Lease Bill providing for all-out aid to the powers at war with the Axis.[24] "The League's position on foreign policy for almost twenty years," Miss Wells stated to the President, "has been consistently against the idea that isolation is possible; so long as wars exist in the world, they will threaten us; the United States should help develop some sort of collective system based on law and order. More recently as such a system has failed to materialize, the League of Women Voters has favored 'A foreign policy as a non-belligerent which permits discrimination against an aggressor and favors the victim of aggression.' " In the same letter Miss Wells notified President Roosevelt: "Basic to our support is acceptance of your own assurance that your policy is not directed toward war, but that its sole purpose is to keep war away from us."

As a rule, however, members of the anti-war bloc maintained that there was no middle ground, that the United States could not depart from neutrality as recognized in international law without a definite risk of war, and that the quarantine doctrine, if actually applied, meant nothing more nor less than setting out on the road to war. Hence they

24. Letter dated February 28, 1941.

spoke and wrote in unequivocal language against it. Public opinion at the time appeared to be arrayed on their side. On the basis of various popular polls taken in the preceding months, it had been reported that about three fourths of the people were opposed to getting into another world war. Indeed in April, 1937, 71 per cent of the persons polled had answered that they thought it had been a mistake for the United States to become embroiled in the first World War.[25] The out-and-out advocates of neutrality for the United States condemned the quarantine speech and declared that attempts to apply it would be more than steps on the way to war with Japan and the other Axis Powers; would be in fact acts of war.

Each of the principal parties to the great dispute had support from interested quarters. Communists, traveling along the Moscow line and now engaged in working up "popular front" against all "Fascists," lustily joined the internationalists in cheering the quarantine speech and calling for action against the aggressors. Meanwhile on the side of nonintervention were German and Italian propagandists employed in enlisting American support for the cause of Hitler and Mussolini. To intensify the controversy, certain powerful journals, while isolationist in respect of Europe, were imperialist in respect of Asia and ready to welcome a war against Japan.

A defender of internationalism and the doctrine that the United States must join Great Britain in preventing any single power from becoming dominant on the continent of Europe, the *New York Times*, on October 6, gave the quarantine speech a warm reception. It declared "unassailable" the President's conclusion that "the only effective assurance of peace is a 'concerted effort' to avert the outbreak of war itself and to uphold the sanctity of treaties." It invited the President to "clarify" the question whether he intended to take a "specific line of action" or was stating general principles.

25. Walter Johnson, *The Battle against Isolation*, p. 19.

Two days later the *Times* informed the President editorially that if "the new policy outlined in the Chicago speech" was to become the policy of the United States, the Neutrality Act should be removed from the statute books, that he must be prepared to face the formidable opposition in Congress, that he must be ready to argue his case for "concerted action" at the bar of public opinion, that he must undertake to convince the nation that its "honor" and "enlightened self-interest" required it to accept a larger share of its responsibilities as "a great world power." [26]

In many parts of the country the quarantine speech met similar approval. The *Raleigh* [North Carolina] *News and Observer* proclaimed it a statement of "fact" and applauded it as a return to the position taken long before by Woodrow Wilson.[27] The *Cincinnati Enquirer* greeted it as a definite sign that the President "is determined to do more than merely speak against aggression." [28] Congratulation came from the *Christian Science Monitor:* "The time for Americans to get into the fight is before it begins. And that is the surest way to keep out." [29] The *St. Paul Pioneer Press* lauded the speech as "definitely" aligning the President with Woodrow Wilson's "viewpoint" as against "isolationist policies." [30] In San Francisco the *Chronicle* hailed it as a warning against isolation and neutrality.[31] To the chorus of praise the *Baltimore Sun* contributed its approbation.[32]

On the front page of the *Foreign Policy Bulletin* for October 15, 1937, Raymond Leslie Buell, head of the Foreign Policy Association in New York, praised the quarantine speech under the caption: "Roosevelt Abandons Isolation." Mr. Buell found in it a rejection of the isolationist philosophy, but inquired whether it was "intended as another 'moral gesture' " or was to be backed by "a positive foreign

26. *New York Times*, October 8, 1937.
27. Quoted in *New York Herald Tribune*, October 6, 1937, p. 3.
28. Quoted in *New York Times*, October 6, 1937, p. 17.
29. October 7, 1937, p. 20.
30. Quoted in *New York Times*, October 6, 1937, p. 17.
31. *Ibid.*
32. Quoted in *New York Herald Tribune*, October 6, 1937, p. 3.

policy." He advised President Roosevelt to refrain from applying the Neutrality Act to the war in the Far East as long as this was "legally" possible and, in case the Act could not be amended soon, as was likely, to prepare for "a Japanese declaration of war" by attempting to coordinate the provisions of the Neutrality Act with the action of the League powers in such a way as to produce an international shipping embargo. Only in this fashion, Mr. Buell thought, could the United States "escape from becoming a virtual ally of Japan."

In the "Washington News Letter" printed in the *Foreign Policy Bulletin* of the same date, a Washington observer said that the State Department had escaped from "an air of unreality, a pleasant complacency, as though we lived in a quaint Alice-in-Wonderland world." With evident satisfaction he welcomed the signs of a new day: "We are in the game of Power Politics. From now on, whether we like it or not, we will be compelled to play the game. The American people have an important stake in whether it is played well, or badly."

The *Nation* heartily endorsed President Roosevelt's quarantine plea and rejoiced that the public reaction to the speech was "amazingly friendly." It declared that the principal objection had come from "the die-hard isolationists and from the Hearst press," and manifested delight in the fact that the President had "definitely" chosen the path of opposition to treaty breaking and aggression. After remarking that isolationists fought shy of collective measures against aggression, "on the ground that they might lead to war," the *Nation* assured its readers that "for such fears there is no reasonable justification." On the contrary, it went on to say, "Japan is far too deeply involved in its adventure in China to dream of waging war against a major power, to say nothing of a general war against all the democratic nations. The real danger of war, as Mr. Roosevelt has so clearly pointed out, lies in the opposite direction." [33]

33. October 16, 1937, pp. 391–392.

Writing in the same issue of the *Nation*, Oswald Garrison Villard expressed regret that President Roosevelt had not used "the words *Japan* and *Italy*" in his quarantine speech, but overlooked the lapse and contended that "if he goes no further, he has rendered a tremendous service to the world. His words will be acclaimed by liberals and peace-lovers wherever they are read. . . ." Incidentally, Mr. Villard revealed the fact that he had some weeks previously telegraphed the President, urging him to speak out on foreign affairs and "to reassume the moral leadership of the world which Woodrow Wilson abandoned when he surrendered to the 'peacemakers' at Paris."

Prominent leaders of the "peace movement" in the United States joined in applauding the quarantine speech. For example, James G. McDonald, formerly head of the Foreign Policy Association and at the moment member of the *Times* editorial staff, hailed it as marking a return of President Roosevelt to internationalism. Apparently having some special information, Mr. McDonald averred that "the President's speech was carefully prepared for weeks, and should be considered as an expression of a new foreign policy being formulated by the State Department." [34]

Dr. Nicholas Murray Butler, President of Columbia University and head of the Carnegie Endowment for International Peace, commended the quarantine speech, called for an international police to maintain world order, and deplored the notion that such use of force involved war. Disposing of the opposition swiftly, Dr. Butler asserted that the "folly" of isolation was exceeded only by its "immorality," and thus drew the line of conflict in opinion between wisdom and morality on his side and folly and immorality on the other side.[35]

Earl Browder, general secretary of the Communist party

---

34. *New York Times*, October 14, 1937, p. 16. This confirmed the view of Drew Pearson, *The Nation*, October 16, 1937, to the effect that the speech "had been planned weeks in advance."
35. *New York Times*, November 12, 1937.

in America, united his plaudits with those of Dr. Butler, Mr. McDonald, and Mr. Villard in acclaiming the quarantine speech. At that time Communists were following the Moscow line of collaboration with "bourgeois" elements in forming a "popular front" against "Fascism." Mr. Browder followed suit. He welcomed President Roosevelt's repudiation of neutrality and promised him "100 per cent unconditional support of the Communist party," if he would let Communists work out things for themselves. "We have been the bitterest critics of Mr. Roosevelt's foreign policy in the past," Mr. Browder said. "His neutrality was unneutral and hypocritical and was designed to help Fascist nations in war. Now we are glad to see it change." [36]

Two days after Mr. Browder had spoken, the *New Masses*, Communist journal of opinion, swelled the chorus of praise by calling the quarantine speech a major pronouncement, "a historic statement of the first rank . . . since we emerged as a major world power." The speech directed American foreign policy away from "isolation" toward "some form of collective security" and was in line with Secretary Stimson's doctrine "that this country would never recognize the territorial gains of an aggression." [37]

Editors of opposition newspapers and weekly journals, especially those of Republican affiliations, in commenting on President Roosevelt's quarantine address, generally concurred with endorsers of the speech in respect of two matters: (1) the speech signified a repudiation of the policy of neutrality and non-entanglement which the President had long followed; and, (2) unless it was to be deemed a mere

36. *Ibid.*, October 18, 1937. Two years later, after Stalin made his pact with Hitler, in 1939, the Communist line became violent in its hostility to President Roosevelt's policy as "war-mongering" and "imperialist." After Hitler declared war on Russia in 1941, the Communist line was again "100 per cent" support for President Roosevelt and against Germany and her satellites in Europe. As Russia did not go to war with Japan until August, 1945, American Communists who took their cue from Moscow were circumspect about the American war in the Pacific which they had once decried, ferociously, as "imperialist" in spirit and purpose. To the old position on "imperialism" they returned, apparently without qualm, after the surrender of Japan in 1945.

37. October 19, 1937.

moral gesture, it called for positive action on internationalist principles. These contestants in the forum of public opinion differed, however, some more, some less, as to the willingness of the President to implement his words and as to the possibility or probability that, if duly implemented, the quarantine doctrine spelled peace or war for the United States.

Continuing in the vein of irony employed long ago by Charles A. Dana, but with no such devastating skill, the *New York Sun*, under the heading "So what, Mr. President?" inquired: "What does Mr. Roosevelt really intend to do about it?" After asserting that the President had showed a propensity for easy generalizations and reluctance to get down to details, the *Sun* accused him of criticizing certain countries in one breath and, in another, declaring that the United States was determined not to become entangled in another foreign war. At this point the author of the editorial said that the affair reminded him of the alarmed schoolmarm who shrieked commands of obedience to bad boys and at the same time vowed that she would never use the rod on them. "Surely," he continued, the President "does not suppose that the United States can impose its own standards of political morality on other nations by the simple process of slapping them rhetorically on the wrist." [38]

About a week later the *Sun* seemed sure of one thing: the President's speech had knocked "the new neutrality" into a cocked hat as a guarantee of non-entanglement for the United States, and the country was "in a fair way to get into the Chinese imbroglio with both feet." Then it offered a lesson from history: Woodrow Wilson had been reelected in 1916 largely because he had kept us out of war and in April of the following year we were at war.[39] The next day, after the President's fireside chat, the *Sun* informed its readers that "in the world as it is, aggressive search for peace seems only less dangerous than aggressive search for war." [40]

38. October 6, 1937.
39. October 12, 1937.
40. October 13, 1937, p. 26.

The *New York Herald Tribune* in commenting on the Chicago speech took a stand similar to that of the *Sun.* It charged the President with resorting to rhetorical effusions and failing to calculate the probable consequences of any strong action designed to give effect to them.[41] It also turned to the pages of history and recalled the outcome of President Wilson's war for democracy.

If [declared the *Herald Tribune*] the Germans have pointedly reminded President Roosevelt of the 'Wilson shipwreck,' he has only himself to thank. The Chicago speech could have been taken very nearly word for word from the impassioned oratory of twenty years ago which heralded the American intervention in the World War. . . .

So Mr. Wilson spoke and the consequence was the expenditure of about 125,000 lives and some $25,000,000,000 "to make the world safe for democracy," with the results now visible in the contemporary world. So Mr. Roosevelt has spoken in turn. What the result will be no one can say; but it is evident that the Chicago speech, if it means anything (always a matter of some doubt with present-day Presidential utterances), means a reorientation of American policy upon Wilsonian lines and a rededication of American life and treasure to the difficult task of enforcing peace on earth.

The President, doubtless, did not intend it quite that way, for his words were guarded with a careful vagueness. But the reaction from Germany and Japan is enough to show how little even the most painstaking equivocation is likely to serve in practice. . . . The essence of Mr. Wilson's earlier policy was to strike a happy compromise between the two courses, encouraging peace on our own terms without accepting the pains and risk of war. The essence of Mr. Roosevelt's policy, as stated at Chicago, is apparently the same. "It is a matter of vital concern to the people of the United States that the sanctity of international treaties and the maintenance of international morality be restored." This, however, is to be achieved without fighting. To the defense of this "vital concern" we are to bring only moralistic exhortation in the

41. October 6 and 9, 1937.

first instance, with, possibly, some kind of blockade or boycott should that fail. It is an easy, relatively painless and attractive prospect.

But before embarking upon it a second time . . . it is worth thinking about what will happen in case both exhortation and boycott fail to conserve this "vital" interest. Could we then say that it was none of our affair and that the interest wasn't really so "vital" after all?

Having incited the League powers to desperate adventure, could we wash our hands of the consequences when they threatened to be bloody? Hardly, and before cheering too loudly for the President's sudden foreign diversion, it might be just as well to get it perfectly straight as to just what these "vital" interests are and just how vital they are in practice likely to prove.[42]

As expected, the *Chicago Tribune* scored the quarantine speech. It charged the President with adopting the policy of Woodrow Wilson, which had brought the United States into war with Mexico and then into the first World War— "the policy which was overwhelmingly rejected by the American people after the war." It contended that Japan would not be easily beaten to her knees, that the threat of a boycott would only inflame Japanese patriotism, and that if the boycott did not work the President would face the question: "What to do then?" It reminded him that President Wilson once found himself with no alternative but war and it asked: "Does not Mr. Roosevelt's policy invite the coming of the day when he, too, may have no alternative but to resort to arms?"[43]

Owing to the large Democratic vote in Boston, opinion in that city was important for any implementation of the quarantine speech. And the *Boston Herald*, on October 6, 1937, after referring to President Wilson's experience, spoke in the

42. Editorial, October 7, 1937.
43. Quotations in the *New York Herald Tribune* and the *New York Times*, October 6, 1937.

manner of a warning: "But this time, Mr. President, Americans will not be stampeded into going 3,000 miles across the water to save them ['the very foundations of civilization,' referred to in the Chicago speech]. Crusade, if you must, but for the sake of several millions of American mothers confine your crusading to the continental limits of America."

The editors of the *New Republic,* then following the isolationist creed, dealt with the quarantine speech in terms of recent history and the long prospect ahead. They were of the opinion that the speech, if seriously intended, meant an abandonment of neutrality and the pursuit of a course that could only lead to the very world war which the President said he feared. Moral lectures to the aggressors, they claimed, would be ineffectual, and only an alliance of the peace-loving powers could defeat those aggressors "after a long and bloody war." [44]

To Raymond Moley, former associate of President Roosevelt in politics and administration, the quarantine speech forecast "a new foreign policy for the United States." He declared that "there are abundant indications that the Chicago doctrine was fathered and partially formulated by William C. Bullitt, United States Ambassador to France," and that the new policy looked to "the sudden assumption of leadership in an effort to regenerate the world by enforced peace." Since much had been made by President Roosevelt and Secretary Hull of the moral obligations to uphold international law, Mr. Moley reminded them that there was one

44. October 20, 1937. In February, 1938, Bruce Bliven, editor of the *New Republic,* opposed the big navy bill then up in Congress on the recommendation of President Roosevelt. Mr. Bliven asserted that the real intention of the bill was not the defense of the United States but an excursion into world politics. Speaking of Walter Lippmann, Secretary Hull, and Admiral Leahy, Mr. Bliven accused them of misrepresenting the real purpose of the proposed naval measure: "I am not so rude as to think that these gentlemen really mean the nonsense they have told us. I believe they know very clearly what they are about, but refuse to make public either their intentions or the reasons behind their intentions." *Hearings before the Committee on Naval Affairs,* 75th Congress, 3d Session (February 9, 1938), pp. 210 ff. In other words, Mr. Bliven took the position that the sponsors of this bill were deliberately deceiving the public as to the real foreign policy they were pursuing and proposed secretly to pursue.

law which they were also bound to uphold, namely, the Neutrality Act of 1937.[45]

While the editor of the *American Mercury* thought that the quarantine performance at Chicago might be a kind of political trick, "extra-hazardous" in any case, he felt sure that it represented a clear reversal of American foreign policy. Referring to history, he remarked that President Roosevelt had been "decisively, almost ostentatiously, in favor of non-intervention, keeping out of other people's business, neutrality, abstention from war and all the rest of it," but now at Chicago he had made "such a quick turn on his record that he left the toes of his shoes still pointing in the opposite direction." [46]

During the remainder of the year 1937, from October 5 to December 31, President Roosevelt made no public pronouncement and took no public action that indicated any change in the foreign policy he had expounded from February 2, 1932, to the day of the quarantine speech. Insofar as the outward signs of his thought and purposes were concerned, his foreign policy for the United States remained the same as it had been since 1932. And American citizens, friends as well as foes of his Administration, who expected him suddenly to apply the quarantine doctrine in practice, were disappointed in their anticipations. If, in fact, the Chicago address was intended to announce a new foreign policy, by the end of the year it seemed that the President had returned to his long proclaimed isolationist position.

On the occasion of sending Norman Davis to the Brussels conference of the signatories of the Nine-Power Treaty, called by the Belgian Government to consider the situation in China, President Roosevelt made a public announcement assuring the country that the United States remained free

45. "Perspective," *Newsweek*, October 15, 1937. Mr. Moley doubtless saw in the quarantine speech a definite relation to Mr. Roosevelt's approval of the Stimson doctrine, which had alarmed him in January, 1933. Above, pp. 136 ff.

46. Editorial, December, 1937.

from commitments. In his statement, the President said: "Mr. Davis, of course, will enter the conference without any commitments on the part of this Government to other governments." [47] After the other Great Powers at Brussels, as well as the United States, declined to join in any form of concerted action against Japan and the conference adjourned,[48] the President accepted the failure without making any open protest in line with the quarantine doctrine.

President Roosevelt's message to the extraordinary session of Congress, November 15, 1937, was confined entirely to matters of domestic legislation. It contained no exposition of his foreign policy and no call for modifications in the Neutrality Act.[49]

After Japanese airplanes had attacked the United States gunboat *Panay* on the Yangtze River, December 12, 1937, the President contented himself with demanding and receiving an apology from the Japanese Government and a check for the indemnity demanded.[50]

In an exchange of telegrams on foreign policy between himself and Governor Alfred M. Landon, December 21, 1937, the President said that "throughout our long history we Americans have rejected every suggestion that ultimate security can be assured by closing our eyes to the fact that whether we like it or not we are a part of a large world of other nations and peoples." But he drew from this proposition no conclusion in harmony with the quarantine doctrine. He merely added, "As such we owe some measure of cooperation and even leadership in maintaining standards of conduct helpful to the ultimate goal of general peace." [51]

As the year 1937 drew toward its close, advocates of collective action against designated aggressors seemed unable to discover any proof that President Roosevelt contemplated an effective application of his quarantine doctrine. In fact,

47. *Public Papers*, 1937 Vol., p. 463.
48. *American Year Book* (1937), p. 84.
49. *Public Papers*, 1937 Vol., pp. 490 ff.
50. *Ibid.*, pp. 541 ff.
51. *Ibid.*, pp. 549 ff.

they lamented the failure to implement the doctrine and laid most of the blame for this outcome on "isolationists," "pacifists," "blind peace groups," and defenders of the Neutrality Act, critics of Great Britain, and "short-sighted people" who insisted that the purpose of the armed forces of the United States was to defend their own country.

For example, on November 30, 1937, the *New York Times* in an editorial deplored "America's Aloofness." It declared that "the United States has lost its leadership in world affairs," and that dictators and treaty-breakers have become convinced that the country would initiate or join in an effective movement to uphold world peace "for no cause short of actual invasion." For this outcome "the 'isolationists' and 'pacifists' in Congress and their vociferous supporters in the country are chiefly responsible." The President, the editorial continued, had recently called for "quarantines" against governments guilty of butchery and aggression, but "pacifist and isolationist groups" had opposed positive action on that line and in so doing had given aid to such enemies of mankind.

Yet, the editors of the *Times* maintained, "our statesmen and leaders of public thought could aid peace mightily" if they would cast off their fear of "blind peace groups" and serve notice on foreign trouble-makers that the great democracies "will stand together" against the enemies of peace. Thus, the editors hoped, the ravishers of weak neighbors and enemies of democracy "will discover that the United States has not become so timorous and so stupid as to abandon its responsibility and imperil its greatness and its freedom."

Professional advocates of peace shared the judgment of the *New York Times*. For instance, the *Chronicle of World Affairs* for December, 1937, published by the League of Nations Association under the editorship of Clark Eichelberger, took the Roosevelt Administration to task for refusing to urge strong measures against Japan at the Brussels conference. The *Chronicle* laid the principal blame for this breakdown to "British moribundity" in the sphere of international action and to the complete lack of any American plan of action beyond moral persuasion. If the United States had taken a firm stand for strong action against Japan, the author of the editorial insisted, "the British bluff" would have been called, and "the United States would have lost nothing." Why had the United States defaulted in its duty? "The trouble seems to be that no plans, practical or otherwise, have been formulated for such efforts. It may be an injustice to say so, but there is every appearance of those at Washington 'sitting around and waiting for something to turn up.'"

If, as the *Chronicle* suggested, the United States had stood squarely for collective action on quarantine principles at the Brussels conference, the British might have had their "bluff called." Judging by comments of the British press on the quarantine speech, however, the British doubted whether the President would in fact venture to act upon it, if he really wished to do so, and were convinced that the American people would not follow him into the League of Nations or any collective agreement to designate aggressors and apply armed force to them in case they refused to yield to threats.

The views of the London *Times, Daily Telegraph,* and *Daily Express* on the quarantine speech were fairly well summed up by the *Fortnightly* of December, 1937, in an effort at metaphorical humor. "The American people," said the *Fortnightly* in discussing President Roosevelt's alleged reversal of policy, "haven't got any further than consenting to let their darling daughter swim in the good old way; but she must not go near the water, indeed, she must not even hang her clothes on a hickory limb. For the moment, a sort of diplomatic strip-tease act is all that will be allowed. American active intervention, like the art of Miss Lee, must wait for happier days." In some respects this prophecy was correct: active intervention did have to wait, but whether the days were "happier" must be submitted to the judgment of history to come.

After scrutinizing the full and open record for 1937, the

Associates of the Geneva Research Center, always on the alert for the slightest deviation in American foreign policy, felt compelled to report that the Government of the United States had not, during the year, departed from the doctrine of isolationism. They noted that "the United States gave increasingly serious attention to world affairs," and that the American ideal of respect for treaties and international law coincided with that of the League of Nations. They greeted with pleasure the President's quarantine speech and spoke gratefully of the cordial cooperation between Washington and Geneva as revealing an "affinity of purpose."

But having made as much as they could of the record, the Associates confessed that no real change had taken place in the relations of the United States to political activities of the League. They wrote that the "affinity of purpose" between the two institutions "did not take concrete form . . . nor imply any change in the different methods followed. The League remained an organization for consultation, negotiation, evaluation, and even enforcement; the United States continued uncommitted except for the uncertain obligations of the Pact of Paris and the Neutrality Act." [52] Contact between the two "tended to become firmer," and yet "no change of principles or obligation took place." There had been cordial cooperation, but "Serious gaps existed in this cooperation . . . due to America's non-membership in the League. Most important was her absence from the two central agencies, Assembly and Council, which both initiate and approve the League's many activities. American participation was not, therefore, fully effective, either as regards initiative or control. The result was disadvantageous both to the United States and the League. . . . America's most striking single absence still remained its non-adhesion to the World Court." [53]

52. There could be no uncertainty as to the fact that the United States assumed no obligations to the League of Nations or to internationalism in the Pact or the Act.

53. *American Year Book* (1937), pp. 92 ff.

At the opening of the new year, 1938, the debate over the quarantine speech seemed to have died away. As the days passed the silence of the White House remained unbroken. Both internationalists and isolationists appeared to regard the issue raised by the President at Chicago on October 5, 1937, as closed: he intended to do nothing in the way of putting it into effect. In his annual message to Congress, January 3, 1938, he referred to America's love of peace, said nothing about his new foreign policy, if he had one, but drew attention to the growing conflicts and disorders abroad as matters of concern to the United States.

Later in the month, January 28, 1938, President Roosevelt sent a special message to Congress calling for increases in naval armaments and for legislation aimed at "the prevention of profiteering in time of war and the equalization of the burdens of possible war." On its face, this message seemed to have no particular significance. The proposed increase of naval expenditures was not so large as to be sensationally out of line with other increases in naval appropriations from time to time since 1933. Schemes for "taking the profits out of war" had been up in Congress frequently since the discovery of the enormous profiteering that had accompanied the first World War; and the "equalization of burdens in war time" had likewise been long discussed by the American Legion and Members of Congress, in connection with conscription or universal service, as "a measure of democratic justice and equality." Now, on January 28, President Roosevelt merely said that he believed the time had come to legislate against war profiteering and in favor of equality in war burdens.

But owing to the fact that the echoes of the quarantine speech were still ringing in the national capital and to certain actions recommended and certain phrases used by the President, his appeal to Congress was taken by watchful critics to be an indication of a purpose to underwrite or implement the quarantine principle, by augmenting the navy and making provisions for an immense army. At all events immediately after the message was made public, a determined opposition began to describe and condemn his proposals as some kind of "search for peace" that connoted intervention in the power politics of Europe and Asia.

This is no place to give a record of all the circumstances which surrounded President Roosevelt's call for the new legislation and the conflict over it in Congress and outside. To do that would be to write a fuller history of those times. But on one point great emphasis was laid by the opposition: Why has the President demanded these new armament measures at this particular moment? The armament program for the coming year had long been under consideration in Congress; and one week before the message of January 28, making new demands, the House of Representatives had passed the largest appropriation bill for the navy ever adopted in the history of peace times—a bill granting substantially every request made by the Navy Department. Why the additional demands? Why had they been postponed and then suddenly advanced? What had happened since the close of 1937 to warrant this precipitate action? Such were the questions asked immediately after the message was sent to Congress and during the months of hearings and debates on the bills, naval and military, projected in implementing the message.

A full exposition of the political implications involved in the President's recommendations would require a review of hundreds of pages of congressional hearings and debates bearing on them. But, to speak with utmost brevity, the demand for more battleships was interpreted to be a call for instruments of action in distant waters rather than for instruments of defense in the American sphere; and the "equalization of burdens" was taken to mean the establishment of a huge army by universal conscription—an action widely deemed unnecessary for defense and as designed for expeditionary operations in a foreign war, as in 1917 and 1918.

The phrases in the President's message which awakened distrust among opponents of intervention in foreign quarrels appeared in the passages justifying his call for increased armaments. He declared that he made his recommendations "specifically and solely because of the piling up of additional land and sea armaments in other countries, in such manner as to involve a threat to world peace and security, . . . It is our clear duty to further every effort toward peace but at the same time to protect our Nation. That is the purpose of these recommendations. Such protection is and will be based not on aggression but on defense."

Taken in connection with the President's declaration at Chicago that the United States could not hope to escape the horrors of the coming war and that peace must be sought through a quarantine, or collective action, against aggressors, these lines of the message were regarded as evidence that he had the idea of quarantine in mind when he wrote them. With insistent reiteration, his critics pointed out that he had made these recommendations *solely* and *specifically* on account of a threat to *world peace and security*, rather than on account of a threat to the peace and security of the United States; and with equal pertinacity they cried out that he had laid it down as our clear duty *to further every effort toward peace*, adding secondarily, at the same time to protect our Nation.

In expounding and defending the proposed program before the House Committee on Naval Affairs, Admiral William D. Leahy, chosen by the President as his spokesman, said early in the proceedings: "The political conditions in the world at this moment, both in Europe and in the Far East, are far more threatening than at any time since 1918, and no improvement is in sight. The major conflict in China has resulted in many grave incidents involving the sovereign rights and interests of the United States and other third powers. The civil war in Spain continues unabated and the threat of a general European conflict is ever present." Only at the end of this recital did the Admiral speak of a possible seizure of the republics of Central and South America by foreign powers as suggesting the need for increased armaments to be used in American waters. Later in the hearing he discussed at some length the operations of Germany, Italy, and Japan as affording justification for greater naval construction by the United States.

Admiral Leahy had not gone very far in his exposition of the political argument for large armaments, when a Republican member of the Naval Affairs Committee raised the issue of foreign policy by asking the Admiral to go into the matter of the relation between the "quarantine" doctrine and "the President's message that led to this bill." The Admiral by-passed the question by saying that the Navy Department had nothing to do with policy and that he had "no idea what the future policy may be."

Subsequently, in the hearings, the issue of the relation between the quarantine doctrine and the battleships was raised again and again by members of the House Committee and by witnesses who appeared before it. Moreover, the whole question of implementing American power politics in the Far East was brought up in connection with battleships designed for operations in distant waters, extending the range of the discussion. Indeed the fate of the bill was put into such jeopardy by protests against its alleged quarantine and imperialist implications that the chairman of the committee, Carl Vinson, went to the White House and reviewed with President Roosevelt the matter of his foreign policy in relation to the measure. Did the President regard the new naval bill as representing a reversal of the non-entanglement and non-intervention policy which he had repeatedly endorsed between February 2, 1932 and "quarantine" day, October 5, 1937?

After the chairman's conference with President Roosevelt, the majority members of the Naval Affairs Committee amended the text of the new naval bill by inserting a long declaration of policy: "It is declared to be the fundamental naval policy of the United States to maintain a Navy in sufficient strength to guarantee our national security, not for aggression, but to guard the continental United States by affording naval protection to the coast line, in both oceans at one and the same time; to protect the Panama Canal, Alaska, Hawaii, and our Insular possessions; to protect our commerce and citizens abroad; to insure our national integrity; and to support our national policies." To this declaration other lines were added, including a provision referring to the possibility of further naval limitations by international agreement.[54] Although these amendments were by no means satisfactory to the opposition, they at least confined American naval policy to the protection and promotion of "national interests" instead of the maintenance and promotion of "world peace and security," as indicated in President Roosevelt's naval message.

At the end of the hearings on the naval bill, a minority of the Naval Affairs Committee, three Republicans and one Democrat, dissented from the report of the majority favoring the President's program.[55] In their own dissenting report the three Republicans maintained that the navy bill was not a defense bill, that its purpose was to implement the President's quarantine policy, that the public had rejected this policy, and that Great Britain had also refused to cooperate with him in giving effect to it. Turning to the Far East in particular, the minority of three maintained that the President's purpose was "to pursue 'power politics' in Asia" and that the amendment attached to the bill "reveals the designs of the universal-quarantine policy and the interventionist policy in Asia and upholds the obsolete British–Mahan sea-power doctrine." In a summation under the head, "This Bill Is a Blank Check," the minority asserted tersely: "If this bill is passed the President will have a blanket authorization, after Congress ad-

54. *Report of the Committee on Naval Affairs*, No. 1899, H. R., 75th Congress, 3d Session (1938), p. 2.
55. *Minority Views*, No. 1899, Pt. 2, H. R., 75th Congress, 3d Session (1938). In this dissent the three Republican members in effect took the line of the old Republicans who had opposed imperialism in the early part of the century even though they would not support William Jennings Bryan and "free silver." As to imperialism itself they were following the Democratic line of 1900.

journs, to apply the universal-quarantine policy and Asiatic interventionist policy."

During the extended debates on the naval bill in the House of Representatives and the Senate, the relations between armament measures and foreign policy were subjected to a scrutiny unusual in the history of naval bills. Supporters of the Administration stuck close to the argument that the naval bill was designed for defense, not aggression, and that it was not intended to implement the quarantine doctrine or any other project for intervention in foreign wars, as the minority maintained. On the other side, advantage was taken of the opportunity to dissect and criticize President Roosevelt's quarantine and interventionist policies and argue that war perils were inherent in the pursuit of such policies.

After prolonged discussion in Congress, the naval authorization bill was passed; but the actions of the President, the Congress, and the Navy Department after the enactment of the law convinced opponents of the measure that they had been correct in their contention that, in spite of disclaimers, the Act was designed to underwrite quarantine, interventionist, and imperialist policies—in other words, to give the President an instrument to use in foreign conflicts. All along the minority insisted that the technical features of the bill supported their case. In the House Minority Report, the opposition pointed out that under the Vinson–Trammell Act of 1934 Congress had authorized a $4,000,000,000 program of naval building, and that there was already in the statutes authorization to build nine new battleships in the next five years (to 1943)—"nine battleships as large and powerful as the naval experts deem necessary to defend America—besides the two now building." In these circumstances, the opposition asked: "Why should Congress authorize three more $75,000,000 battleships when the Navy is not ready to build three battleships that are already authorized?"

In countering this argument, made while the new naval bill was still pending in 1938, sponsors of the bill declared that the battleships contemplated by the measure would be started promptly after the authorization was adopted by Congress. Yet after the naval bill demanded by the President had been carried, Congress did not at once appropriate the money for the ships authorized under the Act.

On the contrary, the Deficiency Act, approved June 25, 1938 (52 Stat. L. 1094) for the fiscal years ending June 30, 1938, and June 30, 1939, simply provided money for commencing two battleships already authorized by the Act approved March 27, 1934. The money so appropriated was to cover the cost of two new ships in addition to the two for which appropriations had been made in 1937 and two more for which appropriations had been made early in the year 1938. This failure to act immediately under the new naval law demanded and secured by President Roosevelt served further to convince opponents of the proposal that it was "a foreign policy" measure, not, as alleged, "a defense measure"; that it was a diplomatic "bluffing" bill and was fraught with perils of war.

Although President Roosevelt was successful in obtaining the enactment of the naval bill called for by his message of January 28, 1938, Congress refused to comply with his request for an "equalization" law or, as he characterized it at a press conference, a "mobilization" measure. Congress was unwilling to pass a thorough-going bill for taking the profits out of war and for establishing universal military service. A serious, if passionate, discussion of the subject took place at committee hearings, in Congress, and in the press. Charges and countercharges were made.[56] It was alleged by opponents that there was only one design behind a universal service measure: namely, preparation of an expeditionary army for a foreign war; that no gigantic army was then needed for purposes purely defensive. On the other side the existence of

56. For example, see *Preventing Profiteering in Time of War and to Equalize the Burdens of War and Thus Provide for the National Defense, and Promote Peace*, No. 1870, H. R., 75th Congress, 3d Session.

any such purpose, in connection with the equalization or mobilization project, was vigorously denied. Whatever the meaning or merits of the proposal, Congress adjourned without enacting a bill for giving effect to it.

In upshot, the "big navy" bill had been passed by Congress; the war mobilization project had died in committee; supporters of the Administration program had doubly assured the country that in adopting the recommendations for increases in naval construction they had in mind only defense, not collective security, quarantine, or intervention in foreign political controversies; and President Roosevelt had issued in connection with the dispute no pronouncements out of accord with the asseverations of his supporters. As a net result, many Americans, if disturbed by the turmoil of the season, were left with the definite impression that the President still stood for defense, security, neutrality, and peace for the United States. If there had been any turn in foreign policy on his part when he wrote his naval message of January 28, 1938, there had been a return at the end of the great national debate.

During the remainder of the year 1938 President Roosevelt certainly made no other public pronouncements that could be construed as departing from the doctrine of no political entanglements and no political intervention abroad which he had set forth on February 2, 1932, and had so frequently reiterated. He did from time to time call the attention of the country to growing war perils in Europe and Asia, and let it be known that he was still seeking peace. He sent a message to Czechoslovakia, Germany, Great Britain, and France on September 27, 1938, in behalf of efforts to find a "peaceful solution of the threat of war," and on the same day he directed a message to Chancellor Hitler in a similar vein.[57]

But in these communications he declared that "the United States has no political entanglements," and that its traditional

57. *Public Papers*, 1938 Vol., pp. 531 ff., 535 ff.

policy has been "the furtherance of the settlement of international disputes by pacific means." Both were in the nature of moral appeals, not threats. The reference to the settlement of disputes by pacific means merely re-echoed sentiments that had often been expressed by Republicans and Democrats for many decades. It was far removed from any advocacy of collective security, sanctions, or coercion. Nor did the President in addresses made with reference to the congressional campaign, then in progress, say anything that might precipitate another storm, such as his quarantine speech of October 5, 1937, or his naval message of January 28, 1938, had brought down upon his head.

From the point of view of internationalists, the pronouncements and actions of the Roosevelt Administration in respect of American foreign policy during the year 1938 were for practical purposes a total loss. In their appraisal for the year the Associates of the Geneva Center could enter on the credit side of the year's ledger nothing in the nature of even a gesture at Washington in the direction of the internationalism which they championed. They wrote pleasantly of the message transmitted "through the American legation at Berne," inviting the League of Nations to organize an exhibit at the New York World's Fair, and of the steps taken to prepare the exhibit. They set down with satisfaction the item that there had been sympathetic cooperation between the United States and the League in technical, labor, and humanitarian affairs and the additional item that the pacific ideals of the United States were akin to those of the League.

Efforts to discover in the public statements and actions of the Roosevelt Administration for the year some real grist for the mill of internationalism taxed the ingenuity of the Geneva Associates to the limit. At the outset, they framed an excuse for the failure of the Administration to move in their direction: "During the critical year of 1938, the opportunity did not offer for the United States to take as large a part in the League's general work as previously." But their partial explanation of this mishap was a notation that European powers, in regard to some highly important matters, were also operating outside the League. In other words, the associates attributed the Administration's lack of opportunity for participation in "the League's general work," in some measure, to the fact that "there developed more and more a tendency to handle such affairs outside the League: Spain, for instance, in part, and Czechoslovakia entirely."

Having proffered this excuse for American neglect of the League, the Geneva Associates were encouraged by what they regarded as evidences that the United States was in "complete accord with the League's underlying philosophy." But they could not report that this "complete accord" had resulted in any political approach to the League which went beyond the genuflections of previous years.

Indeed, they seemed astonished by this contradiction between "complete accord" and actual practice, for they exclaimed: "What was surprising, however, was that, with this complete sympathy of viewpoint and a very considerable degree of actual cooperation, there was only the most cautious suggestion of even a limited reconsideration of a better relationship between the two. . . . Considerable groups within the United States were beginning to feel that the country had become an uncomfortable part of the world scene, insecure, if not positively endangered by outside events. . . . None of this, however, found strong reflection in the Government's attitude toward the League of Nations, nor in any proposal of a freer and more effective method of cooperation with an international agency, however imperfect, dedicated to the advancement of international peace and cooperation." [58]

In sum, what the Geneva Associates ventured to report as possible changes in United States foreign policy during the year 1938 was exceedingly tenuous: "there was only the most cautious suggestion of even a limited reconsideration of a better relationship" between the United States and the

58. "The United States and World Organization during 1938," *International Conciliation*, September, 1939 (Carnegie Endowment), pp. 375 ff.

League; "considerable groups in the United States" were beginning to feel uncomfortable about the business; but neither this discomfort nor anything else had "found strong reflection in the Government's attitude toward the League of Nations"; nor had there been, on the part of the United States "any proposal of a freer and more effective method of cooperation" with the League. Thus, as far as the Geneva Associates could actually find out, President Roosevelt was standing at the end of 1938 where he had stood on foreign policy in his Grange speech of February 2, 1932.

CHAPTER IX

Neutrality, Peace, and Non-intervention Reaffirmed in 1939

WITH the intensity that characterized his quarantine speech of October 5, 1937, President Roosevelt, on January 4, 1939, spoke to Congress of undeclared wars raging "all about us" and of threats of new aggression "all about us." On this occasion and at great length, he admonished Congress that war perils were mounting higher and higher. "Storms from abroad," he said, "directly challenge three institutions indispensable to Americans, now as always. The first is religion. It is the source of the other two—democracy and international good faith. . . . Godfearing democracies of the world . . . cannot forever let pass, without effective protest, acts of aggression against sister nations—acts which automatically undermine all of us." For the moment it looked as if he would take the next step: again summon the democracies to join in applying an effective quarantine to aggressors as enemies of mankind and make an appeal for a new foreign policy.

But the President paused on the brink of such a momentous resolution, if he had the possibility in mind, and made no break with the foreign policy of abstention from interference with arms in the conflicts of Europe and Asia. "Obviously," he continued, the Godfearing democracies "must proceed along practical, peaceful lines. But the mere fact that we rightly decline to intervene with arms to prevent acts of aggression does not mean that we must act as if there were no aggression at all. . . . There are many methods short of war, but stronger and more effective than mere words, of bringing home to aggressor governments the aggregate sentiments of our own people. At the very least, we can and should avoid any action, or any lack of action, which will encourage, assist or build up an aggressor."

And what practical action did President Roosevelt recommend to Congress? He intimated that the neutrality legislation might well be changed, for he declared we have learned that our neutrality laws "may operate unevenly and unfairly—may actually give aid to an aggressor and deny it to the victim." He also emphasized the need of greater preparedness for defense. Yet he did not urge a repeal of the neutrality legislation or any other measure pointed in the direction of action on the part of the United States against aggressors.[1]

If anyone interpreted his message of January 4 to imply that he had modified his conception of the proper foreign policy for the United States, the interpretation was soon disavowed: at a press conference on February 3, 1939, the President said that his foreign policy had not changed and he restated it. A journalist present remarked that "some people seem to have some difficulty understanding foreign policy," and asked the President whether he had "any intention of getting down to the elementary A, B and C's in a statement, or speech, or fireside talk in the near future." The President replied that the foreign policy of the United States had been "thoroughly" covered in his message to Congress, "completely and adequately covered in every way," that there was nothing new about it, and that a great many people, including Senators, Representatives, and newspaper owners were "deliberately" misrepresenting the facts. He then referred to eight or ten newspapers on the desk before him as giving, "to put it politely," an erroneous impression.

Thereupon the President recited the following formulas to the journalists assembled in his conference room:

The foreign policy has not changed and it is not going to change. If you want a comparatively simple statement of the policy, I will give it to you . . .

Number 1: We are against any entangling alliances, obviously.

Number 2: We are in favor of the maintenance of world trade for everybody—all nations—including ourselves.

1. *Public Papers*, 1939 Vol., pp. 1 ff.

Number 3: We are in complete sympathy with any and every effort made to reduce or limit armaments.

Number 4: As a Nation—as American people—we are sympathetic with the peaceful maintenance of political, economic and social independence of all nations in the world.

Now, that is very, very simple. There is absolutely nothing new in it. The American people are beginning to realize that the things they have read and heard, both from agitators of the legislative variety and the agitators of the newspaper owner variety, have been pure bunk—b-u-n-k, bunk; that these agitators are appealing to the ignorance, the prejudice, and the fears of Americans and are acting in an un-American way. . . .

Now, on the question of secrecy, that also is 100 per cent "bunk." [2]

If the President's reply to questioners at his press conference on February 3, 1939, lacked anything in precision with reference to peace, neutrality, and non-intervention, this deficiency was more than made good later in the course of the year. During the spring and summer, while European powers were engaged in the feverish negotiations which threatened to eventuate in a general war, the whole subject of American neutrality and non-intervention became the storm center of a nation-wide controversy. Nominally, this controversy turned on proposals to revise the Neutrality Act, particularly to eliminate the provisions that placed an embargo on the sale of arms, munitions, and implements of war to all foreign belligerents when the President should "find" a state of war existing abroad. Actually the old issue of non-intervention in foreign conflicts as against collective security was the heart of the dispute.

Now confident that no advance toward their goal could be made under the head of "quarantine," many internationalists, with aid from other quarters, concentrated on a repeal of the munitions embargo. In support of their project they contended that, if the President had a free hand in controlling foreign relations and if sales of munitions to England, France,

2. *Ibid.*, pp. 110 ff.

and other democracies could be exempted from embargo, the Axis powers would or might be diverted from their aggressive plans or at least be put at a disadvantage in case war came anyway. On the other side, isolationists felt certain that Executive manipulation of foreign relations, coupled with the munitions traffic, was mainly responsible for getting the United States into the World War in 1917, and that a repeal of the munitions embargo in 1939 was simply another device for involving this country in another world war, already in prospect.

The controversy over neutrality legislation was brought to a head and pointed up by direct action on the part of the Roosevelt Administration. In May, 1939, Sol Bloom, acting chairman of the House Committee on Foreign Affairs, at the instigation of Secretary Hull, introduced in the House of Representatives a "neutrality resolution" providing for revisions of the Neutrality Act and eliminating the embargo on the sale of arms, munitions, and implements of war to foreign belligerents to be applied in time of war. The Bloom resolution was referred to the Foreign Affairs Committee, hearings were held, and in due course the bill was reported to the House for debate and action. But the House, before passing the bill, insisted that an arms embargo provision be inserted in the measure, thus defeating Secretary Hull's plans. In this dilemma, baffled in the House, Secretary Hull turned to the Senate, and in vain; for the Senate committee in charge of neutrality measures by a close vote deferred action on modifications of the Neutrality Act.[3]

On behalf of the Administration's proposal, sponsored by Representative Bloom, it was argued that the embargo provisions of the Neutrality Act tied the hands of the President in conducting foreign affairs and hampered him in his efforts to prevent a general war abroad and if it came to keep the United States out of such a war. Indeed a composite summary of the principal arguments advanced in the House of Repre-

3. *Peace and War*, 1931–1941 (Department of State, January, 1943, text), p. 64.

sentatives in support of a repeal of the embargo on the sale of munitions to belligerents could be correctly entitled "pleas for promoting the neutrality and peace of the United States by means of modifications in the Neutrality Act." A few citations from the debate of the House of Representatives in June, 1939, illustrate the nature of the pleas.[4]

Representative W. O. Burgin, Democrat, of North Carolina:

The United States wants peace. There can be no doubt about that. I believe that feeling exists in the heart of all of our people, regardless of party, race, or creed. We want to keep war out of the United States, and we want war kept out of the world. I believe this will or desire for peace permeates the thinking of every man in public life, from President Roosevelt down to the least and last man. No one, I think, in this House will vote for any legislation except with this in mind. I believe the President's action in the past trying times has been a potent factor in discouraging the spread of the war spirit in other parts of the world. . . .

I realize, as Secretary Hull did, that no law which we can write can be guaranteed to keep us out of war. All we can do is to see to it that our legislation, first, minimizes the chance that war will break out at all—the only really safe way of keeping out of war; and second, if it does break out, that it will not involve us (p. 8178).

Representative Luther A. Johnson, Democrat, of Texas:

. . . I am for the repeal of the embargo because I believe it will help to prevent war. . . . When we passed the neutrality law I said that the arms embargo would not prevent war, but would serve to encourage other nations. I hoped other nations would follow our example and pass similar laws, but they did not do so.

I say to this House that in view of the conditions as they now exist, to leave this law on the statute books is not to discourage war but to encourage war by causing war to break out . . . (p. 8324).

4. These extracts are from the *Congressional Record*, 76th Congress, 1st Session, Vol. 84, Pt. 8 (June, 1939). The number at the end of each extract refers to the page of the volume from which the extract is taken.

Representative E. V. Izac, Democrat, of California:

I want the Members to bear in mind as I go along with my remarks the fact that the American people are demanding some kind of neutrality legislation for the express purpose of keeping us out of war. I am convinced the only reason that the Committee on Foreign Affairs held hearings as early as 1935 and passed a neutrality bill was because of the demand of the American public that we have something more than international law on which to rely in case the world again catches fire as it did in 1914. The present act is an evolution of the act of 1935. We have placed in the act something which I opposed, and which I will always oppose, a partial embargo. Whenever you have a partial embargo it is bound to be unneutral because no two nations are situated alike. . . .

The present act does not mean we are neutral. It does not keep the nations of the world at peace, and therefore we are remiss in our duty to the American people in that we are deluding them that by having this feature in the act we are keeping the peace and keeping this Nation, incidentally, out of war. True, we have kept out of the war, but it was as a result of the action of our President, in my opinion, who had all the opportunity in the world, if he wanted it, to get into a war, but he has not wanted to do so, and I bring that to your attention. He has not wanted to, much as you hear about our President leading us into a war. He has been in power here for six or seven years and during all of that time nations were at war or were at each others' throats, both in the Orient and over across in Europe, and he never resorted to the slightest pretense of going into war. He tried to maintain the dignity of the American Republic in the eyes of the world, and I think he has done so, but here you are tying his hands in not giving to some of the smaller nations the right to defend themselves (pp. 8234–8235).

Representative L. E. Geyer, Democrat, of California:

. . . in my opinion the passage of this bill will serve the interests of peace everywhere, by to some extent lessening the danger of war in Europe. To my mind the best proof that the Bloom bill will have this effect is to be found in the press of those nations which are today mobilizing and preparing for war. The American people and the devotees of peace in every land, will welcome the passage of this bill as a step toward peace. But Rome and Berlin are shrieking that it is a form of "war-mongering," and Hitler and Mussolini, through their controlled press, tell us to vote down the Bloom bill. With whom are you going to vote? With the American people; or with the war lords of fascism?

The Bloom bill is a step toward peace. But in my opinion it is a hesitant step. I would prefer to see this country step out more firmly, more boldly, in the direction of blocking the way of those who prepare the mad adventure of war . . . (p. 8172).

Representative Pete Jarman, Democrat, of Alabama:

. . . the Committee on Foreign Affairs of both the Houses . . . did hold very extended hearings—open hearings—to which all concerned were invited. . . . After these hearings a bill was dropped in the hopper by the acting chairman of our committee. . . . I have not asked Chairman Bloom who wrote that bill. It bears his name. But I do say this: . . . It is natural to look to the Secretary of State . . . I am perfectly willing to follow the suggestions of Secretary of State Cordell Hull in such matters, particularly at a time so serious as we fear this to be. . . . I do not believe we have ever had a Secretary of State or a President of the United States who would deliberately lead us down the road to war for an ulterior purpose. . . . At any rate, this bill, no matter who authorized it, we think in the Committee is a good bill, which will contribute toward the peace of America (pp. 8148–8149).

Representative J. W. Wadsworth, Republican, of New York:

I believe the existence of that embargo against the exportation of munitions in the permanent law is a source of danger. With all my heart I hope it will be eliminated.

Many people are of the belief, and I honor their beliefs, that in neutrality laws lies safety. I disagree. I think the safety and the peace of the people of the United States lie in their retention of the right to do what is best for America when the time comes.

My plea is for freedom of action, and that is all. Freedom to do what is best for us, no binding rules, no inflexible regulations, maintain our self-respect, work our best for peace, but be forever free.

I feel that way about these neutrality acts, just as I did about the Covenant of the League of Nations . . . (pp. 8158–8159).

In opposition to any weakening of the Neutrality Act, especially the repeal of the embargo on the sale of munitions to belligerents, a major proposition was asserted and reasserted during the debate in the House of Representatives over the Bloom bill: It was by the sale of munitions and extension of credits to the Entente Allies that the United States became involved in the first World War, step by step; if the embargo on munitions is repealed and the selling of munitions and the extension of credits are started again, the United States will repeat the old story and get into the next general war, step by step; and the best way to keep the United States out of all foreign wars is to maintain the Neutrality Act in full force, strengthen it if need be, and adhere to neutrality as proclaimed under it when and if a general war breaks out in Europe.

Illustrations of this line of argument follow:

Representative Martin J. Kennedy, Democrat, of New York:

At this time I want to make it clear that my decision to oppose this resolution has been reached after careful study and consideration. Deep down in my heart I believe it would be a serious mistake to adopt the present resolution, but if we must have a change I believe it would be far better to repeal the entire law. The people of my district are scared to death that this resolution will lead to war. God knows they have enough to worry about without this problem. For all of these reasons, I hope the resolution will not be adopted (p. 8173).

Representative G. H. Tinkham, Republican, of Massachusetts:

I was educated to be a professor and writer of history. I am thoroughly convinced, with my 50 years' experience in Europe and my reading of history, that if this bill is approved by this House and finally becomes law it means war for the United States. . . .

I say to this House that the issue of war is now before us and that we should not allow ourselves to be deluded by fallacious arguments into taking absolutely wrong positions as we did 20 years ago (pp. 8160–8161).

Representative P. W. Shafer, Republican, of Michigan:

Mr. Chairman, the American people do not want to be dragged into another European war which is now in the making. This Bloom bill . . . is a war-promotion bill clothed in the robes of neutrality. This bill is just what the international bankers, international war-mongers, and war profiteers desire.

The present Democratic administration is in control of the same international forces which plunged America into the World War in the name of "Making the world safe for democracy," and "A war to end all wars." The fathers and mothers of America do not want their sons slaughtered or maimed on foreign battlefields in order to pull foreign nations' chestnuts out of the fire and make blood money for international bankers, munitions makers, and war profiteers (p. 8318).

Representative J. M. Vorys, Republican, of Ohio:

The real issue in this bill arises from a fundamental difference as to the way to peace. The President's policy is to use the threat of our power to preserve a balance of power in Europe. Opposed to this is the traditional American belief that the way to peace is for us to be neutral, not biased; friendly, and not threatening. The President's theory is that if we stop war from starting we will not get into war. If we make a strong enough bluff we can prevent war from starting. The President has no more intention of taking us into war than he had six years ago of taking us into debt; but we have learned that despite good intentions, if you spend enough you get into debt, and if you threaten enough you get into war. The road to war is paved with threats.

I have two criticisms to make of this policy. First we have no assurance that the threat of our force will be sufficient to stop war in Europe. No one can give us that assurance.

Second, if the bluff does not work, we will inevitably go into war. When any international incident takes place on the faith of our promise to one side or threat to the other, the pressure to make good our bluff, to back up our commitment will be irresistible. If you think that our eventual entry into the next war is inevitable, then vote for the Bloom bill as is. . . .

America has come to believe that the sale of arms to belligerents is immoral, un-Christian and leads to war. Most experts on international law favor retention of the arms embargo. . . . Mr. Hull says that he can see no difference between the selling of arms to belligerents and the selling of anything else they may need. That is because he thinks of neutrality in terms of helping or hindering some other nation and not in terms of helping ourselves. I emphasize this particularly: There is no principle of international law that requires us to sell arms to anybody (p. 8151).

Representative J. M. Robsion, Republican, of Kentucky:

I am against this Bloom so-called neutrality bill. Its major purpose is to repeal the present law that contains an embargo against the shipment of arms, ammunitions, and munitions of war to nations engaged in war. This Bloom bill will permit the shipment of these arms, ammunitions, and war materials from this country to warring nations. This action will involve us in another World War just as it did in 1917. This bill is unneutral and President Roosevelt who is charged with the carrying out of this law is not neutral. It, therefore, is not a neutrality bill to promote peace but it is rather a bill to promote another World War and involve us in that war (p. 8486).

Unable to secure from Congress the modification of the Neutrality Act which had been sought through the mediation of Secretary Hull, President Roosevelt, in a special message to that body on July 14, 1939, made a personal appeal for action in favor of the Administration's program. The main part of his message consisted of a long statement on the subject by the Secretary of State, Cordell Hull, which, the President said, "has my full approval." On his own part, he assured Congress that he asked for the modification of the law in the interest of peace, security, and neutrality; "It has been abundantly clear to me for some time that *for the cause of peace and in the interest of American neutrality and security*, it is highly advisable that the Congress at this session should take certain much needed action." [5]

Secretary Hull's statement coincided with the opinion thus briefly set forth by President Roosevelt in the introductory part of his message. "In substance and in principle," Mr. Hull declared clearly and emphatically, *"both sides of the discussion agree on the following* points:

1. Both sides agree that *the first concern of the United States must be its own peace and security*.
2. Both sides agree that it should be the policy of this Government *to avoid being drawn into wars between other nations*.
3. Both sides agree that this nation should at all times *avoid entangling alliances or involvements with other nations*.
4. Both sides agree that *in the event of foreign wars this nation should maintain a status of strict neutrality*, and that *around the structure of neutrality we should so shape our policies as to keep this country from being drawn into war*.[6]

Here, in a few plain and unmistakable words, Secretary Hull, with the unequivocal endorsement of President Roosevelt, expounded to Congress and the country the doctrine of non-entanglement, non-involvement, neutrality, and peace for the United States, which had been so often proclaimed by the President himself since February 2, 1932. This was the very position which nationalists and even the most intransigent isolationists had been taking all along and were taking at the very moment when Secretary Hull squarely committed the Administration to it again.

In principle, therefore, the contending parties agreed. The

5. *Public Papers*, 1939 Vol., pp. 381 ff. (Italics supplied.)
6. *Ibid*. (Italics supplied.)

only difference between them, Secretary Hull explained, was over the method of achieving this supreme end for the United States. On his part, Secretary Hull argued at great length for modifications of the Neutrality Act and for entrusting more power to the President and the Secretary of State in conducting foreign affairs in the interest of the United States. This, he pleaded, is the best way to attain the objective claimed by both contestants in the debate; that is, to keep the country out of war.

But the Senate was obdurate. The votes necessary to pass the President's proposal could not be marshaled, despite the large Democratic majority in the chamber. Not even at a White House conference between President Roosevelt and leaders of both parties in the Senate could the deadlock be broken. And Congress adjourned in August, leaving the munitions embargo on the statute books.[7]

On September 1, 1939, the German dictator, Adolf Hitler, then in league with the Russian dictator, Josef Stalin, ordered his battalions of death forward into war against Poland, and Great Britain and France responded by declaring war on Germany. On September 3 President Roosevelt spoke to the nation over the radio, and, besides warning the people of grave difficulties at hand, informed them of the policies he planned to pursue:

Let no man or woman thoughtlessly or falsely talk of America sending its armies to European fields. At this moment there is being prepared a proclamation of American neutrality. This would have been done even if there had been no neutrality statute on the books, for this proclamation is in accordance with international law and in accordance with American policy.

This will be followed by a Proclamation required by the existing Neutrality Act. And I trust that in the days to come our neutrality can be made a true neutrality. . . . We seek to keep war from our own firesides by keeping war from coming to the Americas.

7. Charles A. Beard, "The Neutrality Deadlock," *Events*, September, 1939, pp. 161 ff.

For that we have historic precedent that goes back to the days of the administration of President George Washington. . . .

This nation will remain a neutral nation, but I cannot ask that every American remain neutral in thought as well.

I have said not once but many times that I have seen war and that I hate war. I say that again and again.

I hope the United States will keep out of this war. I believe that it will. And I give you assurance and reassurance that every effort of your Government will be directed toward that end.

As long as it remains within my power to prevent, there will be no black-out of peace in the United States.[8]

Two days later, September 5, the President issued his neutrality proclamations: one under general international law and another under the Neutrality Act of 1937, which provided for an embargo on arms and munitions. His oft-repeated prophecy that a more terrible war was coming had been fulfilled. That was now beyond debate. But what of the future of the United States?

On September 13, 1939, having already entered into personal communication with Winston Churchill, then serving in the British Admiralty,[9] President Roosevelt called Congress in an extraordinary session. In his message to Congress on September 21, he made an argument for the repeal of the embargo on munitions in line with the plea of Secretary Hull on July 14 and reassured Congress and the nation again that his primary objective was to protect the neutrality of the United States and keep the country out of war:

At the outset I proceed on the assumption that every member of the Senate and of the House of Representatives, and every member of the Executive Branch of the Government, including *the President and his associates, personally and officially are equally and without reservation in favor of such measures as will protect the neutrality, the safety and the integrity of our country and at the same time keep us out of war.*

8. *Public Papers,* 1939 Vol., pp. 460 ff.
9. For Mr. Churchill's account of this exchange of messages, see *London Times,* April 18, 1945.

Because I am wholly willing to ascribe an honorable desire for peace to those who hold different views from my own as to what those measures should be, I trust that these gentlemen will be sufficiently generous to ascribe equally lofty purposes to those with whom they disagree.

Let no man or group in any walk of life assume exclusive protectorate over the future well-being of America, because I conceive that regardless of party or section *the mantle of peace and of patriotism is wide enough to cover us all.*

Let no group assume the exclusive label of the "peace bloc." We all belong to it. . . .

For many years the primary purpose of our foreign policy has been that this nation and this Government should strive to the utmost to aid in avoiding war among nations. But if and when war unhappily comes, the *Government and the nation must exert every possible effort to avoid being drawn into the war.*

The Executive Branch of the Government did its utmost, *within our traditional policy of non-involvement,* to aid in averting the present appalling war. Having thus striven and failed, *this Government must lose no time or effort to keep our nation from being drawn into the war. In my candid judgment we shall succeed in these efforts. . . .*

I seek a greater consistency through the repeal of the embargo provisions, and a return to international law. I seek reenactment of the historic and traditional American policy which, except for the disastrous interlude of the Embargo and Non-Intercourse Acts, has served us well from the very beginning of our Constitutional existence.

It has been *erroneously said that return to that policy might bring us nearer to war. I give to you my deep and unalterable conviction,* based on years of experience as a worker in the field of international peace, *that by the repeal of the embargo the United States will more probably remain at peace than if the law remains as it stands today.* I say this because with the repeal of the embargo *this Government clearly and definitely will insist that American citizens and American ships keep away from the immediate perils of the actual zones of conflict. . . .*

These perilous days demand cooperation among us without trace of partisanship. *Our acts must be guided by one single hard-headed thought—keeping America out of this war. In that spirit,*

I am asking the leaders of the two major parties in the Senate and the House of Representatives to remain in Washington between the close of this extraordinary session and the beginning of the regular session on January 3, 1940. They have assured me that they will do so, and I expect to consult with them at frequent intervals on the course of events in foreign affairs and on the need for future action in this field, whether it be executive or legislative action.

I should like to be able to offer the hope that the shadow over the world might swiftly pass. I cannot. The facts compel my stating, with candor, that darker periods may lie ahead. The disaster is not of our making; no act of ours engendered the forces which assault the foundations of civilization. Yet we find ourselves affected to the core; our currents of commerce are changing, our minds are filled with new problems, our position in world affairs has already been altered.

In such circumstances our policy must be to appreciate in the deepest sense the true American interest. Rightly considered, this interest is not selfish. Destiny first made us, with our sister nations on this Hemisphere, joint heirs of European culture. Fate seems now to compel us to assume the task of helping to maintain in the Western World a citadel wherein that civilization may be kept alive. *The peace, the integrity and the safety of the Americas— these must be kept firm* and serene. . . .[10]

During the congressional discussions of proposed modifications in the neutrality legislation, including the repeal of the embargo on munitions-selling and the introduction of other provisions, the familiar types of argument were restated or repeated, with variations. On behalf of changes in the law, it was said that they would be more effective in keeping the country out of the war and that the purpose of President Roosevelt in advocating them was to maintain neutrality and peace for the United States. In opposition to certain modifications, especially the embargo repeal, it was avowed that they were steps on the road to war and that President Roosevelt, like Woodrow Wilson in 1917, was leading the country on the way to war.

10. *Public Papers*, 1939 Vol., pp. 512 ff. (Italics supplied.)

Thus supporters of President Roosevelt's policy and opponents of that policy were united on a basic principle: the neutrality of the United States must be maintained and the country kept out of the war then raging. And for long weeks they hammered this principle into the minds of American citizens.

Typical views expressed by advocates of modifications in the neutrality legislation, especially the repeal of the munitions embargo, during the debates in the House of Representatives, follow:

Representative Luther A. Johnson, Democrat, of Texas:

. . . we are receiving letters demanding that we make no change in the present law and in that way keep us out of war. If the present partial neutrality law is not changed or amended, the United States is certain to be in this war, and that within a very short time.

President Roosevelt is to be commended for acting promptly on the outbreak of war in Europe by calling Congress into special session to pass an adequate and a complete neutrality law to safeguard in every way our interests and to prevent our involvement in the war. It is not the fault of President Roosevelt and Secretary Hull that such legislation was not passed at the last session of Congress. If Congress had passed such a bill at the last session of Congress, there would have been no necessity for this session of Congress and there is a possibility that there might not be any war at this time in Europe. . . .

Some of these opponents charge that the President is trying to get us into war because he is suggesting changes in the present partial and wholly inadequate neutrality law. This is in line with the charge made by the same gentlemen at the last session of Congress when President Roosevelt was trying to have legislation passed. When he talked about war being imminent and need for neutrality legislation they called him a war-monger, and stated that he was simply stirring up strife and that there was no likelihood of any war. Now, when war has broken out and he tries to get legislation to keep us out of war, they say he is simply doing that, not to keep us out of war, but to get us into war. . . .

The resolution now being considered is an improvement . . .

and in my judgment should be less objectionable and be more effective in keeping us out of war. . . .

Those who think that an arms embargo alone to belligerent nations will keep us out of war have not given thoughtful consideration to this subject. I assert, Mr. Speaker, that the retention of the arms embargo will not keep us out of war, and its repeal will not get us into war. . . .[11]

Representative Sol Bloom, Democrat, of New York:

The aim of all neutrality legislation has been to keep the country out of war. No matter how many points are covered, no matter what is put in or left out, no law is good if it falls short of what law can do to keep us out of war. The best that any country can do is to deal with realities and shape its course accordingly, for the purpose of maintaining its peace.

Regardless of differences of opinion as to details, Congress reflects the determination of the people to avoid war. . . .

When House Joint Resolution 306 was passed by this body last June there was peace in Europe. . . . It was contended at that time that repeal of the embargo upon arms, ammunition, and implements of war would have a tendency to encourage foreign war into which the United States might be drawn. . . .

Undoubtedly many Members of the House voted to retain the embargo in the belief that they were helping to maintain peace in Europe. . . . Unfortunately for these Members, and unfortunately for the world, war did break out. The retention of the embargo did not stop it. . . .

If there was any reason to hope that the embargo would tend to prevent the outbreak of war in Europe, that hope no longer exists. We are now dealing with actual war conditions abroad. We are trying to avoid being drawn in. We are keeping all American ships and citizens from the areas of warfare.[12]

Representative R. L. Doughton, Democrat, of North Carolina:

11. *Congressional Record*, 76th Congress, 2d Session, Vol. 85, Pt. 1 (October 12, 1939), 338–339.
12. *Congressional Record*, 76th Congress, 2d Session, Vol. 85, Pt. 1 (October 31, 1939), 1119 ff.

We were told by those who opposed the removal of the embargo, in the last session of the Congress, that it would prevent war, and that as long as it was maintained there would be no war in Europe. These same persons now tell us that unless the embargo is kept intact it will constitute a first step that will lead to our involvement. Their first prediction did little to advance their reputation as prophets, and their opposition, resulting as it did in inaction on this important question, in my opinion, undoubtedly was a contributing factor to the outbreak of war in Europe.

In the meantime, both our great President and our capable Secretary of State warned that a European war was likely, and might break with little notice. They urged that we prepare ourselves by removing from our statutes the present ineffectual neutrality legislation, and replacing it with something along the lines of the pending bill. Persons from every walk of life, without regard to partisan policies and their positions upon other very controversial questions, concurred in this opinion. . . .

In conclusion, I repeat, the controlling desire of all of us is to keep our country from becoming involved in the war in Europe. Our great President and Secretary of State, who have larger official responsibilities and also a better and more thorough knowledge of all factors relating thereto, have urged and recommended the policy outlined in the pending bill.

In my judgment, their position has the endorsement and support of an overwhelming majority of the American people without regard to political affiliations or connections. From North, South, East, and West come conclusive evidence of such support, and it is my studied, deliberate, and confident belief that the enactment of the pending measure will be taking the safest course possible at this time to promote and safeguard the peace, well-being, and happiness of the American people.[13]

Representative Mary Norton, Democrat, of New Jersey:

. . . It is my confident belief that the proposed neutrality act will be the means of keeping us free, that America shall remain at peace. This is now and shall continue to be my most fervent prayer.

13. *Congressional Record*, 76th Congress, 2d Session, Vol. 85, Pt. 2 (November 1, 1939), 1193.

May I say to my colleagues, as one who went through a World War, who saw all of its horrors, who worked day and night in the interest of our boys, that I would not stand here today and urge that we repeal the present Neutrality Act if it were not my honest conviction that it is the best way to keep us out of war. I sincerely hope that my colleagues, however they may vote today upon the question of the best means to keep us neutral, will join with me in telling the women of America that this Congress, by its vote, will never consent to send American boys to fight in a European war.[14]

Representative J. W. Wadsworth, Republican, of New York:

There can be no doubt, however, that an overwhelming majority of our people expect the Congress to enact legislation which, if legislation can do it at all, will keep us from being involved in the present conflict. I believe the Senate bill approaches this difficult problem in a realistic way. . . . I believe the Senate in its cash-and-carry provision at least approaches this difficult problem realistically and that if legislation can keep us out of war, this particular provision will do more in this direction than any other provision that can be drafted. . . .[14a]

Illustrations of the views set forth in the House of Representatives by opponents of President Roosevelt's foreign policy, as exemplified in his call for modifications of the embargo provisions, are given in the following excerpts from the debates:

Representative Louis Ludlow, Democrat, of Indiana.

Mr. Speaker, in this country of ours we have two ideologies in respect to war. Those ideologies have come to the point where they are clashing violently and where America must choose between them. If we adopt as our permanent policy one ideology,

14. *Ibid.*, p. 1192.
14a. *Congressional Record*, 76th Congress, 2d Session, Vol. 85, Pt. 2 (November 2, 1939), 1311.

sometimes contemptuously referred to as "isolation," but which is not isolation at all, we may safely count on remaining at peace with the world. If we adopt as our policy the other ideology, the interventionist ideology, it will simply be a question of time when it will drag us into war.

I have said that isolation is a misnomer, and it is. The isolation ideology does not suggest or even intimate that America should isolate itself from the world. It merely suggests that we should isolate ourselves from the wars that are eternally brewing in the cockpit of Europe and in other foreign trouble areas of the globe. This we are fortunately able to do because of our detached geographical position. . . .

The Bloom so-called neutrality bill . . . runs counter to the general wish of our people that America should keep out of war. It is a shining example of the interventionist ideology. It is based on the theory that it is to the best interest of the United States to line up on the side of certain great powers and against certain other great powers. It would plunge America into power politics up to the hilt. No candid champion of the bill, however ardently he might favor it, ever claimed that it is a neutrality bill. Its proponents frankly admit that it is a bill in the interest of England and France, and its effect would be to make America an ally of the British Empire and France in any future war in which they choose to engage, because it would establish the United States as the arsenal and storehouse of supplies and credits for those countries that control the seas. . . .

We can never keep out of war if we have an enormous stake in the game. Our stake must be in peace and not in war, if we are to remain safe and secure. . . .[15]

Representative V. F. Harrington, Democrat, of Iowa:

Only one consideration is facing us today: The best way to keep us out of war. Last June the House said to the world: "We think the best way to keep from becoming involved in any war is to keep the arms embargo." We voted to retain it. This embargo principle had been established as a national policy over a period of four years, and we reaffirmed it only ninety days ago.

15. *Congressional Record*, 76th Congress, 2d Session, Vol. 85, Pt. 1 (October 16, 1939), 485 f.

The world was then at peace. Now, great nations are at war. I believe that if we try to change the law now, after war has been declared, we will commit an act of unfriendliness—yes, an act of aggression, if you please, and I would be opposed to the embargo today if a gigantic and cruel war were not in progress. That was my opinion last June and is my opinion today. Change the law then? Yes; a thousand times. Change it now? Ten thousand times no.[16]

Representative E. M. Dirksen, Republican, of Illinois:

They say that the arms embargo of itself is not important and that of itself it will not involve us in war or keep us wedded to peace. If that be true, why were we called here to repeal it? . . . If the arms embargo is unimportant, who will contend that it will involve us in war? If the arms embargo is unimportant, who will contend that it will shatter the peace we now enjoy? If the arms embargo is unimportant, why does not the President announce to the Nation and to the world that it is unimportant, and then and there pass it by as befits the agenda of a busy man? . . .

By the very force of the drive for its repeal, they have bestowed dignity upon the issue and persuaded the American people as nothing else could have done that it is important. The argument answers itself. . . . I like the candor with which Senator Austin, of Vermont, Senator Burke, of Nebraska, have spoken on the subject. Their observations were stripped of all pretense. Frankly they averred that the arms embargo should be repealed that we might affirmatively aid one side in the present conflict. . . . It is not a case of neutrality. It is not a case of whether under all concepts of international law and the precedents of our own State Department we do or do not have a lawful right to do so. It is not a case of stimulating employment or aiding national defense. It is not a case of returning to international law. It is not because the embargo violates international law or impairs our peaceful relations with other countries. The case for repeal consists of a policy of giving every possible aid and assistance to one side in the present controversy without actually being embroiled in war. Can we do it successfully? That

16. *Congressional Record*, 76th Congress, 2d Session, Vol. 85, Pt. 2 (November 1, 1939), 1196.

is where the issue is finally joined. Those who favor repeal of the embargo are willing to gamble with that chance. Those who oppose the repeal of the embargo are persuaded that it is the first step on the road to a baptism of blood for the youth of America.[17]

Representative Dewey Short, Republican, of Missouri:

Sir, we who want the embargo on arms, munitions, and implements of war retained do not claim its repeal would immediately lead us into another conflict but we are convinced in our own minds, "amateurish" as they are, and are forcibly told by the consciences that we possess, that repeal would be the first step on the road that leads ultimately to involvement. It is not the last blow that is struck, but the first one that usually precipitates a battle. Woodrow Wilson was a man of high ideals and certainly did not want America to be dragged into the last World War, but the initial steps taken by our Government with all their unpredictable eventualities finally led him against his own will into the conflict.

Last Thursday night, Mr. Roosevelt said, "the United States, as I have said before, is neutral and does not intend to get involved in war." [18] Mr. Speaker, I wish to call the attention of all Members to the word "intend." After all, our intentions and motives do not count for as much as the practical and inevitable results of our acts. I repeat, sir, that none of us wants this Nation to go to war, . . . but by taking certain steps—and the repeal of the arms embargo is one of these steps—we shall be led inexorably and inescapably into the heart of the conflict. Are we who honestly and conscientiously believe this way to be branded as "fakers" by anyone who disagrees with us? [19]

Representative J. W. Ditter, Republican, of Pennsylvania:

Those who oppose lifting the embargo believe that a program of neutrality is the pathway to peace, and that it conforms to the long-established policy urged upon us in the early life of the

17. *Congressional Record*, 76th Congress, 2d Session, Vol. 85, Pt. 1 (October 27, 1939), 1045–1047.

18. Below, p. 261.

19. *Congressional Record*, 76th Congress, 2d Session, Vol. 85, Pt. 2 (November 1, 1939), 1167.

Republic to avoid "entangling alliances." Such a program we believe is one of realism rather than idealism. It profits by our past experiences instead of gambling on future experiments. It restrains us from attempting another enthusiastic enterprise "to make the world safe for democracy" or to engage in "a war to end war." . . . We are convinced that our intervention in the quarrels of Europe will neither cure the ills nor remove the causes. We believe that our duty at home is greater by far than our responsibility abroad. We believe that the peace of America is something more than to be hoped for. We believe it must be planned for—and that plan, we believe, must rest upon an impartial treatment of all belligerents.[20]

The following extracts from the debates in the Senate on modifications in the neutrality legislation show how supporters of President Roosevelt's proposal in that chamber expressed the principle that the purpose of the project was to keep the country out of war.

Senator Tom Connally, Democrat, of Texas:

Mr. President, our objective, and our only objective, is to keep out of this terrible war. We are not responsible for it. God knows if the American people could have had any influence, it would never have occurred. . . .

We want to keep out of the war. What is the most practical, the most sensible, and the plainest course for us to pursue? I submit, Mr. President, that the joint resolution gives the greatest possible assurance of any measure that can be devised by any legislative body. It makes sacrifices, it makes sacrifices of our shipping and entails sacrifices upon our people greater than have ever been made by any people in all the history of warfare, . . . We are doing it willingly; we are doing it as a domestic regulation; we are doing it in order to save the necessity for facing the issue as to involvement or non-involvement in the war. We want to stay out of the war, and we are going just as far as any people can go in this legislation to stay out of the war.[21]

20. *Congressional Record*, 76th Congress, 2d Session, Vol. 85, Pt. 2 (November 2, 1939), 1304.
21. *Congressional Record*, 76th Congress, 2d Session, Vol. 85, Pt. 1 (October 4, 1939), 92.

Senator L. B. Schwellenbach, Democrat, of Washington:

At first blush it is apparently a perfectly logical thing to say, "I believe in peace; therefore I believe that our Government should stop the export of arms, ammunition, and implements of war to any belligerent nation." But when we come to a realization that by that act our Government takes on an obligation which the authorities at least agree is more likely to get us into war than any other policy or process that we might use, then certainly we must pause and hesitate. . . .

Another phrase has also attracted the attention of our people. It was the one given over the radio by the very distinguished and brilliant and eloquent Senator from Idaho [Mr. Borah]: "This is the first step toward war." All the arguments and all the oratory since have been based upon it. I know that neither the Senator from Idaho nor anyone else in opposition to the pending joint resolution consciously believes or consciously argues that those of us who believe in the joint resolution have any intention of taking this Nation toward war. If we did have, certainly we would not have presented the Pittman joint resolution, which not only is not a step toward war but, in my opinion, is the most orderly and complete retreat from war that any nation has ever taken. . . .

Mr. President, I receive mail each day accusing the President of the United States of wanting to take this first step to get us into war, and then plan on other steps. . . . Do you think that if we had some ambition to take the first step toward war we would have attempted to write into our statutes the most completely restrictive statute that this or any other nation ever saw to prevent us from getting into war? . . . .

So I believe the objections which have been advanced to the repeal of the arms embargo, when analyzed in the light of the experience of this country and the experience and knowledge of the neutral nations of the world, fall to the ground. It is not a changing of rules after the game begins. It is not the first step toward war. It is not a matter of becoming an arsenal for one side with the danger of becoming a target for the other. It is a careful, painstaking effort to try to keep this Nation out of war.[22]

22. *Congressional Record*, 76th Congress, 2d Session, Vol. 85, Pt. 1 (October 5, 1939), 125, 131.

Senator Robert Wagner, Democrat, of New York:

After the most careful study of the legislative details which divide us, I am convinced that the changes in our neutrality law reported by the committee give the best promise of keeping America out of war and keeping war away from America. . . .

I am indeed mindful of the sincerity and earnestness with which the embargo provision has been supported by able and distinguished Senators; but I find myself unable to agree either that the arms embargo represents the moral judgment of the American people, our indispensable defense against war, or the symbol of our neutrality. . . .

In closing, Mr. President, I sincerely believe that the deep yearning of all America for uninterrupted peace will be fully realized through the enactment of the joint resolution under consideration. But even within the framework of that law, incidents may arise and propaganda will undoubtedly be forthcoming to disturb our peaceful pursuits and shake our neutral purpose. In the difficult times that lie ahead, increased measures for national defense and unswerving unity of national effort will keep this Nation in the path of peace. Under the experienced and inspiring leadership of a President who has proved equal to every crisis, we face calmly what the future may bring, secure in our democratic strength and confident in our national destiny.[23]

Senator E. R. Burke, Democrat, of Nebraska:

. . . Repeal of the arms embargo will, therefore, not operate equally. To defend repeal upon that ground alone does not carry conviction. For myself, I have crossed that bridge. I speak no more of repeal of the arms embargo as an expression of strict neutrality, for it is not that. It checks the belligerent who now has a great advantage, takes that advantage away, and checks the belligerent which I, speaking for myself personally, want checked. It favors the belligerents that I want favored, by giving them the chance of coming here with their ships and buying our goods. However, I base my defense of repeal not on these preferences. We should repeal the arms embargo and adopt the other

23. *Congressional Record*, 76th Congress, 2d Session, Vol. 85, Pt. 1 (October 10, 1939), 240–243.

provisions of the substitute, with some minor modifications, because such action will greatly further the best interests of the United States. . . . There are many reasons why this is so. I shall now set forth a few of them.

First, this policy gives the largest measure of assurance attainable that we will not become involved in the war.

There is no doubt of the overwhelming desire of Americans to remain out of war. I respect the views of all who differ from me as to the best method of accomplishing that end. At the same time, I resent the statement or implication by anyone that those with whom they do not agree are trying to take us into war. As matters stand today, there is not the remotest possibility that we will ever send another American expeditionary force to Europe. Certainly no person of sense wants to do that or desires that this country should take any direct part in the war that is how under way or in any foreign war.

It is whispered that the President is consciously moving in the direction of war, that Secretary Hull is favorable to such a course, that some Senators and others are willing that such action should follow. That is calumny of the basest sort. . . .

Mr. President, we are justified in proceeding on the assumption that Congress, the Chief Executive, all of our people, are united in a common purpose to protect the safety and integrity of our country and keep us out of war. How is the pending measure adapted to secure that result?

First, by going to extreme lengths in keeping American ships, American citizens, and American goods out of danger zones. . . .

Second, repeal of the arms embargo will shorten the war. I have no doubt that in the end the democracies will prevail in their struggle against the totalitarian powers, whatever action we take. But without repeal it may easily be a long-drawn-out war, costly in human life and in the destruction of the accumulated values of centuries of effort. Moreover, the longer the war lasts the greater the danger of our involvement. Every day that the war is shortened means just that much less possibility of our participation. . . .[24]

Senator Francis Maloney, Democrat, of Connecticut:

24. *Congressional Record*, 76th Congress, 2d Session, Vol. 85, Pt. 1 (October 11, 1939), 290.

At the moment some good people of our country are going through a period of hysteria. Added up, or boiled down, however, the unanimous desire and demand is that we take the path away from war. . . .

It is my opinion that the pending measure will in no way increase the danger to us, while almost all admit that there are features of it which add to our protection against war. . . .

I have patiently waited for an argument which might, even to a slight degree, strengthen the contention that the passage of the joint resolution would be the first step toward war. That presentation is still delayed, and my own conviction becomes the stronger. . . .

Let me say at this time, Mr. President, that if there is reason for any nations in Europe to believe, or to entertain the serious hope, that at some later date we may enter this war, no ground for such belief has been afforded by those who favor repealing the arms embargo. The encouragement, if there is any—and I hope there is none—has been given, unintentionally, of course, by those who are opposed to the pending measure.[25]

Senator W. R. Austin, Republican, of Vermont:

I think one of the marked differences in the approach to the problem before us, and the widest cleavage we find between those who favor the joint resolution and those who oppose it, is the assumption which is now made by the distinguished Senator from Michigan; namely, that the citizens of the United States and their representatives in the Congress of the United States are no longer free agents; that they are no longer intelligent; that they no longer are men of character and fidelity; and that they are incapable of putting restrictions and regulations upon commerce which commonly goes free without taking another step and sending our boys across the sea.

That is the grave difference in attitude between us; and it is a difference upon which we will never agree, for I believe that those who favor the joint resolution are as eager and firm in their decision that our boys shall not be sent across the sea to do battle as any group in the United States. What is more, I believe that

25. *Congressional Record*, 76th Congress, 2d Session, Vol. 85, Pt. 1 (October 17, 1939), 500–501.

they have character enough and fidelity enough to truth to carry out that purpose, and that they are not so helpless that they must be dragged in. Dragged in by whom? You cannot have war with us unless you attack us, unless we are willing to declare war—and we are unwilling to declare war. When it comes to a matter of defense, we are not obliged to cross the seas with armed forces to defend ourselves. Our plan does not involve that.[26]

Senator J. E. Murray, Democrat, of Montana:

Mr. President, if the American people in this war maintain their neutrality, not on a basis of taking sides but on a just and legal basis—a basis which conforms to international law as we have known it for hundreds of years—no belligerent nation can justly take offense. If we do this, I believe it is as certain as any event of such nature can be certain that sooner or later this country will be asked to exercise its good offices for peace. When that time comes, it will not be difficult for the President of the United States to suggest the terms which will establish justice between the warring countries, and, in fact, between all the nations of the Old World. . . .

I think it must be manifest to any impartial, intelligent American, to any student of the realities of the situation, that the Pittman joint resolution presents the correct American policy of neutrality. . . .[27]

Senators opposed to President Roosevelt's request for a repeal of the embargo on munitions took cognizance of numerous pronouncements made by the President and his supporters in Congress, which assured the country that their purpose was *to maintain neutrality* and peace for the United States; but they insisted that he and his supporters were in fact pursuing in this respect a course that would inevitably lead to an involvement of the United States in war.

Excerpts from speeches delivered in the Senate setting forth the opposition views follow:

26. *Congressional Record,* 76th Congress, 2d Session, Vol. 85, Pt. 1 (October 19, 1939), 600.
27. *Congressional Record,* 76th Congress, 2d Session, Vol. 85, Pt. 1 (October 26, 1939), 911.

Senator W. E. Borah, Republican, of Idaho:

Our Secretary of State, Mr. Hull, has declared, speaking of the act of August 1935: "The Neutrality Act of last August, in embargoing exports of finished war commodities to belligerents, was to keep us out of war."

If the purpose of the Embargo Act then was to keep us out of war, what is the purpose of repealing it; to get us into war? Oh, no; I would not say the purpose but the inevitable effect of repealing it, in my judgment, would be to get us into war. If the enactment of it, as stated by the distinguished Secretary, was to keep us out of war, what kind of logic is it that says its repeal will keep us out of war?

We passed this law because we wanted to stay out of European conflicts. . . .

I am following the course which I am following solely because of my desire to stay out of the European war. I can see nothing in this program contributing to the cause of peace. On the other hand, it seems clear to me that we are moving rapidly to participating in this war. Arms, munitions, and implements of war are things with which to fight, to destroy life, to win battles; they are fit for nothing else. To furnish these things in the midst of a war to the advantage of one side or with the intent of assisting one side, is to help in the destruction of life and to win battles. All the debates in the world, in parliament, or on the stump, will have no effect as against the passion, the deep-seated war spirit of those who are on the field. To them the manufacturer, the salesman, the carrier, all who participate in getting the instrumentalities to the scene of conflict, will be regarded and treated as enemies. We will be in the war from the time the machinery is set in motion which carries these instrumentalities to the seat of war.[28]

Senator A. H. Vandenberg, Republican, of Michigan.

. . . In the midst of foreign war and the alarms of other wars, we are asked to depart basically from the neutrality which the American Congress has twice told the world, since 1935, would be our rule of conduct in such event. We are particularly asked to depart

28. *Congressional Record*, 76th Congress, 2d Session, Vol. 85, Pt. 1 (October 2, 1939), 69 ff.

from it through the repeal of existing neutrality law establishing an embargo on arms, ammunition, and implements of war. We are asked to depart from it in violation of our own officially asserted doctrine, during the World War, that the rules of a neutral cannot be prejudicially altered in the midst of a war. We are asked to depart from international law itself, as we ourselves have officially declared it to exist. Consciously or otherwise, but mostly consciously, we are asked to depart from it in behalf of one belligerent whom our personal sympathies largely favor, and against another belligerent whom our personal feelings largely condemn. In my opinion, this is the road that may lead us to war, and I will not voluntarily take it.

Mr. President, millions of Americans, including many Members of the Congress, believe—rightly or wrongly—this action not only breaks down our will to peace but also relatively faces toward our involvement in this war. Therefore millions of Americans and many Members of the Congress, regardless of their belligerent sympathies, earnestly oppose the inauguration of such a trend. The proponents of the change vehemently insist that their steadfast purpose, like ours, is to keep America out of the war, and their sincere assurances are presented to our people. But the motive is obvious, and the inevitable interpretation of the change, inevitably invited by the circumstances, will be that we have officially taken sides. . . .

No matter how earnestly the proponents of the change may seek to cushion it for peace, and they have made every effort, the cold, stark fact of fundamental change itself remains. No matter what new insulating devices are created, the greatest of all protections against our involvement is stricken down. Of course, it is not intended as a step toward war. But definitely, under existing circumstances, it is not and cannot be a step toward peace. The consequences . . . are a monstrous speculation. . . .

. . . I do not speak of peace at any price. I reject that doctrine as wholly un-American. I speak of peace only at the price of scrupulous neutrality and an incorrigible effort to maintain it. While perfecting the national defense of a people that shall be invincible in the righteousness of their democracy, I simply plead that peace shall have the benefit of every doubt.

This brings us squarely to the pending issue. Are we less likely to become involved in this new World War and its consequences if we faithfully maintain the neutrality code which we said two years ago would govern our attitudes in the event of alien war, and if, under this code, we refuse all arms, ammunition, and implements of war to all belligerents? That is one point. Or are we less likely to become involved if we change the code, for the admitted benefit of one belligerent against the other, and if we become armorers for one against the other?

It seems to me that the question answers itself. I cannot escape the profound conviction that the change must inevitably be less safe, less insulated, less calculated to achieve the American detachment to which we all say we are devoted. I do not say repeal precipitates us into war. That is not necessary to prove my point. I say that as between the two alternative courses available to us as to arms, ammunition, and implements of war it must obviously be relatively safer for America to pursue neutrality precisely as we solemnly declared two years ago we intended to pursue it under just such circumstances as we confront today; . . .

But from whatever viewpoint the problem is assessed, Mr. President, I find myself always driven back to the proposition that no matter what else is involved in this bill, the repeal of the arms embargo, which is the all-controlling symbol of an attitude, is not the way to encourage America's non-involvement in this war and in all of its disastrous consequences. Because of the reasons assigned to repeal, it is the way, rather, to encourage ourselves to progressively believe that our appropriate national course is to tie our destiny with one belligerent against the other and to progressively act upon that theory as our favorite's subsequent vicissitudes may require. That is not the road to peace.[29]

Senator H. C. Lodge, Republican, of Massachusetts:

Most of those who urge me to repeal the embargo, however, do so because they want to help England and France by safely selling them supplies, while not wanting to do so strongly enough to go the whole distance. These people are perfectly willing to abandon neutrality because of their belief that by helping England and France they will promote the peace of the United States. . . .

29. *Congressional Record*, 76th Congress, 2d Session, Vol. 85, Pt. 1 (October 4, 1939), 95, 98, 103.

They further contend that repeal of the embargo will promote peace for America on the ground that if England and France "crack," we will surely enter the war; we should, therefore, help them to win in órder to keep ourselves out. I submit that the chances of England and France being defeated are slim indeed. The choice seems to be between a defeat of Germany on the one hand and a stalemate on the other. I further contend, however, that even if Germany were victorious and desired to conquer the United States, she never could do so. No European power can occupy or vanquish the United States, and it is fanciful to suggest that it could. Fortunately, our national safety is not at stake. . . .

We should wait to repeal the embargo until the first overt act has been committed against us. Let us then use repeal of the embargo as a weapon of military strategy and as an act of self-defense. When we have done so, let us follow it up with still more direct and effective measures. If a great and damaging overt act is committed against America, we should not only give our Allies groceries on a cash-and-carry basis; we should jump in with both feet and fight for our country and our God shoulder to shoulder with them. Not for us will be a vacillating policy called "short of war"; not for us will there exist a counsel of being half in and half out, of bringing in by the back door what we are ashamed of at the main gate; . . . No! Once the war becomes our war, whether for economic, military, or moral grounds, let us get into it, and get really in. But until we have cause to get in, let us stay out.[30]

Senator B. C. Clark, Democrat, of Missouri:

. . . when I see that . . . there is an attempt to throw over the embargo provision which we know from experience is an absolutely necessary safeguard if we are going to erect adequate bulwarks against involvement in war, I cannot keep silent. I must lift my voice in protest against any efforts on the part of anyone to enact a policy that in any degree increases our chances of getting into war.

. . . I will tell you why we must keep the arms embargo. In the first place, it keeps us from engaging in the bloody, unholy,

30. *Congressional Record,* 76th Congress, 2d Session, Vol. 85, Pt. 1 (October 10, 1939), 250.

immoral business of being an arsenal for death-dealing weapons, or dealing in instruments of death. Furthermore, Mr. President, it is necessary to keep the arms embargo to all belligerents, because the armaments trade is the one trade which depends most on war for profits. . . . We must keep the arms embargo, because we adopted the embargo on arms to all belligerents in 1935 and reenacted it in 1936 and 1937 as our national policy, as a strong protective measure to insure our peace; . . . because we did not want to permit the growth of a vested interest in the arms trade which would inevitably endanger the determination of the country to keep out of foreign war.

I submit that the strongest protection for our people against involvement in war will be afforded by a strong cash-and-carry law in addition to the absolute ban on the sale or shipment of arms, ammunition, and implements of war. . . . Why can we not have both? We need both if we are to stay out of war. . . .

On the one hand are those who believe that we can "eat our cake and keep it too," that we can actively aid Great Britain and France by measures short of war, and still avoid ultimate participation in the struggle. On the other side are those of us who believe that the relaxation of our policy of strict neutrality by the repeal of the arms embargo, and the establishment of the United States as a reservoir for slaughterhouse weapons is only the first step which must inevitably lead to war. . . .

There are, in this country, perfectly honorable and patriotic men and women who conceive that our interests are so inextricably interwoven with those of Great Britain and France and Poland that we should step forward openly and frankly as a partner and ally. . . . With such a view I am in passionate disagreement, and I believe that the American people when they completely understand the issue will be in overwhelming disagreement. But, Mr. President, while I violently and completely dissent from the judgment, I respect such opinions when openly and candidly expressed.[31]

Senator G. P. Nye, Republican, of North Dakota:

But if the question is, Is the arms embargo repeal a symbol of the first step on the part of the United States on a steady tramp,

31. *Congressional Record*, 76th Congress, 2d Session, Vol. 85, Pt. 1 (October 11, 1939), 270, 275, 280.

tramp, tramp into war program? then the answer is most definitely, "Yes"; again and again, "Yes." Any man who can give his mind and his time to an honest, open study of what trade in munitions did to the United States back in 1914, 1915, and 1916, and say that embargo repeal at this time is not symbolic, is utterly ignoring so well-written a record of truth that it is unfortunate.

Mr. President, there is one lone issue in this debate, and it involves this question, Will helping the Allies keep us out of war? The President thinks it will. I am sure it will not. . . .

I deny with all the emphasis at my command that helping the Allies is neutrality. Others have denied it. We affirm that embargo repeal is a step toward war. We deny that the British Navy and the French Army are America's first line of defense. We affirm that neutrality is our first line of defense. We deny that the United States can make the world safe from Hitlerism by becoming the silent partner of the British Empire. We affirm that America's participation in this war, in any form, would bring no more democracy, no more justice, no more lasting peace to Europe than our last credulous crusade "to make the world safe for democracy." [32]

Senator W. J. Bulow, Democrat, of South Dakota:

To preserve the peace of our country, my administration contends that we should now repeal the arms embargo and sell guns and ammunition to fighting nations to be used for human destruction. It is contended that if we become a peddler of bullets, powder, and guns to other people, by so doing it will make America safe for peace. I cannot subscribe to that doctrine. The Congress enacted the Arms Embargo Act, which was signed by the President, committing this country to a policy of neutrality. . . . It is now proposed that we must repeal that act . . . It is contended that we must repeal the arms embargo and return to international law in order to safeguard our destiny of peace. . . .

Mr. President, if we repeal the Embargo Act it is our first step to war, and will be followed by other steps in quick succession that inevitably lead to participation on European battlefields. Within the memory of every one of us here we have had one sad

32. *Congressional Record*, 76th Congress, 2d Session, Vol. 85, Pt. 1 (October 13, 1939), 360.

and costly experience in our attempt to settle European bound-
ary disputes and have learned to our sorrow that that cannot be
done.[33]

Senator R. M. LaFollette, Progressive, of Wisconsin:

Mr. President, I regard the issues presented in this legislation as
of vital importance to the future of this Republic. I intend to discuss these issues at some length, but I shall first state them briefly:

Repeal of the embargo, in the present circumstances, and the
sale of arms, ammunition, and implements of war is a significant
step toward participation in the European war.

The several discretionary loopholes in the pending joint resolution are sufficient to allow for incidents which may lead us into
war.

It is not in the best interest of American democracy to gamble
everything of value which we possess in return for some temporary profits together with a permanent participation in a post-war
chaos most certain to be revolutionary in character. . . .

Mr. President, I am impressed by the fact that many people in
official life in Washington justify the repeal of the arms embargo
privately on the ground that our national interest requires a
policy which will assure victory for Great Britain and France
in this European war. This is the only real justification they give
for repeal of the arms embargo. . . . They argue that we must
take sides, to see one group of belligerents win. But once we take
sides since war is declared, knowing we are taking sides, repeal
can only be interpreted at home and abroad as an official act taken
by our Government for the purpose of partial participation in the
European war. . . .

Our patriotic course is clear. It is to stay out of Europe and the
Far East, which would drain our blood, our manhood, and our
wealth forever. It is to concentrate on making democracy function here in the last great industrial nation which has a chance of
making it function in the modern machine world. . . .

We have a great opportunity to build up an intercontinental
economy in this hemisphere. We can provide an army and navy
to defend it for a fraction of the cost of our involvement in war

33. *Congressional Record*, 76th Congress, 2d Session, Vol. 85, Pt. 1 (October
12, 1939), p. 315.

abroad. We do not have to accept as the solution of our problems the employment resulting from trade produced by slaughter and destruction of human beings on another continent.

We can utilize our idle manpower, productive capacity, and idle capital to restore our natural-resource base; to rehabilitate and conserve our human resources; to develop our Nation and this great and rich hemisphere. Here is a program that will give us a dynamic America, and restore that equality of economic opportunity that characterized the development of our own physical frontier. Here is a program which gives this generation "a rendezvous with destiny" in this hemisphere instead of with death in some other.

I put this program up against the program of taking sides; against the program of selling arms; against the program of intervention in a long, weary war, which will probably end abroad in revolution, and, if we become involved, may end here in dictatorship.[34]

Senator Arthur Capper, Republican, of Kansas:

Mr. President, I am opposed to the United States taking any part in the present European war. It is not our war. I am opposed to our taking the first step toward participation in this war, which is not our war. I am emphatically opposed to repeal of the arms embargo. . . . Repeal of the embargo unquestionably means involvement in the European controversy; it is the first step toward war. That is the main reason why I am opposed to repeal of the embargo against sale and shipment of arms, ammunition, and implements of war to nations at war. . . .

I do not want the United States dragged into the war, or bribed into the war with "cash and carry at a profit," or led into the war by the mistaken enthusiasm of some of our own leaders.

There is just one safe place for the United States in this war and that is in the United States. I am convinced the surest way for us to keep out of involvement is to stay on our own ground and mind our own business, and selling arms, ammunition, and implements of war to be used in this war is not staying at home and minding our own business. . . .

In 1935, in 1936, President Roosevelt was in favor of United

34. *Ibid.,* pp. 321 ff.

States neutrality; he thought he was opposed to the United States taking part in Europe's wars. He wanted peace; he regarded neutrality as an essential part of a peace program.

But in 1937 the President's ideas on the part the United States should play in world affairs began to enlarge. He saw things going on in Europe that he did not like—and in that respect I will say that I myself and most other Americans had no more liking for these things than did President Roosevelt.

But President Roosevelt, who in 1936 saw in neutrality the safe path for peace, and who saw in the arms embargo an effective expression of neutrality at least—President Roosevelt in 1937 felt an urge to meddle in European affairs. . . .

From that time on the United States was bound to pursue conflicting foreign policies. . . . As plainly it is difficult to maintain neutrality and at the same time take sides, of course it became necessary for the President to work for the repeal of the arms embargo, so that the Presidential urge to help Britain and France could be satisfied without violating the law of the land. . . .[35]

Senator D. I. Walsh, Democrat, of Massachusetts:

Because a war crisis in Europe has actually developed it is now proposed that we repeal the measures heretofore made to resist our involvement. The present issue, therefore, is . . . Shall we change our policy of non-intervention to intervention—to the extent of supplying to one of the belligerents destructive war weapons? . . .

Mr. President, candor compels me to state that I think of nothing, now that war has swept over Europe, that threatens more certainly to involve us in the present holocaust than deliberately to reverse our present policy of positive refusal to sell war weapons to any or all belligerents, and by solemn enactment offer the output of our munitions' factories for sale, knowing that only one group of belligerents can be our customer. No living being contends that we are morally bound to sell implements of war to any nation at any time. . . .

Instead of pleading here in the Senate of the United States for

35. *Congressional Record*, 76th Congress, 2d Session, Vol. 85, Pt. 1 (October 17, 1939), 461, 462.

traffic in arms or war profits, we should be militantly resisting every possible step that will lead to traffic in human lives, the lives of the youths of America. . . .

Mr. President, who are those urging the repeal of our arms embargo aside from the Chief Executive and the State Department, whose motives, like our own, we concede to be actuated by what they conceive to be the best interests of the Nation? Others, however, disclose motives that seem to me to be based on other considerations than neutrality. I refer to those Americans who believe we should at once enter the war and who are for repeal of the arms embargo as the first step. They, of course, frankly concede they are opposed to the policy of neutrality. They are for war.[36]

Senator Hiram Johnson, Republican, of California:

With embargo repeal we are half in and half out of war. We know from our bitter experience in the past how easy it will be to shove us along until we are fully in, and this is the nub of the matter. We will be shoved along and pushed about in relation to the present European war once we repeal the embargo, until we will not be sure where we stand or what we do. We will be pushed about and shoved along by those wily men who play the game of power politics, which some of our people, some of those who are snobbish, imagine they can play better than the diplomats of Europe, but when they indulge in the game of power politics with Europe they have as much chance as I would have trying to play poker with the Senator from Nevada. . . .

You may say that you will not go to war. You may say—and you may mean it—that you will not vote for a declaration of war, or to send a single boy across the sea. Who ever believed that we were sending 2,000,000 men across the sea when we voted for a declaration of war before? No! No! No! You must steel your hearts against the first false step. You must say to yourselves that you will not take a single step toward war, or you will find you cannot resist when the time comes.[37]

36. *Congressional Record*, 76th Congress, 2d Session, Vol. 85, Pt. 1 (October 17, 1939), 494.
37. *Congressional Record*, 76th Congress, 2d Session, Vol. 85, Pt. 1 (October 20, 1939), 630, 631.

After the debate on neutrality had gone on for about a month, President Roosevelt intervened. On October 26, 1939, the President said in a radio broadcast:

In and out of Congress we have heard orators and commentators and others beating their breasts and proclaiming against sending the boys of American mothers to fight on the battlefields of Europe. That I do not hesitate to label as one of the worst fakes in current history. It is a deliberate setting up of an imaginary bogey man. The simple truth is that no person in any responsible place in the national administration in Washington, or in any State Government, or in any city Government, or in any county Government, has ever suggested in any shape, manner or form the remotest possibility of sending the boys of American mothers to fight on the battlefields of Europe. That is why I label that argument a shameless and dishonest fake. . . .

The fact of the international situation—the simple fact, without any bogey in it, without any appeals to prejudice—is that the United States of America, as I have said before, is neutral and does not intend to get involved in war.[38]

At length Congress yielded to the President's plea for the repeal of the munitions embargo in the interest of peace and neutrality for the United States, but it coupled with the repeal several stringent amendments which materially strengthened the neutrality legislation in other respects. The new bill was signed by President Roosevelt on November 4, 1939. In commenting later on actions of Congress, the President said: "The adoption of these recommendations offered greater safeguards than we had before to protect American lives and property from destruction and in that way tended to avoid the incidents and controversies likely to draw us into conflict, as they had done in the last World War." [39]

Under the new Neutrality Act which permitted the sale of munitions to belligerents, President Roosevelt issued a

38. *Public Papers*, 1939 Vol., pp. 556 f.
39. This comment appears in the Introduction to his *Public Papers*, 1939 Vol., p. xxxviii, dated July, 1941.

new proclamation of neutrality on the day he signed the bill, November 4, 1939; and on December 2, 1939, he issued a statement urging American airplane makers not to sell planes to nations guilty of bombing civilians. In this statement, he said: "The American Government and the American people have for some time pursued a policy of wholeheartedly condemning the unprovoked bombing and machine-gunning of civilian populations from the air. This Government hopes, . . . that American manufacturers and exporters of airplanes, aeronautical equipment and materials essential to airplane manufacture will bear this fact in mind before negotiating contracts for the exportation of these articles to nations obviously guilty of such unprovoked bombing." [40]

The large vote cast in Congress for the new neutrality bill, despite the vigor and persistence of the opposition, indicated that the Democratic managers in the national legislature had affairs well in hand. The outcome had been foretold by an anonymous writer in an article which appeared in the scholarly British magazine, *Round Table*, September, 1939. This article, evidently prepared some time in advance of publication, that is before the war began, was entitled "America and the World Crisis." It made a bold prophecy: "If war is actually precipitated, President Roosevelt will call a special session of Congress . . . and will seek the practically guaranteed repeal of the arms embargo. . . . The full economic, industrial, agricultural resources of the United States would then be at the disposal of Great Britain . . . though perhaps on a 'cash and carry' basis." The article continued: "How, when, or whether the United States would actually be drawn into the conflict is, naturally, a question that cannot be answered, but if one is estimating

40. *Ibid.*, p. 589. At this time, Russia, under the pact with Hitler, had occupied Estonia, Latvia, Lithuania, and large parts of eastern Poland; and had also begun a war on Finland. On December 6, 1939, President Roosevelt, in greetings to Finland on the anniversary of its independence, voiced "the whole-hearted esteem felt for them [the Finnish people] and their government by the people and government of the United States." *Public Papers*, 1939 Vol., p. 595.

the probabilities they are that the history of 1914–17 would be foreshortened and repeated . . . the precise pattern of participation might be very different from that of 1917, but it might be none the less effective." [41]

Among the managers of the President's cause in Congress, Senator James F. Byrnes was outstanding. It was generally recognized in Washington that the Senator had extraordinary powers and abilities in making compromises, adjustments, and an efficient distribution of executive patronage; and his services were appreciated as far away as London. In the issue for December, 1939, *Round Table* reported on the tactics employed in putting through the modification of the Neutrality Act: "In September, the President had Senator James F. Byrnes—a skilled and highly popular negotiator—poll his colleagues at their homes in all parts of the country by lavish use of the long-distance telephone. Striking early, Senator Byrnes obtained ample commitments to repeal of the embargo before ever the Senators returned to Washington for the special session. Similarly, practical methods were employed in the House, where the 'solid south' of Democratic representatives and the machine-controlled city blocs of representatives were all whipped into the party camp. . . . It was a triumph of sanity and legitimate political organization. . . ." [42]

By the end of the fateful year 1939, in which the general war in Europe flamed up, basic guarantees of peace for the United States had been written into the record by President Roosevelt and supporters of his Administration.

In his message to Congress on July 14, incorporating formulas devised by Secretary Hull, the President had informed the American people that his purpose was to maintain the

41. Quoted in Porter Sargent's *Getting Us into War* (Porter Sargent, 1941), p. 122.

42. Quoted in Sargent, *op. cit.*, pp. 204 f. Senator Byrnes was highly useful to President Roosevelt later: in qualifying the anti-war plank in the Democratic platform of 1940 and in putting through the Lend-Lease Bill of 1941. In June, 1941, Senator Byrnes was appointed Justice of the Supreme Court of the United States.

neutrality of the United States and so shape his foreign policy as to keep the country out of war.

On September 3, after the European war had begun, in a broadcast to the nation, he had warned citizens against "falsely" talking about sending American armies to Europe and had vowed: "This nation will remain a neutral nation."

In his message to Congress in September, calling for a repeal of the munitions embargo, he had informed the American nation that he and his associates in the Government were "equally and without reservation in favor of such measures as will protect the neutrality, the safety and the integrity of our country and at the same time keep us out of war," and had informed the people that "Our acts must be guided by one single hard-headed thought—keeping America out of this war."

Again and again during the debate that raged from June to November over modifications in the Neutrality Act, President Roosevelt and his supporters in Congress had assured and reassured the American people that their purpose was to preserve the neutrality of the United States and avoid being drawn into foreign wars.

In a radio broadcast to the country, October 26, 1939, while the issue of the embargo repeal was still pending, President Roosevelt had declared that the United States "is neutral and does not intend to get involved in war."

After members of the opposition had many times asserted that a repeal of the embargo on munitions was a step in the direction of war and would lead in due time to the sending of American boys to fight on European battlefields, President Roosevelt had denounced them in severe language—in his broadcast of October 26. He had branded their assertion as "a shameless and dishonest fake." He had invited the people's trust by testifying that no responsible person in the Government had "ever suggested in any shape, manner or form the remotest possibility of sending the boys of American mothers to fight on the battlefields of Europe."

CHAPTER X

Peace Promises in the Election Year 1940

In terms of time, President Roosevelt's pronouncements on foreign policy in 1940 fell into four periods, each marked by special characteristics. The first extended from January 1 to the summer season of the party conventions. The second included June—when the Republican convention was held in Philadelphia, and July—when the Democratic convention met at Chicago. The third period ran from the end of July to early September, during which the President refrained from campaigning in the ordinary sense of the term, as if confident of winning the election without indulging in customary politics; while the Republican candidate, Wendell Willkie, was making political capital and raising the issue of "no war." The fourth period opened on September 11 when the President, warned by his advisers against expecting easy victory by default, took to the stump, and it closed with his final campaign speeches on the eve of the balloting in November; in this period he made several speeches, some of them brief; while Mr. Willkie kept challenging him by assertions that his policy meant war for the United States.

President Roosevelt's declarations on foreign policy and war after the opening of the campaign season were in some respects framed to meet Mr. Willkie's charges that he was taking the country on the road to war—charges that grew more explicit and more vehement as election day drew nearer. On the other hand, Mr. Willkie's arguments and contentions were frequently shaped with reference to countering the President's replies and charges. In other words, all along reciprocal influences were at work giving form and point to campaign promises on both sides as allegations and denials, arraignments and contradictions proceeded apace amid the heated competition for the people's suffrages. But a weighing or appraisal of these reciprocal influences involves judgments likely to be controversial at best. So, with a view to avoiding the possible introduction of such polemics, a plan of treating merely seriatim the peace pledges on both sides of the party battle, with reference to the special periods of the year, has been adopted for the following pages.

President Roosevelt's Statements on Peace
Prior to the Democratic Convention

Between January 1, 1940, and the meeting of the Democratic convention at Chicago in July, terrible events occurred in Europe; by the first of July Hitler's armies had flooded out in all directions; France had fallen; the British had been driven off the Continent and stood alone battling heroically for existence; Belgium, Holland, Denmark, and Norway had come under the sway of German tyrants; Italy had struck falling France in the hour of her deep distress; the utter triumph of the Axis Powers in Europe seemed imminent.

Although there had been a lull in the European war on the Western front after it began in September, 1939, signs that its fury would be soon renewed were on the horizon when President Roosevelt delivered his annual message to Congress on January 3, 1940. If there was to be a reversal of the foreign policy which he had hitherto espoused, the occasion seemed appropriate, but no such reversal was announced in the message.

It is true that he pleased internationalists by chiding "American ostriches in our midst" and remarking that "it is not good for the ultimate health of ostriches to bury their heads in the sand." And he referred, with impatience, to "those who wishfully insist, in innocence or ignorance, or both, that the United States of America as a self-contained unit can live happily and prosperously, its future secure, inside a high wall of isolation, while, outside, the rest of civilization and the commerce and culture of mankind are shattered."

At the same time, however, the President adhered strictly

to his old line of defense, neutrality, and peace for the United States. "I can understand," he said, "the feelings of those who warn the nation that they will never again consent to the sending of American youth to fight on the soil of Europe. But, as I remember, nobody has asked them to consent—*for nobody expects such an undertaking.*

"The overwhelming majority of our fellow citizens do not abandon in the slightest their hope and their expectation that the United States will not become involved in military participation in these wars. . . . there is a vast difference between keeping out of war and pretending that this war is none of our business.

"We do not have to go to war with other nations, but at least we can strive with other nations to encourage the kind of peace that will lighten the troubles of the world, and by so doing help our own nation as well.

"I ask that all of us everywhere think things through with the single aim of how best to serve the future of our own nation. . . . it becomes clearer and clearer that the future world will be a shabby and dangerous place to live in—yes, even for Americans to live in—if it is ruled by force in the hands of a few. . . ."

As if anticipating the partisan efforts of the campaign to divide the country into a war party and a peace party, the President spurned the tactics: "The time is long past when any political party or any particular group can curry or capture public favor by labeling itself the 'peace party' or the 'peace bloc.' That label belongs to the whole United States and to every right thinking man, woman, and child within it. . . .

"The first President of the United States warned us against entangling foreign alliances. The present President of the United States subscribes to and follows that precept." [1]

Speaking to the Young Democratic Clubs on April 20, 1940, President Roosevelt told the members that "Your Government is keeping a cool head and a steady hand. We are

1. *Public Papers,* 1940 Vol., pp. 1 ff. (Italics supplied.)

keeping out of the wars that are going on in Europe and in Asia, but I do not subscribe to the preachment of a Republican aspirant for the Presidency who tells you, in effect, that the United States and the people of the United States should do nothing to try to bring about a better order, a more secure order, of world peace when the time comes." [2]

When he called on Congress for additional appropriations for national defense, May 16, 1940, the President said: "Our task is plain. The road we must take is clearly indicated. Our defenses must be invulnerable, our security absolute. . . . *Our ideal, yours and mine, the ideal of every man, woman, and child in the country—our objective is still peace—peace at home and peace abroad.* Nevertheless, we stand ready not only to spend millions *for defense* but to give our service and even our lives *for the maintenance of our American liberties.*" [3]

In another message to Congress asking for additional appropriations for national defense, July 10, 1940, the President again assured the members: "That we are opposed to war is known not only to every American, but to every government in the world. We will not use our arms in a war of aggression; *we will not send our men to take part in European wars.* But, we will repel aggression against the United States or the Western Hemisphere." [4]

Mr. Willkie's Statements on Peace Prior to His Nomination by the Republicans

Before the year 1940 had advanced far, it became known that a new contender had entered the lists for the Republican nomination—Wendell Willkie of New York City, and

2. *Ibid.,* p. 168.
3. *Ibid.,* p. 204. (Italics supplied.)
4. *Ibid.,* pp. 288 f. (Italics supplied.) It may be noted here that on June 18, 1940, Mr. Willkie had declared in an address in Brooklyn: ". . . despite our whole-hearted sympathy for the Allied cause, we must stay out of war. . . . We do not intend to send men from the shores of this continent to fight in any war. . . ."

that a powerful organization was preparing to storm the Republican convention on his behalf. Mr. Willkie had been until recently a Democrat, not a Republican; and he was primarily a man of business, not of politics. His fundamental quarrel with President Roosevelt, such as it was at the moment, appeared to involve domestic policies affecting "big business," rather than foreign policies relative to peace and war.

Born and reared in Indiana in humble circumstances, Mr. Willkie had risen to distinction and wealth as a public utility lawyer. As the legal, or rather publicity, representative of a great utility concern, with offices in New York City, Mr. Willkie had come into a public collision with President Roosevelt over federal legislation and actions in respect of corporate interests, special and general. To Republicans who regarded President Roosevelt as an inveterate foe of "economic royalists," Mr. Willkie seemed to be a godsend, just the man to lead America's chosen people out of the New Deal wilderness, despite the fact that he had long been affiliated with the Democratic party. In "the instant need of things" they overlooked his record in matters of foreign policy, or perhaps deemed it negligible or accepted it as offering promises to interventionists.

At all events Mr. Willkie's record on the issue of foreign policy was known to students of public affairs. As if to make it doubly clear in history, he later described it in an article written in 1944 for John Temple Graves, columnist of the Birmingham *Age-Herald*, a leading Democratic paper in Alabama. In the opening paragraph of his letter, Mr. Willkie exulted in what he called a recent revival of interest in Woodrow Wilson, and declared that he was among those who had found their "first strong political ideology in devoted support of Wilson's gallant but tragic fight for the League of Nations." Thereupon Mr. Willkie recited at length a story of how year after year he had associated himself with Newton D. Baker, outspoken champion of President Wilson's internationalism, and had himself preached to "all who would listen," in his locality in Ohio, the doctrine that "only through such an instrumentality as the League [of Nations] could future wars be prevented." [5]

According to the recital in his article, Mr. Willkie had later, as a delegate to the Democratic national convention of 1924, zealously supported Mr. Baker in his valiant struggle to wring from the convention an endorsement of the League of Nations.[6] "The story has an epilogue," Mr. Willkie continued. He invited remembrance of the fact that Governor Franklin D. Roosevelt, while a candidate for the Democratic nomination in 1932, had "publicly repudiated the League of Nations." [7] He stated that he and other "Baker boys" thereafter started a movement to win the nomination for Mr. Baker—"the leader who almost alone through the dark isolationist twenties had fought consistently for world cooperation." The Baker boys made a desperate effort at Chicago in 1932 to defeat Governor Roosevelt and nominate Mr. Baker; but they lost. As Mr. Willkie interpreted their defeat, John N. Garner, William Randolph Hearst, William G. McAdoo, Joseph Kennedy, and James A. Farley "got together," and they were little interested in "world cooperation"; Governor Roosevelt, who had publicly denounced the League of Nations, won the nomination.

Mr. Willkie closed his article of 1944 with a postscript. The Democratic party not only had rejected the League of Nations but after 1932 it had begun to violate Woodrow Wilson's "philosophy of government"; that is, his emphasis on economic individualism. After his discomfiture in battles for the League of Nations and after President Roosevelt had gone in heavily for social reform by government action, Mr. Willkie dissociated himself from the Democratic party as then constituted and led or, to use his own words, "I left the

5. Reprinted in *The United States News*, September 8, 1944, with an introductory note by David Lawrence, an ardent interventionist, who was hostile to the "socialism" of the New Deal. See above, p. 100.

6. For an account of the nature of this contest in 1924, see above, pp. 50 ff.

7. For Governor Roosevelt's repudiation of the League, February 2, 1932, see above, pp. 75 ff.

Democratic party—or, perhaps the Democratic party left me."

It was, therefore, a strange political figure whom the Eastern Republicans put forward as an aspirant for the nomination early in 1940. Mr. Willkie had once been a stout and regular Democrat but he had not, like President Roosevelt, publicly cast off his allegiance to the League of Nations. His record on internationalism up until 1940 had been thoroughly satisfactory to those Republicans and Democrats who abhorred the New Deal and yet openly or secretly hoped for American intervention in the European war. But Mr. Willkie's chief rivals for the Republican nomination were known to be opposed to involvement in that war, if not outright isolationists, and during the weeks before the Republican convention assembled Mr. Willkie laid before the country his own offerings on the theme of peace and war.

Writing early in the year 1940 on the subject of aiding the Allies at war with aggressors and at the same time keeping the United States out of war, Mr. Willkie declared that the double objective could be effected.

Now we have been sure for a great number of years that we don't want to have any part in anybody's war. We have had some wars of our own in the past. We now think we have outgrown them. If we and our neighbors on this hemisphere are left to ourselves, we can get along very nicely without any military activity. And we don't think that we should be called upon to settle the boundaries of a less fortunate continent. Also, we have a vague feeling that if the situation were reversed, if the hostilities were over here, we should not see any country in Europe coming over to stand beside us on the battle line. . . .

And, clearly, we have a right to lend, buy, sell, or borrow, with respect to any country we designate. We might well drop that right for the sake of peace. Yet we must remember that no foreign nation wants to have the U. S. as its enemy or will contrive to find a cause for hostility with this country. In fact, its tendency will be the other way—to overlook annoyances in the hope of keeping us neutral. If the aggressive countries today—

the U.S.S.R.,[8] Germany, and Japan—were looking for quarrels to pick with the U. S., they could find plenty of excuses. The government, for instance, has encouraged the sale of military equipment to England and France. It has also expressed its vigorous opposition to certain of the policies of Germany, the U.S.S.R., and Japan. It has even gone so far as to call for a "moral embargo" against Japan. It has refused to recognize the state of Manchukuo, which the Japanese took from China, and it has similarly refused to recognize Germany's conquest of Czechoslovakia or the conquest of Poland. It has withdrawn our Ambassador from Germany. . . . No one of those things involved us in a war, and neither will a loan to Finland, however the Finns use the money.

It does not seem to us that our foreign policy need be complicated by the obsessions of the extremists on either side. Our political foreign experts should get rid of the habit of whispering through the window and slipping things down the back alley. Our foreign policies should be forthright and clear. We are opposed to war. But we do not intend to relinquish our right to sell whatever we want to those defending themselves from aggression. And we are not so foolish as to believe that these sales of products at our ports, with our ships withdrawn from combat areas, can possibly involve us in hostilities.[9]

In a press interview, May 4, 1940, Mr. Willkie made the following statement on foreign policy, which was interpreted in some quarters as substantially identical with President Roosevelt's:

. . . despite the views of the narrow isolationist, America does have a vital interest in the continuation in this world of the English, French and Norwegian way of life. *We must at all hazards*

8. Russia, associated by a pact with Hitler's Germany, had been at war with Finland for some time. In February, 1940, President Roosevelt had said: "The Soviet Union, as everybody who has the courage to face the fact knows, is run by a dictatorship as absolute as any other dictatorship in the world. It has allied itself with another dictatorship, . . ." *Public Papers,* 1940 Vol., p. 93.

9. Wendell L. Willkie, "We, the People," *Fortune,* XXI, 4 (April, 1940), p. 172.

stay out of war, but I doubt whether we will stay out of war merely by putting our head, like the ostrich, in the sand and allowing the democracies to be defeated in their fight against the totalitarian States. It may well be that the most effective way of us keeping out of this war will be by helping the democracies in every way possible, *within the limits of international law.*

Also, we should on all occasions as a nation give our complete moral support to the democracies, for if the totalitarian States prevail the odds are very substantial that we shall have to meet them in armed conflict when they have been victorious *over the democracies* and are truculent and strong.[10]

Speaking before the Indiana Bankers Association, May 15, 1940, Mr. Willkie warned his auditors against the dangers to "the American system of free enterprise" of a German victory in Europe and added: "I think it is fair to say that those who have the peace of America at heart must want to do *anything short of war* which would strengthen the forces of France, England, Holland and Belgium."[11]

While engaged in his quest for the nomination, Mr. Willkie, speaking at a "Hoosier" box supper in New York City, May 21, 1940, maintained that the only way the United States could avoid war was to build up its strength so that it would be respected abroad. "In my judgment," he declared, "a man who thinks that the results in Europe will be of no consequence to him is a blind, foolish and silly man. . . . Hitler knows only strength. He will stand aghast when we start the wheels of our industry turning and put 10,000,000 men back to work."[12]

According to a report of a press interview at the La Guardia airport, June 8, 1940, after his return from a western trip, Mr. Willkie took the stand that "isolation" necessarily involved a flat refusal to approve any aid whatever to the Allies. After thus reducing isolationism to these terms, he disclaimed any sympathy with it:

10. *New York Times*, May 5, 1940. (Italics supplied.)
11. *Ibid.*, May 16, 1940. (Italics supplied.)
12. *Ibid.*, May 22, 1940.

"During my trips across the country in the past few weeks I have found no material difference of opinion between people in the West and Far West and in the East on the European outlook," Mr. Willkie said. "An overwhelming number of people in this country believe that we should give all possible aid, *short of war*, of course, to the Allies. . . ."

When asked if he thought it possible that the Republicans would write in an isolation plank in their platform, Mr. Willkie said:

"I don't think there is any chance that the Republicans will adopt any isolation plank. I haven't been able to find any strong isolation groups in the Republican party and I am sure that the country is overwhelmingly in favor of granting immediate *aid to the Allies*." [13]

Answering questions at a press conference in Washington, June 12, 1940, Mr. Willkie said respecting his own attitude:

As to foreign affairs, as far as assistance to the democracies is concerned, *I am in accord with the National Administration*. I think the President is too secretive and too emotional about the details of his foreign policy, but generally I am in full accord with his program. Generally speaking, as far as entering the war is concerned, it should be the duty of the President to act as a resistant and a deterrent force, and a restraining influence upon impulses to go into this or any war. His position should be that we are not to go in unless absolutely compelled to. [14]

To 8,000 Republicans assembled at Boston, Mr. Willkie presented his views on peace and war in three brief paragraphs:

Many persons have asked me whether, if I were nominated and elected, I would lead the United States to war.

My reply is that the Chief Executive should not lead the people to war unless and until the people insist upon that action. It is the

13. *Ibid.*, June 9, 1940. (Italics supplied.)
14. *Ibid.*, June 13, 1940. (Italics supplied.)

duty of the Chief Executive to prevent war if he can possibly do so. In that awful decision he should not push Congress. Congress should push him. In a democracy only the people have a right to decide upon war. The duty of a President is to be the restraining and the calming influence in all periods of crisis.

And, personally, *in spite of my belief that we would help the Allies in every possible way, I have been against getting into this war, or any other war, and I still am.*[15]

In an address to Connecticut delegates about to depart for the Republican convention, Mr. Willkie declared that he favored aid to the Allies "short of war," and explained later that he would favor extending credits to them if necessary. He summed up his case tersely: "I am one of those who favor giving every material assistance we can to the democracies of Europe in these critical times. *But by the same token talk of sending American boys over there when we have no material or equipment is sheer nonsense.*" [16]

Speaking in Brooklyn, June 18, 1940, Mr. Willkie reiterated his endorsement of aid to the Allies but made his emphasis on keeping the country out of war more decisive in letter and tone:

. . . despite our whole-hearted sympathy for the Allied cause, we must stay out of war. In the stress of these times, when our hearts are confused with emotion, we must keep our heads clear. We do not intend to send men from the shores of this continent to fight in any war. This is not mere selfishness on our part; we shall not serve the cause of democracy and human freedom by becoming involved in the present war; we shall serve that cause by keeping out of war. I believe in national defense, not as a step toward war but as a protection against it.

It is the duty of the President of the United States to recognize the determination of the people to stay out of war and to do nothing by word or deed that will undermine that determination. No man has the right to use the great powers of the Presidency

15. *Ibid.*, June 15, 1940. (Italics supplied.)
16. *Ibid.*, June 16, 1940. (Italics supplied.)

to lead the people, indirectly, into war; only the people through their elected representatives can make that awful decision and there is no question as to their decision.[17]

In a press interview at the opening of the Republican convention in Philadelphia, Mr. Willkie was asked by reporters whether he approved aid to the Allies. His answer was: "I favor all possible aid to the Allies without going to war." A woman bystander interjected the question: "Doesn't that mean war?" This inquiry he turned aside by saying: "That's a matter of opinion." [18]

The Peace Pledge of the Republican National Convention

Long before the Republican convention met at Philadelphia late in June, 1940, accounts of conflicts within the party over a foreign policy plank for the platform appeared in the press. Reports from the West carried the news that delegates from that region were coming prepared to write into the platform an unequivocal pledge against involving the country in foreign war. In the East, however, Republican sentiments were not so uniform. In that section especially were many Republicans who believed that the United States should intervene in the European war immediately or sometime in the near future. So far they had carried on their propaganda under the slogan: "Defend America by aiding the Allies." But nowhere in the Republican party was there a considerable body of members who maintained openly and frankly that they were in favor of putting the United States into the war by constitutional methods—a declaration of war by Congress. Republicans who cherished interventionist designs did not often venture to disclose them publicly as yet and they adopted the strategy of working for an anti-war plank, with an escape clause, and for a plank emphasizing aid to the Allies that might carry the country on the road to war.[19]

One of the trial suggestions broached before the Republi-

17. *Ibid.*, June 19, 1940.
18. *Ibid.*, June 23, 1940.
19. Johnson, *The Battle against Isolation*, especially chap. v.

cans assembled—a scheme ascribed to Governor Alfred M. Landon—was a projected foreign policy plank for the platform to read as follows: "We favor all proper aid to the Allies that does not involve any commitment that will take us into war unless the vital interests of America are threatened in a tangible and concrete way." To the editors of the *New York Times*, the proposition attributed to Governor Landon was "a straightforward statement." It seemed to meet the *Times* requirement that the Republicans "speak openly and plainly" instead of dodging the issue by a statement that could mean different things to different persons.[20]

Mr. Landon's plan for starting with "all proper aid" encountered snags in the platform committee then at work in preparation for the convention the next week. "Old-time isolationists" would have nothing whatever to do with it. Taking a middle course, Dr. Glenn Frank urged the adoption of an anti-war plank with an escape clause: a declaration against involvement in the European war, *unless* American interests were "vitally and concretely concerned," a denunciation of President Roosevelt's policies as leading the country to war, and an approval of aid to the Allies "through the normal channels of trade," with safeguards against military commitments.[21]

While the Republican platform-makers were wrestling with the foreign policy plank, President Roosevelt spread consternation in their ranks by appointing Henry L. Stimson as Secretary of War and Frank Knox as Secretary of the Navy. Both were orthodox Republicans known to be in favor of powerful aid to the Allies and a strong policy in dealing with the Axis countries; that is, in favor of marching as if to war, perhaps to war itself. President Roosevelt's stroke, the *New York Times* reported, "changed the whole pattern of the convention." Interventionists engaged in advocating "aid to Britain" were embarrassed. Isolationists and even those in the middle of the road took the appointments

20. Editorial, *New York Times*, June 19, 1940.
21. *New York Times*, June 19, 1940, p. 1.

to signify preparations for war and were inclined to make an attack on the Democrats as the war party and to line up the Republicans as the peace party.[22]

For practical purposes, President Roosevelt's action in putting Mr. Stimson and Mr. Knox at the head of the war agencies in his Administration created difficulties for the Republican interventionists who had hoped to insert a plank in favor of unconditional aid to the Allies. But the interventionists were still undaunted and what was more they had money to dispense for campaign purposes. So the compromisers went to work on the proposal that the matter of foreign policy be treated briefly and vaguely in the platform, and that the party's stand on that subject be left largely to the candidate nominated for President. As expected this design drew fire from the isolationists, who threatened to take the fight from the committee room to the floor of the convention. Furthermore to neither factions did there seem to be much sense in a campaign if the Republicans played a "me too" game for President Roosevelt.[23]

Despite the efforts of reporters for interventionist papers to make it appear that the Republicans would agree upon a compromise plank which was strong on aid to the Allies and weak in opposition to war, nothing in the records of the convention shows that such a project was possible at any moment. A large majority of the Republican delegates at Philadelphia were in favor of some kind of aid to the Allies, but the phrase was meaningless without definitions of the "aid" and the methods of giving it. Moreover, the resolve of the anti-war group at Philadelphia was so inexorable that no vague definition of the "aid" and the methods could have escaped its watchful eyes and its determination to put the party on record against the war. In fact, it was reported by William Allen White, on what he called "fairly good authority," that the Republicans were in negotiation with anti-

22. *Ibid.*, June 21, 1940.
23. *Ibid.*, June 25, 1940, Sec. I, p. 3.

war Democrats with an idea of getting their support if the Democrats at their own coming convention "went too far toward war." [24]

As the hours ticked off, the anti-war Republicans at the convention seemed to gain in force. They could not defeat all references in the platform to aid for the Allies; nor did a majority of them so desire apparently. Yet they were staunch in their resolve to make the anti-war plank stiff in its terms and pin "the label of 'war party' on the Democrats." While the contest over the platform was still on, the sentiments of the anti-war majority were expressed by Herbert K. Hyde, chairman of the platform committee, and avowed with striking brevity: "We intend to keep faith with the fathers and mothers of this nation and guarantee to them that the youth of America will never be called upon to cross any man's sea to settle European or Asiatic quarrels. Instead of saving the world for democracy, we propose to make democracy real and effective for the American people in the United States. We can't police the world." [25]

In an address to the convention on June 25, 1940, Ex-President Herbert Hoover presented three axioms of policy for the Republicans to consider. First, the "immediate dangers" to the United States are not to be over-exaggerated. Second, preparedness must be "competent." Third, the supplying of materials and munitions to nations fighting for their freedom must be facilitated, subject to two limitations: no action of the kind that "takes us to war" should be permitted and "as liberty lives by law we must act within the law." [26]

Mr. Hoover's speech upheld the hands of the anti-war Republicans at the convention and led to modifications in the plank, which made it a still stronger manifesto against getting the United States into the war and in support of better preparedness for defense in this hemisphere. The modifications

24. "Republicans Act Like Democrats," *ibid.*, June 25, 1940.
25. *New York Times*, June 25, 1940, p. 1.
26. *Ibid.*, June 26, 1940.

also sharpened the attack on the Roosevelt Administration as leading the country on the road to war. When interventionist Republicans sought to weaken these changes by inserting words of double meaning, the anti-war bloc again threatened to take the fight to the floor of the convention where they felt sure of winning immediate and full endorsement. Some trimming of phrases was effected by compromise but, as the *New York Times* reported, "the non-interventionists were flushed with victory." Even Governor Landon, despite his position in the party, yielded to the "isolationists" and did not risk a conflict with them before the whole body of delegates.[27]

At length the bloc of Republicans in favor of adopting a strong foreign policy that might justify or lead to war gave up the struggle in the resolutions committee and a foreign affairs plank that represented a victory for the non-interventionists was unanimously reported to the convention. One of the chief leaders of the non-interventionist bloc, C. Wayland Brooks, of Illinois, called upon the convention to adopt the entire platform "so that the party might offer itself to the country as the instrument for keeping the United States out of war." Hamilton Fish, ranking Republican member of the Foreign Affairs Committee of the House of Representatives, declared that the platform made the Republican party the peace party, and the Democrats a war party.[28]

As to participation in war, the Republican platform was unequivocal: "The Republican party is firmly opposed to involving this nation in foreign war." To this affirmation was added no "escape" clause, such as *unless* or *except* this or that. After this anti-war pledge came a denunciation of the Roosevelt Administration as responsible for national confusion, weakness, and the dangers of involvement in war.

To appreciate the full force of the Republican manifesto, the foreign policy and defense section of the platform must be studied in detail. It read:

27. *Ibid.,* June 26, 1940, p. 1.
28. *Ibid.,* June 27, 1940, pp. 1-4.

The Republican party is firmly opposed to involving this nation in foreign war.

We are still suffering from the ill effects of the last World War—a war which cost us a twenty-four billion-dollar increase in our national debt, billions of uncollectible foreign debts and the complete upset of our economic system, in addition to the loss of human life and irreparable damage to the health of thousands of our boys.

The present National Administration has already spent for all purposes more than fifty-four billion dollars, has boosted the national debt and current Federal taxes to an all-time high, and yet by the President's own admission we are still wholly unprepared to defend our country, its institutions and our individual liberties in a war that threatens to engulf the whole world, and this in spite of the fact that foreign wars have been in progress for two years or more and that military information concerning these wars and the rearmament programs of the warring nations has been at all times available to the National Administration through its diplomatic and other channels.

The Republican party stands for Americanism, preparedness and peace. We accordingly fasten upon the New Deal full responsibility for our unpreparedness and for the consequent danger of involvement in war.

We declare for the prompt, orderly and realistic building of our national defense to the point at which we shall be able not only to defend the United States, its possessions and essential outposts from foreign attack, but also efficiently to uphold in war the Monroe Doctrine. To this task the Republican party pledges itself when entrusted with national authority.

In the meantime, we shall support all necessary and proper defense measures proposed by the Administration in its belated effort to make up for lost time; but we deplore explosive utterances by the President directed at other governments, which serve to imperil our peace, and we condemn all Executive acts and proceedings which might lead to war without the authorization of the Congress of the United States.

Our sympathies have been profoundly disturbed by invasion of unoffending countries and by disaster to nations whose ideals most closely resemble our own. We favor the extension to all peoples fighting for liberty, or whose liberty is threatened, of such aid as shall not be in violation of international law or inconsistent with the requirements of our own national defense.

We believe that the spirit which should animate our entire defensive policy is determination to preserve not our material interests merely, but those liberties which are the priceless heritage of America.[29]

The lines relative to aid for the nations fighting for liberty deserve special scrutiny. They read, to repeat: "We favor the extension to all peoples fighting for liberty, or whose liberty is threatened, of such aid as shall not be in violation of international law or inconsistent with the requirements of our own national defense." The word "international" as used to qualify "law" was highly significant. It meant, without any quibbling, that the aid given to one or more belligerents in the war must be furnished by private persons and concerns in the form of munitions, goods, and services, at their own risk, financial and otherwise; and in no case by the Government of the United States at its expense and risk. International law, as then understood by all persons familiar with it, characterized as an act of war the supplying of munitions by a neutral government to any government engaged in war with another. The anti-war Republicans who inserted this restriction on aid to the Allies in the platform knew exactly what they were doing. They proposed to keep the Government of the United States out of the business of aiding belligerents in Europe by supplying them the sinews of war at public expense, by resorting to acts of war.

The Peace Pledge of the Democratic National Convention

When the Democratic delegates assembled for their convention at Chicago in mid-July, they had before them indubitable evidences of a large anti-war sentiment in the country. The Republicans at Philadelphia had declared without quibbling: "The Republican party is firmly opposed to involving this nation in foreign war." Public opinion polls

29. *Ibid.*, June 27, 1940.

had recently indicated that the Republicans had correctly gauged the temper of the American people in general, despite the existence of a wide-spread desire to aid the Allies in their war with the Axis Powers. Either on their own motion or in response to the demands of their constituents, a very large majority of the Democrats at Chicago shared this sentiment and were dead-set against any platform planks that would authorize actions on the part of the Federal Administration at all likely to eventuate in American participation in a foreign war.

If advocates of a foreign policy slanted in the direction of intervention were first in gathering their forces at the Republican convention in Philadelphia, the tables were turned among the Democrats at Chicago in July. Circumstances were different, of course. It was well settled among the Democrats that President Roosevelt would be nominated for a third term, despite the tradition against it. Moreover, in accordance with the custom followed in nominating a president to succeed himself, it was assumed that President Roosevelt would provide at least a draft of a platform for the convention to adopt if with modifications here and there. In fact, Democrats opposed to the President's policies were in a quandary. It was not definitely known or at least officially declared that Mr. Roosevelt would accept the nomination for a third term and there was no other leader in the party who, in the opinion of party experts, could easily carry the country if nominated at Chicago. It seemed, therefore, that President Roosevelt would want to "write his own ticket and platform," to quote the old political adage.

At the outset it appeared that immemorial party custom would prevail at Chicago. Press reports before the convention assembled ran to the effect that the non-interventionist Democrats were wasting their time in discussing the foreign policy planks of the Democratic platform, "for this part of the prospective campaign document is understood to have been virtually written already. According to word brought by Senators from Washington, the language of the foreign affairs declaration was outlined in rough several days ago by President Roosevelt, Secretary Hull, and congressional leaders, and in substance is a short paraphrase of the President's latest defense message to Congress," [30] July 10, 1940.

President Roosevelt's message of July 10, 1940, had followed the line that he had adopted at least as early as the autumn of 1939 when the repeal of the embargo on the export of munitions had been at issue. It represented the country as in dire peril from the threats of Axis aggressors, demanded more and bigger armaments "for defense," but offered assurance to the people against involvement in war. In respect of such assurance, the President had said in that message: "That we are opposed to war is known not only to every American, but to every government in the world. We will not use our arms in a war of aggression; we will not send our men to take part in European wars." [31]

After a search for the nature of President Roosevelt's proposed foreign policy plank for the party platform, a *New York Times* representative reported: "Some Senators who have insisted that the party must take a strong, unequivocal stand against military involvement in the current European conflict and say they have been informed as to the content of the proposed plank prophesied tonight that it would close the Democratic ranks tightly on this issue. They said Senator Wheeler and his followers would be satisfied." [32]

The *Times* reporter also took note of the fact that Senator Wheeler, who had recently threatened to bolt the party if it failed to take a firm stand against involvement in war, was

30. *Ibid.*, July 13, 1940. See above, p. 268.
31. President Roosevelt, well aware of popular hostility to shedding American blood in another European war, had devised sometime before 1940 what seemed to be a definite anti-war formula to the effect that "Whatever happens, we won't send troops abroad." *Events*, May, 1940, p. 332. Joseph Alsop and Robert Kintner, *American White Paper: The Story of American Diplomacy and the Second World War* (Simon & Schuster, 1940). Although this formula allayed the alarms of many citizens who were opposed to going into the war, anti-war Democrats, such as Senator Burton K. Wheeler, held that it was not a sufficient pledge against war in view of various measures promoted and acted upon by the President.
32. *New York Times*, July 13, 1940.

active at Chicago and had already delivered a public address in which he had announced that the platform would contain a clear-cut plank against intervention.[33] The same dispatch added: insistent demands were being made that "the Democratic party pledge itself to a policy of non-intervention in the European war and center its energies on national defense and re-employment."

This news story also contained the information that the first witness before the platform-drafting subcommittee, Philip Murray, head of the Congress of Industrial Organizations, had taken a strong stand against war. "We cannot accept or adopt any policy," Mr. Murray said, "which may lead toward involvement of the United States in the European or Asiatic war. Peace must be preserved for the people of the United States." [34]

As the Democrats on the subcommittee in charge of drafting the platform began work, they encountered trouble in dealing with President Roosevelt's representatives in their midst. The anti-war sentiment among the delegates was so strong as to be stunning. Anne O'Hare McCormick, the veteran journalist for the *New York Times*, reported: "To any one who questions the delegates, it is clear that the anti-war pledge is 100 per cent popular. The non-interventionist sentiment reflected here seems more general and more vocal than it was in Philadelphia [among the Republicans]." [35]

33. It was Senator Wheeler's conviction that President Roosevelt's measures "short of war," if not blocked, would finally lead to involvement in the war and the sending of American boys to fight in Europe.

34. In making this statement Mr. Murray had the support of the Communists in the labor movement, for at this time Stalin and Hitler were allies under their agreement of the previous year and, according to the Communist "line" during the Communist–Nazi alliance, the war in Europe and Asia was simply "an imperialist war" in which the United States should take no part. Until Hitler and Stalin made their compact in 1939, American Communists had been agitating in favor of a common "front" against Fascism; but after the compact, they besought the American people to stay out of the war, to maintain peace for the United States. After Hitler attacked Russia, in June, 1941, the American Communists again changed their line to conform to the Moscow line and carried on an equally vigorous agitation in favor of "aid to the Allies" and American participation in the war.

35. *New York Times*, July 18, 1940.

When President Roosevelt's party managers at Chicago insisted that his formula, "keep American boys out of war," was sufficient to meet all the demands of the anti-war Democrats, the latter replied that it was a "dodge" which would let him travel "on the road to war" and finally get to war.

But the non-interventionists faced the fact that they had no alternative to the renomination of President Roosevelt and they were many times informed that the platform planks on foreign affairs and defense had to meet his specifications. After attending the first hearings held by the subcommittee on the platform, a shrewd political commentator for the *New York Times*, Turner Catledge, reported: "The general assumption has been all along that President Roosevelt would practically write these declarations [on foreign policy and defense] himself, particularly *if he is to accept third-term nomination*, but he may have considerable trouble in gaining unanimous acceptance of the language he is understood to favor. What the President wants is a virtual repetition by the party of his assurances to Congress last week that no American soldiers will be sent over seas to fight in Europe's wars. That statement is not satisfactory to the strict non-interventionists. . . ." [36]

The "strict non-interventionists" were confirmed in their convictions by efforts of interventionists to force into the platform what was regarded as a war plank. For example, Clark M. Eichelberger, one of the outstanding advocates of "collective security," appeared before the subcommittee as secretary of the Committee to Defend America by Aiding the Allies, and appealed for "the fullest possible aid short of war to Great Britain in her fight with Germany." [37] It was common knowledge that many members of this committee, whatever its public professions, favored "all-out aid" to Britain no matter how great the peril of war might be in this procedure. [38] And Senator Wheeler charged Mr. Eichel-

36. *Ibid.*, July 16, 1940. (Italics supplied.)
37. *Ibid.*
38. Johnson, *op. cit.*

berger with "sneaking up on the people"; that is, with sailing under false colors.

While the subcommittee on the platform was still wrestling with the defense and foreign policy planks, William Bankhead, Speaker of the House of Representatives, delivered a keynote address to the convention which ranks among the political curiosities of the age. If party custom was followed, Mr. Bankhead was speaking for President Roosevelt, whose renomination was then a practical certainty; and yet there was not a word in his address that could have offended or disturbed the stoutest anti-war Democrat in the convention or the country. On the contrary it was a bid to the delegates on behalf of the President to follow him as the great champion of peace and neutrality for the United States. It neither defended nor mentioned President Roosevelt's decisions and actions in foreign affairs which had pleased internationalists and awakened the suspicions of isolationists.

The editors of the *New York Times* were indignant after they read Speaker Bankhead's address; and under the caption "Democratic Keynote, Eclipse of a Foreign Policy," they characterized and condemned it, at the same time that they revealed their own interpretation of the "all-out aid to Britain" movement:

. . . There was not one word in the keynote address last night to the Democratic party, assembled in national convention, about a single one of these policies, a single one of these efforts, of the Roosevelt Administration. There was nothing to suggest that the Administration has been even remotely interested in the problem of collective security. There was not one word about a "quarantine," or a "concerted effort," or "methods short of war." There was not a word about "the material resources of this nation" being made available to democracy in Europe. There was not a word about help for the British people in this hour of their extremity—help at "full speed ahead," or half speed, or even quarter speed. There was, on the contrary, such a discussion of foreign affairs and of foreign policy as many of the President's critics in the Senate might well have undertaken.

It was a remarkable performance, which must have had the President's approval. It was so remarkable a performance that at times, in his effort to prove a point, Speaker Bankhead seemed almost to shade the record. Thus, apparently in order to prove that Mr. Roosevelt has always been a staunch advocate of neutrality legislation, he quoted, as if they ran together, two widely separated sentences of the President's statement of August 31, 1935—leaving out a great deal in between, in the course of which the President said that "the inflexible provisions" of the very law that he was signing "might drag us into war instead of keeping us out." Thus, again, he described the cash-and-carry provisions of the present law as the work of the Administration, whereas it is well known that the Administration compromised on cash-and-carry in order to get repeal of the arms embargo. He even failed to note that, thanks to the Administration, the arms embargo—so staunchly defended by the opponents of the President —had so much as been repealed.

It was not the foreign policy proclaimed by the President at Chicago in 1937, and again in the 1939 message, and again at Charlottesville only a few weeks ago, that Speaker Bankhead espoused last night. It was a very different foreign policy, convention style, 1940. The transformation from old to new is one of the most complete, and certainly one of the swiftest, on record.[39]

During the day that followed Mr. Bankhead's keynote address, it was reported in Chicago that the non-interventionists had triumphed in the subcommittee on platform and had written their own foreign policy plank for the convention to adopt. According to press reports, Senator Wheeler was pleased with it. So was Senator McCarran. Senator Walsh, equally non-interventionist in his opinions, declared that the proposed plank would "meet the objections of those people most scrupulous in their desire to keep this country out of war." Even some of President Roosevelt's managers at Chicago seemed willing to approve the plank that so delighted the isolationists.[40]

By a reporter for the *New York Times*, the satisfaction of

39. Editorial, *New York Times*, July 16, 1940.
40. *New York Times*, July 17, 1940.

the strict anti-war Democrats with their triumph "was taken to mean that unless President Roosevelt were to intervene to have the subcommittee's action modified tomorrow, the platform would emerge with an anti-war plank which might be more restrictive of future Executive action than the one adopted by the Republican convention at Philadelphia." [41] Indeed if the *Times* reporter had sat in the secret meetings of the subcommittee, his observations on this development could scarcely have been more accurate and penetrating. And for the moment his conclusion was correct: the non-interventionists had temporarily forced the adoption of a plank that, if finally approved by the full committee and the convention, would have given a party guarantee to the President's formula—sending no boys to fight in foreign wars—by adding what one of the delegates in the convention called privately "a clincher."

At this juncture in the development of the foreign policy plank of the platform, Anne O'Hare McCormick admitted that President Roosevelt had been "outmaneuvered" by the "die-hard isolationists or known non-interventionists." She reported: "The Roosevelt supporters will now be satisfied, it is said, with a generalized declaration that will enable the head of the ticket to interpret it as he pleases or as circumstances dictate. . . ." [42]

The victory of the determined non-interventionists was, however, short-lived. As a result of negotiations between President Roosevelt's managers and the opposition, the "clincher" for pledging the party to keep the country out of war was modified by the addition of what became known as "the escape clause"—"except in case of attack." Commenting on the final form of the plank, Anne O'Hare McCormick correctly adjudged the outcome. She reported that the apparently plain word "attack" might "easily be extended to mean any assault on American interests, wherever it takes place," and that, according to the assumption of observers on

41. *Ibid.*
42. *Ibid.*

the spot, the President "means to disregard the work of the convention and announce his own views. . . . There is no reason why the document voted on tonight should be more binding than the platforms adopted by previous conventions."[43]

Although the newspaper reports on the maneuvers that accompanied the making of the foreign policy and defense planks for the Democratic platform were substantially correct as far as they went and indeed amazingly shrewd in divination and prophecy, they by no means gave the whole history of those maneuvers. President Roosevelt and his representatives at Chicago, as the newspapers correctly stated, took an active part in planning and writing the platform before and during the convention; but they went further, as the newspapers did not report, and sought to force specific kinds of statements into the platform.[44]

At the very first meeting of the subcommittee engaged in drafting the platform, a United States Senator, closely affiliated with the President's own group of supporters, introduced a proposed plank which opened with a caustic denunciation of the Axis dictators and closed with a declaration that all Americans, young and old, whatever their occupations, should be marshaled in solid array, each in his place, for national defense.[45]

This project was immediately assailed by non-interventionists as meaning nothing short of totalitarianism for the United States. The Senator who presented it, when asked to

43. *Ibid.*, July 18, 1940. In this prognostication, Mrs. McCormick proved to be a true prophet as well as a competent reporter for political conventions accustomed to making "solemn pledges" to the people of the United States.

44. The account here given is based on unpublished materials in my possession which I believe to be authentic and reliable; but for the present I am not at liberty to disclose the sources from which these materials came.

45. This proposal had been hinted at in the President's message of July 10, 1940, calling upon Congress for new appropriations for national defense. In the last paragraph of that message he had said: "So large a program means hard work—the participation of the whole country in the total defense of the country. This nation through sacrifice and work and unity proposes to remain free."

give the origin of the scheme, replied that it came from the White House. Even so, it was rejected by an almost unanimous vote. At a second session of the subcommittee on the same day, a member of the President's cabinet revived the scheme in a different form, only to encounter an equally disastrous defeat. Then the original copy of the memorandum was torn to shreds, lest it fall into the hands of the press.

Thereafter Senator Wheeler, encouraged perhaps by the sharp rebuff that had just been administered to representatives of President Roosevelt, laid before the subcommittee the following anti-war plank: "We will not participate in foreign wars, and we will not send our Army, naval or air forces to fight in foreign lands outside of the Americas." With alacrity the subcommittee adopted this resolution and incorporated it in the draft of the platform to be reported to the full committee in charge of the matter.

As soon as the Wheeler resolution came before the full committee on the platform, it was fiercely assailed by men belonging to the interventionist wing of the Democratic party, but it was carried by a substantial majority in that committee. Defeated in their effort to expunge the Wheeler resolution, opponents of the plank proposed a compromise in the interest of party "harmony," by adding to it the apparently innocuous words "except in case of attack." As all the members agreed that the United States would fight if attacked, Senator Wheeler accepted the amendment and the amended plank was finally adopted by the committee and in due course by the convention.

According to a report which I believe to be well founded,[46] President Roosevelt was kept informed about the struggle over the anti-war plank; news of the compromise proposal was communicated to him and to the Secretary of State, Cordell Hull, and they both demanded modifications in it; Mr. Hull was especially hostile on the ground that it

46. Information at my command from sources I believe to be thoroughly reliable is confirmed in certain fundamental respects by Arthur Krock's column on "The No-war Pledge in the 1940 Democratic Platform," *New York Times*, October 29, 1941.

would interfere with his operations in the Orient. At all events, James Byrnes, the famous adjuster of things in the Democratic party, demanded changes in the compromise. He informed Senator Wheeler that if the anti-war plank, even though made conditional by the escape clause, "except in case of attack," was not modified, President Roosevelt might not accept the nomination, and urged the Senator to approve another revision of the proposal. Senator Wheeler replied that if the anti-war proposal as adopted by the full committee was changed in any vital respect he would walk out of the convention.

That was an ultimatum to Mr. Byrnes and other spokesmen for President Roosevelt which was not to be treated lightly. In 1924 Senator Wheeler had displayed his independence, taken his political life in his hands, walked out of the Democratic party, and, as candidate for Vice-President, associated himself with Robert M. La Follette, Sr., in a revolt against both of the old parties. Democratic "regulars" at Chicago in 1940 could scarcely forget that. They knew full well that Senator Wheeler, right or wrong in his views, had powerful backing in the country; that he had the courage of his convictions; and that, if he went out of the convention, the Democratic party would encounter new hazards at the polls in November. Confronted by the Senator's ultimatum, President Roosevelt's agents finally surrendered. The anti-war plank with the escape clause went into the Democratic platform.

This turn of affairs at Chicago was, not unnaturally, displeasing to President Roosevelt, all the more for the reason that Senator Wheeler was largely responsible for it—the man who had taken the lead three years before in the fight on his plan for reconstructing the Supreme Court. It is true that in his message to Congress in January, 1940, the President had assured the people that "nobody expects such an undertaking" as "the sending of American youth to fight on the soil of Europe." But here was the pledge, written down in the Democratic platform, with no restriction save the "escalator" clause, "except in case of attack." And that clause, binding in good conscience, made it necessary for the President, if he felt moved to call upon Congress for a declaration of war in case of no attack, to refrain from it; to avoid, as Justice Frankfurter later phrased it, "even the appearance of an act of aggression on our part."

Apart from the anti-war plank, the Democratic platform of 1940 was profuse and eloquent in its praise of President Roosevelt's measures. The preamble stated that "for years our President has warned the nation that organized assaults against religion, democracy and international good faith threatened our own peace and security. Men blinded by partisanship brushed aside these warnings as war-mongering and officious intermeddling. . . ." It contained a pledge to extend to "the peace-loving and liberty-loving peoples wantonly attacked by ruthless aggressors . . . all the material aid at our command, consistent with law and not inconsistent with the interests of our own national self-defense, all to the end that peace and international good faith may yet emerge triumphant."

But in spite of the laudations in the preamble, according to reports circulating among responsible journalists in Washington, President Roosevelt was deeply disturbed by the anti-war plank of the Chicago platform. Some evidence to this effect was provided by his acceptance speech of July 19, 1940. In that pronouncement he departed from the time-honored practice, usually followed by party nominees, of approving and agreeing to stand by the platform. He ignored the platform. Although, in the rivalry of the campaign, he later renewed his own anti-war pledges, he failed to mention them in his acceptance address. In passages displaying deep feelings he declared that he would not soften the condemnation he had from time to time expressed against acts of aggression, nor recant the sentiments of sympathy he had proclaimed for free peoples, nor begrudge the material aid given to them. "I have pursued these efforts," he exclaimed, "in the face of appeaser fifth columnists who charged me with hysteria and war-mongering." Then, as if rising above his party and its anti-war plank, the President appealed to the people: "All that I have done to maintain the peace of this country and to prepare it morally, as well as physically, for whatever contingencies may be in store, I submit to the judgment of my countrymen." [47]

On July 19, 1940, in his acceptance speech, President Roosevelt manifested no inclination to make terms with "the Wheeler crowd" or reaffirm his often-expressed resolve to keep the country out of war. On the contrary, he warned Americans of "whatever contingencies may be in store." Not until the autumn of the campaign year did the President, stirred to combat by the anti-war speeches of his opponent, Wendell Willkie, appeal to the anti-war plank of his party's platform and, bidding as high as Mr. Willkie did for the peace votes, categorically assure the country that the United States would stay out of the war. [48]

Party Platforms Compared

A comparison of the two party platforms of 1940 reveals striking similarities and distinctions. The Republicans went on record as "firmly opposed to involving this nation in foreign war." The Democrats made a declaration of will: "We will not participate in foreign wars, and we will not send our Army, naval or air forces to fight in foreign lands outside of the Americas, except in case of attack." Since everybody except strict pacifists was prepared to fight "in case of attack," the Democratic "no-war" pledge appeared to be the stronger of the two; but both definitely reflected the "no-war" sentiment.

Both political parties pledged aid to peace-loving peoples in their struggles against aggressors, but with a fundamental difference. The Republicans insisted that such aid should "not be in violation of *international* law." On the other hand, the Democrats promised all aid "consistent with law," not

47. *Public Papers,* 1940 Vol., pp. 301 f.
48. See below, pp. 312 ff.

merely international law; and that left the way open for the Government of the United States to make its own law—if need be, in defiance of international law—and supply one or more of the belligerents with munitions, money, food, or anything else at public expense—a form of action directly contrary to international law. That single word, "international," omitted from the Democratic platform, was the crux of the whole matter.

Democratic	Republican

Anti-War

Democratic	Republican
We will not participate in foreign wars, and we will not send our Army, naval or air forces to fight in foreign lands outside of the Americas, except in case of attack.	The Republican party is firmly opposed to involving this nation in foreign war.

Aid to Liberty-loving Nations

Democratic	Republican
We pledge to extend to these [liberty-loving] peoples [wantonly attacked] all the material aid at our command, consistent with law and not inconsistent with the interests of our own national self-defense . . .	We favor the extension to all peoples fighting for liberty, or whose liberty is threatened, of such aid as shall not be in violation of international law or inconsistent with the requirements of our own national defense.

National Defense

Democratic	Republican
We favor and shall rigorously enforce and defend the Monroe Doctrine. The direction and aim of our foreign policy has been, and will continue to be, the security and defense of our own land and the maintenance of its peace. . . . We	We declare for the prompt, orderly and realistic building of our national defense to the point at which we shall be able not only to defend the United States, its possessions and essential outposts from foreign attack, but also efficiently to

Democratic	Republican
propose to provide America with an invincible Air Force, a Navy strong enough to protect all our seacoasts and our national interests and a fully equipped and mechanized Army.	uphold in war the Monroe Doctrine.

Recriminations

For years our President has warned the nation that organized assaults against religion, democracy and international good faith threatened our own peace and security. Men blinded by partisanship brushed aside these warnings as warmongering and officious intermeddling. The fall of twelve nations was necessary to bring their belated approval of legislative and Executive action that the President had urged and undertaken with the full support of the people. It is a tribute to the President's foresight and action that our defense forces are today at the peak of their peacetime effectiveness.	The present national Administration has already spent for all purposes more than fifty-four billion dollars, has boosted the national debt and current Federal taxes to an all-time high, and yet by the President's own admission we are still wholly unprepared to defend our country. . . . We accordingly fasten upon the New Deal full responsibility for our unpreparedness and for the consequent danger of involvement in war.[49]

Mr. Willkie's Peace Pledges as Candidate for President

During his quest for the Republican nomination, Mr. Willkie had underlined the general proposition that he favored aid to the Allies, short of war, and was opposed to involving the United States in the war. In his address accepting the Republican nomination, however, delivered in In-

49. *New York Times*, July 18, 1940.

diana on August 17, 1940, he tendered no absolute promises such as he had more than once made while seeking that place of Republican leadership. He quoted President Roosevelt as saying "we will extend to the opponents of force [abroad] the material resources of this nation and at the same time we will harness the use of those resources in order that we ourselves in America may have equipment and training equal to the task of any emergency and every defense." And Mr. Willkie expressed agreement with these principles—"as I understand them—and I don't understand them as implying military involvement in the present hostilities." It was from Mr. Roosevelt's methods rather than from these policies that Mr. Willkie dissented. He accused the President of dabbling in "inflammatory statements," of courting "a war for which this country is hopelessly unprepared and which it emphatically does not want," of concealing facts and objectives from the American people.

But in his acceptance speech Mr. Willkie did not commit himself to the formula: no political entanglements in Europe; defense, neutrality, and peace for the United States. On the contrary, while declaring that he understood Mr. Roosevelt's policies as not implying military involvement in the war then raging, Mr. Willkie, after picturing the horrors of the European war, said, . . . "we know that we are not isolated from those suffering people. . . . No man is so wise as to foresee what the future holds or to lay out a plan for it. No man can guarantee to maintain peace. . . . We must face a brutal but terrible fact. Our way of life is in competition with Hitler's way of life. . . . I promise, by returning to those same American principles that overcame German autocracy once before, both in business and in war, to outdistance Hitler in any contest he chooses in 1940 or after. And I promise you that, when we beat him, we shall beat him on our own terms, and in the American way." By no warrantable construction could these words be interpreted to mean a solemn pledge to keep the United States out of the war. Even in referring with approval to President Roosevelt's

policies of aid to the Allies as implying no military involvement in the war, Mr. Willkie declared: "No man can guarantee to maintain peace," and thus he seemed to sound a war
note.

As the campaign got under way and the question of peace
or war became a paramount issue, Mr. Willkie at first showed
an inclination to "go along" with President Roosevelt on the
matter of aid to the Allies without considering the probable
consequences of that policy. This attitude was displayed in
connection with a discussion of the arrangement which President Roosevelt had made for exchanging American over-age
destroyers for British bases in the Western Hemisphere.
Taking up that subject early in September, Mr. Willkie
merely deplored again the President's methods: "The country will undoubtedly approve of the program to add to our
naval and air bases and assistance given to Great Britain. It is
regrettable, however, that the President did not deem it necessary in connection with this proposal to secure the approval
of Congress or permit public discussion prior to adoption. . . ."

Apparently Mr. Willkie favored the "deal" but disap-
proved the methods employed in consummating it. He was
then asked point-blank by a reporter: "Do you think transfer
of warcraft to a belligerent nation constitutes an act of war?"
Mr. Willkie refrained from venturing an opinion and hedged
by replying: "That is one of the things debate and discussion
would have completely clarified." [50]

A few days later in September, at a great open-air meeting
in Indiana, Mr. Willkie declared that the Republican party
was the party of peace and that when he limited all possible
aid to Great Britain by the phrase "short of war," he was prepared to guarantee peace to the American people if elected:

Secretary Wallace, the New Deal candidate for Vice President,
said that the Republican party was the party of appeasement.

50. *Ibid.*, September 4, 1940.

. . . If Mr. Wallace means that the Republican party is the party of peace, he speaks the truth.

If I am President I shall never lead this country into war.

When I say that I mean it. I never say anything by indirection. That's not what I was taught in Indiana. I was educated in a plain public school, but that is what I learned.

I believe that the United States should give all possible help to Great Britain, short of war. And when I say short of war I mean short of war. And when I am President you will never hear of any great event after it has happened. . . .[51]

A week afterward, in two addresses given in Chicago, Mr. Willkie made an unconditional pledge of peace and explained positively that by defense he meant defense and not offense, not preparation for a foreign war:

. . . I know what it is to serve in the Army and I know what it is to be in Europe and serve in the Army. Let me say to you, if you elect me President of the United States, no American boys will ever be sent to the shambles of the European trenches. I will make this country so strong economically, I will build a defense program so great, I will teach the doctrine of national unity so much, that no dictator ever will dare to strike or touch this great free land of ours. . . .[52]

And let me say in conclusion that I saw service during the entire period of the last war and I know what it is to send men to the shambles of trenches.

If you elect me President I will never send an American boy to fight in any European war. . . .[53]

While on tour in Illinois Mr. Willkie repeated his pledge that, if elected, he would send no American boy to the shambles of a European war and doubly assured his auditors, and the country, that in giving this pledge he meant it. Then he turned on President Roosevelt. "If you elect my oppo-

51. *Ibid.*, September 8, 1940.
52. *Ibid.*, September 14, 1940.
53. *Ibid.*

nent," he said, "you will have no such guarantee." In what a *New York Times* reporter called "an impassioned appeal," Mr. Willkie added: "Please, please, without regard to me, do not vote to send American boys to the shambles of a European war." [54]

At this stage in the campaign, Mr. Willkie had to reckon with the fact that President Roosevelt, after a long silence, had taken the offensive and in an address before the Teamsters Union on September 11 had spoken disparagingly of attempts to frighten the people into believing that his defense measures represented efforts "to lead us into war," had pledged his allegiance to the peace plank of the Democratic platform. About a week later, at Los Angeles, Mr. Willkie commented caustically on this pledge, insinuated that such promises were not to be trusted, and made his own peace covenant with the people. "I hope and pray," Mr. Willkie declared, "that he [President Roosevelt] remembers the pledge of the 1940 platform better than he did the one of 1932. If he does not, you better get ready to get on the transports. Now let me say to you as a candidate for President of the United States in the year of 1940 that if you elect me President of the United States no American boy will ever be sent to the shambles of any European trench." [55]

Again employing retaliatory tactics, Mr. Willkie, at Cleveland, October 2, bluntly declared that President Roosevelt's policy had stirred up hostility against the United States. Mr. Willkie expressed a lack of confidence in the ability of the Administration to protect "our peace," and arrayed himself with the people in their determination to keep out of war:

A few days ago there was announced in Berlin a pact between three nations . . . It is clear enough, I believe, that Germany, Italy and Japan are thinking of the United States in terms of war, in terms of our participation in some bloody conflict of the future. Either they have aggressive designs against us or else they suspect us of having aggressive designs against them.

54. *Ibid.*, September 15, 1940.
55. *Ibid.*, September 20, 1940.

I am shocked by this fact, and I know that you people are. The American people do not want war. They have no idea whatever of joining in any conflict, whether on the Atlantic or the Pacific. They are determined to keep America at peace.

In this determination I stand with them. I am for keeping out of war. I am for peace for America.

And I want to ask this question . . . What have we done, overtly or secretly, to cause the most ruthless States in the world to make this aggressive declaration? . . . For my part I have little confidence that the policy of the last seven and a half years has been the policy best calculated to promote peace.

I have still less confidence that the policy at the present time is calculated to preserve peace. And I have no confidence at all in the ability of the present Administration to protect our peace with an adequate defense system. . . . I say that the first plank of our foreign policy is a defense system. . . . The reason that we are unprepared is because the present Administration has played politics with preparedness. It has played politics with our safety. . . .

Until I had built up the strength of America, I would refrain from inviting aggressive pacts against the American people. I would continue my efforts to aid the heroic British people—the only people in the world today who are fighting with their lives for liberty. I would aid Britain even if it meant the sacrifice of some speed in building up our own air fleet. I would do so because the longer Britain holds out, the more time we have in which to prepare ourselves. . . .

We must not rashly move. Any man who involves us in the risk of war, while we are thus unprepared, betrays his country.

The task before us is grim and hard. But we can still lead the world out of depression and disaster and despair and war. We can still lead the world toward prosperity and progress and peace and hope.

Oh, believe me, we can. The goals before us are distant. But this is the time, now, before it finally is too late, to stop, to think, to define those goals and to become competent to achieve them.

I have called this the Battle of America. . . . It is a battle to create a society strong enough and effective enough to maintain itself in peace. In that battle I promise you victory. . . .[56]

56. *Ibid.*, October 3, 1940.

When he reached Philadelphia on October 4, 1940, Mr. Willkie placed himself without reservations at the head of those Americans who were resolutely determined to stop the drift toward war:

The results of incompetence are written upon the history of the last few years. Incompetence invites bold actions on the part of other powers. The longer the United States remains incompetent to defend itself, the closer we are drawn to war.

We must stop that drift toward war. And in order to do that we must stop this incompetent administration.

Fellow Americans, I want to lead the fight for peace, the fight for peace through the establishment of competence in government. I know how to lead that fight; I will lead this nation back to work.

The first step toward peace is to put a job in every home.

The second step toward peace is to mobilize American industry for the production of armament. . . .[57]

In a radio broadcast given the form of questions and answers, October 8, 1940, Mr. Willkie elaborated his policy in respect of aid to Great Britain and followed it by a declaration that "we should keep out of war at all hazards":

Question:
Would you, if elected, discontinue our efforts for preparedness; would your policy be one of appeasement toward the iniquitous dictators of Europe?
Mr. Willkie:
. . . under no circumstances would I appease the dictators. . . . Europe proves today that appeasement is not a successful means of assuring peace. Indeed, the search for peace through appeasement has resulted in the destruction of the appeasers. In this matter as in all other matters we must be realistic and not sentimental and remember that to the dictators of all people actions speak louder than words. I do not, however, believe in shouting provocative insults at dictators or any one else. Such statements

57. *Ibid.*, October 5, 1940.

get no place. Dictators cannot be quarantined with words, and a dagger in the back speech does only harm. . . .
Question:

Many letters have come in, Mr. Willkie, asking if you think it is in the best interests of the United States to aid Great Britain, and if so, what kind of aid you would give to Great Britain.
Mr. Willkie:

I do think it is in the interest of the United States to aid Great Britain because Great Britain is our first line of defense. . . .

This subject leads directly to my position on going into war. I believe we should keep out of war at all hazards. We are being edged toward war by an Administration which is alike careless in speech and in action.

For us to go to war, particularly in view of our unpreparedness, would be the height of folly. We would not help Britain by going to war today. That distinguished British spokesman H. G. Wells made that clear in his statement to the American press just the other day. We are so unprepared for war that should we go to war we would have to keep all the war supplies we could produce for ourselves. Only by remaining at peace can we give effective aid to Britain and prepare ourselves.

Let me make it clear. I am in favor of giving aid to Britain, but I am first in favor of protecting these United States.[58]

Speaking in the Bronx on the same day, October 8, 1940, Mr. Willkie questioned the sincerity of President Roosevelt's peace pledges and strongly intimated that the President had secret understandings[59] with other countries for putting the United States into the war:

I want to put some questions tonight to the President of the United States and to you people here. . . . Is there any one here

---

58. *Ibid.,* October 9, 1940.

59. By this time allegations were afloat to the effect that President Roosevelt had, after war began in 1939, entered into a secret exchange of messages with Winston Churchill, then in the British Admiralty, and had continued the practice. On August 25, 1940, the *New York Times* had published a brief account of the Kent-Ramsay case in Great Britain that later was made the basis of a libel suit by Captain Ramsay against the *Times.* This case was related to the exchange of messages between Mr. Churchill and Mr. Roosevelt.

who really thinks that the President is sincerely trying to keep us out of war? . . .

An administration that is not telling the truth is not qualified to head the country in time of crisis or any other time. I want to ask the President, and I demand an answer: Are there any international understandings to put America into the war that we citizens do not know about?

Maybe we people will not approve of them but we should know about it. We don't belong to the government, the government belongs to us. I have been repeatedly asked in my trips throughout the country if such secret understandings exist. The only answer I can give is that I do not know, but I want to know. If this country has to fight, public officials do not have to do the fighting. It is the people of this country who will have to fight. If you elect me, the people of the United States will be the ones to decide whether they will be involved in any war. . . .[60]

As if forecasting the solemn and unqualified pledge against sending American boys to fight in foreign wars soon to be made in Boston by President Roosevelt, Mr. Willkie, on October 11, 1940, made a statement to the people of that city which was equally specific:

. . . All around us the world is at war. All around us a hostile system of government has grown up. The three most powerful states have made an alliance against us.

The next administration will bear the awful responsibility of keeping us at peace.

And we can have peace. But we must know how to preserve it.

To begin with, we shall not undertake to fight anybody else's war. Our boys shall stay out of European wars.

But by the same token we will appease no one. We stand for our democratic institutions and we stand ready to defend them with our lives, if necessary.

How, then, shall we stay out of war and avoid appeasement? There is only one way. We must become strong. We must build ourselves an air force, a navy, an army so strong that no dictator

60. *Ibid.*, October 9, 1940.

will dare to tamper with our commerce, our interests or our rights.[61]

Moving out to St. Louis, "the center of America," Mr. Willkie once more asserted that his election would mean sending no American boys "over there again":

Those oceans are indeed broad. We can say with the utmost confidence, standing here in the center of America: We do not want to send our boys over there again. And we do not intend to send them over there again. And if you elect me President we won't.

But by the same token I believe if you re-elect the third-term candidate they will be sent. We cannot and we must not undertake to maintain by arms the peace of Europe. . . .

What is the role under these circumstances that the United States should play in this war-torn world? . . .

Is it that we should send an expeditionary force over there? Is it that we should join again in a foreign war? Is that the role to which the New Deal thinks itself indispensable? Is that the reason for the provocative statements, the gratuitous insults, the whispers, the rumors that keep coming out of Washington? . . .

We cannot send an expeditionary force out to that rim. We have no such force. And even if we had that force it would do no good. It isn't what those people need. It isn't even what they've asked us for. . . .

[On election day] the people choose their government for the next four years. On that day let them not choose a government for which peace is just a word; a government of attitudes and poses, a government whose promises still are, and will remain, on order. Let them choose rather a government that will make peace a reality; . . .[62]

With only a few days left for his campaign, Mr. Willkie, in an address before 25,000 people in Chicago on October 22, 1940, raised again the issue of good faith and challenged the "truthfulness" of his opponent's peace promises:

61. *Ibid.,* October 12, 1940.
62. *Ibid.,* October 18, 1940.

As we look out upon the world today there is one blessing that we all profoundly pray for and desire. We desire to remain at peace. The New Deal promises to keep us out of war. The third-term candidate said that he hates war. He said on September 11: "I have one supreme determination, to do all I can to keep war away from these shores for all time."

That is the promise. My fellow-citizens, in the light of the record I challenge its truthfulness. The third-term candidate has not kept faith with the American people. How are we to know that he will begin to keep it now?

If his promise to keep our boys out of foreign wars is no better than his promise to balance the budget they're already almost on the transports.

Men and women of America, it is my ambition to re-establish good faith between the American people and those in high office.[63]

On the same day, October 22, 1940, in the same city, Chicago, Mr. Willkie, in a question-and-answer broadcast, avowed that his determination to stay out of war distinguished his foreign policy from that of President Roosevelt:

Interlocutor:
What is the difference, then, Mr. Willkie, between your foreign policy and that of the Administration?
Mr. Willkie:
One difference is my determination to stay out of war. I have a real fear that this Administration is heading for war, and I am against our going to war and will do all that I can to avoid it. . . .
Interlocutor [reading from a letter]:
"Is there any reason to assume that the youth of the country would be more protected from the ravages of war if you were elected President than if Roosevelt were re-elected? . . ."
Mr. Willkie:
. . . The greatest obligation of any man who seeks the high office of President is the safety of our sons. And if I am elected President that will be my greatest obligation; and my greatest effort will be to do all that is humanly possible to avoid war.

63. *Ibid.*, October 23, 1940.

Interlocutor:

But what can be done to keep us out of war, Mr. Willkie?

Mr. Willkie:

There are three things we can do. First, avoid acts of war. Second, make our country a prosperous and unified nation. And third, build our defense so strong, so powerful, that no nation would dare attack us.

Interlocutor:

Those are important points. Could you explain them a bit further, Mr. Willkie?

Mr. Willkie:

Certainly. When I say we should not commit any act of war, I mean that we should not meddle in affairs that are none of our business. And we should not use warlike words and invite war. Those are things to avoid. . . .[64]

Two days later, October 24, 1940, at Harbor Creek, Mr. Willkie repeated his questioning of President Roosevelt's good faith:

Last night the third-term candidate, referring to the Democratic platform of 1940, quoted this language from that platform: "We will not participate in foreign wars and we will not send our Army, naval or air forces to fight in foreign lands outside of the Americas, except in case of attack."

I hope, I hope sincerely, that that pledge made last night by the third-term candidate, based upon the 1940 platform of the Democratic party, is remembered by him longer than he remembered the same pledge that he made with reference to the provisions of the Democratic platform of 1932.

If he does not remember it longer, then shortly our boys will be on the transports, sailing for some foreign shore.[65]

A similar charge against his opponent was made by Mr. Willkie the following day, October 25, 1940, in a broadcast address at Wilkes-Barre:

Now in his talk last Wednesday the third-term candidate made us another promise, a most serious promise, a promise that con-

64. *Ibid.*
65. *Ibid.*, October 25, 1940.

cerns every man, woman and child in America. He said that he was working for peace. He said that he would stand by the Democratic platform of 1940, and he quoted this pledge in that platform: "We will not participate in foreign wars and we will not send our Army, naval or air forces to fight in foreign lands outside of the Americas except in case of attack."

I hope, I hope, oh, so sincerely that that pledge by the third-term candidate based upon the 1940 platform of the Democratic party is remembered by him longer than he remembered the honor of the credit of the United States which was based upon the Democratic platform of 1932.

I sincerely hope that on some future occasion the third-term candidate will not tell the reporters that as of the day he made that pledge he had no intention of going to war.[66]

To the people of Indiana, October 28, 1940, Mr. Willkie gave his plighted word: "My most solemn promise to you people in Indiana is that if you elect me President of the United States I will so guide your affairs as to keep this great nation functioning and keep your boys from ever getting involved abroad. They will never go to a foreign war under my direction." [67]

Even when he spoke of aid to Great Britain, as well as when he promised peace to the people of the United States, Mr. Willkie proposed to outdo President Roosevelt. For example, in a radio talk broadcast from Charleston, West Virginia, Mr. Willkie made this tender. According to the report in the *New York Times*, "He asserted that he had been accused unfairly by the President of 'me tooing' on aid to Great Britain. He declared that he was for aid to Great Britain before he anticipated being a candidate and that, while he did not want to send troops, he favored getting production going so that effective aid to Britain would not be limited 'to a few old destroyers and a thin line of airplanes.' " [68]

As the campaign drew toward a close, Mr. Willkie became

66. *Ibid.*, October 26, 1940.
67. *Ibid.*, October 29, 1940.
68. *Ibid.*, October 30, 1940.

even more fervid in asserting that the reelection of President Roosevelt, despite his promises that American boys would not be sent to fight in foreign war, meant war for the United States. At Cumberland, Maryland, October 30, 1940, he expressed the hope that President Roosevelt would keep his pledge to follow the anti-war plank of the Democratic platform of 1940. "If he does not," Mr. Willkie exclaimed, "some of these Maryland boys who are being called today in the draft will shortly be loading onto the transports. You can only judge of a man's future actions by his past actions, and if he repudiates the planks of the 1940 platform the same as he did those of 1932, what way do you people have to protect these boys who are being called into service today?" [69]

In Baltimore, later the same day, October 30, 1940, Mr. Willkie went almost to the limit in attacking the good faith of President Roosevelt. There he took up a recent speech by Ambassador Joseph Kennedy to the effect that the United States had no commitments with Great Britain. There he referred to the fact that in 1932 Senator Carter Glass had got up from a sick bed to assure the country that Mr. Roosevelt would keep his sound money pledge. There, to the audience, which the *New York Times* reported as "wildly cheering," Mr. Willkie exclaimed: "Now I put it to you and let him nail this on the barn door or the front door. Mr. Third-Term Candidate, is your pledge about peace and the acceptance of the Democratic platform in 1940 more or less sacred than the pledge you made about sound money in 1932? Are you kidding Joe Kennedy the same way you kidded Carter Glass? On the basis of his past performance with pledges to the people, if you re-elect him you may expect war in April, 1941. Now, Mr. Third-Term Candidate, has Wendell Willkie falsified the record about that?" [70]

69. *Ibid.*, October 31, 1940.
70. *Ibid.* This statement by Mr. Willkie was so sweeping and delivered with such force that, coming as it did near the end of the campaign, it made a great sensation. Here was a specific charge that if the people reelected President Roosevelt, they could expect war by April, 1941. A little more than three months afterward, namely, on February 11, 1941, Mr. Willkie appeared

Since Mr. Willkie's speech at Baltimore on October 30, 1940, was to receive so much publicity at the moment and the following year, its essential passages relative to peace and war are quoted here at length:

We reject the fatal doctrine of indispensability. One-man rule always leads to the road to war. . . .

In protecting America, the maintenance of peace in the Western Hemisphere will be my objective. The President must be dedicated to the objective of peace in our part of the world.

Aid to Britain to the limits of prudence for our own safety is essential to that objective.

I have given you my pledge many times over: I will work for peace. We are against sending our boys into any war other than the defense of our own country.

The third-term candidate has also pledged himself to peace. Some nights ago he said, and I quote: "I repeat again that I stand on the platform of our party: that we will not participate in foreign wars, and we will not send our Army, naval or air forces to fight in foreign lands outside of the Americas except in case of attack."

That is his pledge . . . I ask you whether his pledge for peace is going to last any longer than his pledge for sound money.

On the basis of his past performance with pledges to the people, you may expect we will be at war by April, 1941, if he is elected.

That is the first requirement for the protection of America, a pledge to work for peace and good faith in that pledge; and another requirement has to do with our relationship with other nations. This is the field of diplomacy. . . .

. . . our diplomacy should be circumspect, wise and con-

before the Senate Committee on Foreign Relations to support the Lend-Lease Bill, while still expressing a desire to keep the country out of war. On that occasion Senator Nye read to Mr. Willkie the following line from the campaign speech of October 30, 1940: "On the basis of his past performance with pledges to the people, you may expect we will be at war by April, 1941, if he is elected." The Senator then inquired of Mr. Willkie: "Do you still agree that that might be the case?" Mr. Willkie replied: "It might be. It was a bit of campaign oratory (Laughter). I am very glad that you read my speeches, because the President said he did not (Laughter)." Thereupon Senator Nye concluded: "That is all." Senate Hearings on the Lend-Lease Bill, Pt. 3, pp. 901–905.

sistent. During the last eight years the third-term candidate has made reckless flights into the field of diplomacy. These flights were made entirely on his own initiative. And they have contributed to the confusion of the world.

Statements of the third-term candidate made in 1939 led British observers to publish opinions that the United States would participate in a European war. These statements of the third-term candidate were probably made with good motives. But they had that misleading effect.

The interests of the United States would have been better served if the third-term candidate had been outspokenly for peace and nonparticipation at that time, instead of waiting to pledge it in an election.

Even as late as June 10, 1940, he startled the world. He declared of Italy that the hand that held the dagger "has struck it into the back of its neighbor." In the capitals of Europe this bit of oratory was not taken as a move to keep the United States at peace.

On October 5, 1937, the third-term candidate called for the quarantine of aggressors. But his policy with regard to aggressors has really tended to strengthen rather than to quarantine them. . . .[71]

Mr. Willkie's final commitment to the nation on the subject of peace was made in a radio broadcast to the women of America on the very eve of the election:

We have a great national defense effort ahead of us. That defense effort will have only one object—to keep us out of war.

Women will play a large part in our defense program. In every community you will be called on to keep social life secure and industrial life running efficiently. You will hold jobs of many kinds. But above all, you will keep our eyes fixed on our true goal, and that true goal is peace, peace.

I happen to know about war at first hand and I hate war. I saw the damage done by a war, at home and abroad—the loss of security and the extinction of civil liberties even in this land of the free.

I have not forgotten that lesson. My every act as President will

71. *New York Times*, October 31, 1940.

be to keep this country out of foreign wars and to keep it at peace. I promise, as I have promised many times before, not to send your husbands and sons and brothers to death on a European or Asiatic battlefield.

I will avoid bringing about a condition of affairs that will make war necessary. And I will never take this country into war until your representatives in Congress declare it.

The Army we will build will be the soundest, the healthiest and the strongest force in the world. But it will be an Army for defense and for nothing else. . . .

My purpose is to keep America out of war and to preserve American values—values that go back to every community and to every fireside. . . .[72]

President Roosevelt's Peace Pledges during the Campaign

Although in accepting the Democratic nomination President Roosevelt dwelt at length on the perils of war on the horizon and refrained from mentioning the no-war plank of the platform, he came back to the theme of peace for the United States a few weeks later and continued to emphasize it in one speech after another. Even after he had consummated the exchange of American destroyers for British naval and air bases in this hemisphere, he declared: "This is not inconsistent in any sense with our status of peace. Still less is it a threat against any nation. It is an epochal and far-reaching act of preparation for continental defense in the face of grave danger. Preparation for defense is an inalienable prerogative of a sovereign state. Under present circumstances this exercise of sovereign right is essential to the maintenance of our peace and safety." [73]

Addressing the national convention of the Teamsters Union on September 11, 1940, the President once more referred to war perils and the need for national defense in the interest of which various measures had been adopted. Then he said to the teamsters' officials and delegates:

72. *Ibid.*, November 5, 1940.
73. *Public Papers*, 1940 Vol., p. 391.

In all these plans for national defense, only those who seek to play upon the fears of the American people, discover an attempt to lead us into war. The American people will reject that kind of propaganda of fear, as they have rejected similar types which are "occasionally" spread forth near election time. . . .

Weakness in these days is a cordial invitation to attack. That's no longer a theory; it's a proven fact, proved within the past year.

I hate war, now more than ever. I have one supreme determination—to do all that I can to keep war away from these shores for all time. I stand, with my party, and outside of my party as President of all the people, on the platform, the wording that was adopted in Chicago less than two months ago. It said:

"We will not participate in foreign wars, and we will not send our Army, naval or air forces to fight in foreign lands outside of the Americas, except in case of attack." [74]

At Dayton, Ohio, October 12, 1940, President Roosevelt expounded his foreign policy under the head of Hemisphere Defense: "We arm to defend ourselves . . . in cooperation with the other American Republics, to help defend the whole hemisphere. We are building a total defense on land and sea and in the air sufficient to repel total attack from any part of the world."

But, he said, "there are some in every single one of the twenty-one American Republics who suggest that the course the Americas are following is slowly drawing one or all of us into war with some nation, or nations beyond the seas."

Taking up this charge, the President made reply: "The clear facts have been stated over and over again. This country wants no war with any nation. This hemisphere wants no war with any nation. The American Republics are determined to work in unity for peace just as we work in unity to defend ourselves from attack. For many long years every ounce of energy I have had has been devoted to keeping this nation and the other Republics at peace with the rest of the world. That is what continues uppermost in my mind today —the objective for which I hope and work and pray. We

74. *Ibid.,* p. 415.

arm to defend ourselves. The strongest reason for that is that it is the strongest guarantee for peace." [75]

Despite the fact that President Roosevelt had so often told the country that his policy was security, defense, non-entanglement, and peace for the United States, for this hemisphere, peace with all nations, his opponent and Republican critics kept insisting that he was in reality on the high road that meant war. Stung by this accusation, he announced from the White House, October 18, 1940, that he intended to make five speeches dealing with "deliberate or unwitting falsifications of fact."

In the first of these speeches on "falsifications," at Philadelphia, October 23, 1940, the President took up the Republican accusation that he had entered into secret commitments with foreign nations, "pledging in some way the participation of the United States in some war." [76] This accusation he denied in language that admitted of no misunderstanding: "There is no secret treaty, no secret obligation, no secret commitment, no secret understanding in any shape or form, direct or indirect, with any other Government, or any other nation in any part of the world, to involve this nation in any war or for any other purpose."

Near the close of his Philadelphia speech, the President dealt with the charge that "this Administration wishes to lead this country into war." Again he was clear-cut in the defense of his policy as a peace policy:

That charge is contrary to every fact, every purpose of the past eight years. . . . my every act and thought have been directed to the end of preserving the peace of the world, and more particularly, the peace of the United States—the peace of the Western Hemisphere. . . .

When war came, I used every ounce of the prestige of the office to prevent its spread to other nations. When that effort failed, I called upon the Congress, and I called upon the nation, to

75. *Ibid.*, p. 464.
76. See Mr. Willkie's statements on this subject, above, pp. 303 f.

build the strong defenses that would be our best guarantee of peace and security in the American Hemisphere.

To Republicans and Democrats, to every man, woman and child in the nation I say this: Your President and your Secretary of State are following the road to peace.

We are arming ourselves not for any foreign war.

We are arming ourselves not for any purpose of conquest or intervention in foreign disputes.

Then the President quoted the pledge of the Democratic platform against participation in foreign wars "except in case of attack," and ended on the note of peace: "It is for peace that I have labored; and it is for peace that I shall labor all the days of my life." [77]

In his second address on "falsifications," at New York City, October 28, 1940, President Roosevelt accused Republican leaders of "playing politics with the national security today," replied to the charges that his administration was "hysterical" and was "manufacturing panics and inventing foreign dangers," and presented his case. Having gone into the Republican charges and his own record, he said: "I am asking the American people to support a continuance of this type of affirmative, realistic fight for peace." The alternative, he continued, is to risk the future of the country in the hands of those who have displayed timidity and weakness or "in the inexperienced hands of those who in these perilous days are willing recklessly to imply that our boys are already on their way to the transports.[78] This affirmative search for peace calls for clear vision. It is necessary to mobilize resources, minds and skills, and every active force for peace in all the world. We have steadily sought to keep mobilized the greatest force of all—religious faith, devotion to God. Your Government is working at all times with representatives of the Catholic, Protestant, and Jewish faiths. . . ." [79]

77. *Public Papers,* 1940 Vol., pp. 488 ff.
78. See Mr. Willkie's charge, above, pp. 307 ff.
79. *Public Papers,* 1940 Vol., pp. 499 ff.

At Boston, October 30, 1940, President Roosevelt discussed the Republican treatment of his defense measures and Republican insinuations as to his intentions in respect of peace for the United States. By this time his chief opponent, Mr. Willkie, had gone far beyond the terms of his acceptance speech and definitely promised the voters that one of his prime objectives would be to keep the country out of war. At Philadelphia the President had attached to his peace pledge the conditional clause of the Democratic platform, "except in case of attack." At New York he had not gone beyond committing himself to "an affirmative search for peace" and impugning the allegation that "our boys are already on their way to the transports." [80]

In his address at Boston President Roosevelt made an unqualified declaration on war and peace:

And while I am talking to you mothers and fathers, I give you one more assurance.

I have said this before, but I shall say it again and again and again:

Your boys are not going to be sent into any foreign wars.

They are going into training to form a force so strong that, by its very existence, it will keep the threat of war from our shores.

The purpose of our defense is defense.[81]

President Roosevelt's campaign address at Brooklyn on November 1, 1940, was devoted mainly to a review of the domestic measures which he had devised in the interest of the people, but the question of peace for the United States was

80. The Burke-Wadsworth bill providing for selective compulsory military training in peacetime was passed by Congress on September 14, 1940, and was signed by President Roosevelt two days later.

81. *Public Papers*, 1940 Vol., p. 517. To this address President Roosevelt or his collaborator, Mr. Rosenman, prefixed the title: "We Are Going Full Speed Ahead." From the prefatory analysis all reference to the anti-war pledge was omitted. The analysis is as follows: "(Rebuilding the navy and naval bases—Expanding and training the army—Defense contracts—Defense housing—Our air power is growing—Planes for Britain—Production capacity—Progress of American agricultural recovery—Republican opposition to aid to farmers.)," p. 514. The President's Introduction to the 1940 Volume of his *Public Papers* is dated White House, July 17, 1941.

not overlooked. In concluding this address, he declared: "I am fighting to keep this Nation prosperous and at peace. I am fighting to keep our people out of foreign wars, and to keep foreign conceptions of Government out of our own United States. . . . And I will not stop fighting." [82]

The following day, November 2, 1940, in "extemporaneous remarks" at Rochester, President Roosevelt said: "Your national Government down in Washington, in all of its component parts, is equally a Government of peace—a Government that intends to retain peace for the American people. As your great Secretary of State said last night: 'Outstanding is the wholly unwarranted and utterly vicious charge that the President is leading us into war.' And then he said, 'We are creating the weapons and the organization needed, first to discourage would-be assailants and, secondly, should we be assailed, to repel assailants.' That is our policy today." [83]

That same day, November 2, 1940, in a brief speech at Buffalo, President Roosevelt cited one of the "vicious misrepresentations" that were being made about the Government of the United States, namely, that the President was already taking certain steps that would lead to war with Japan. This he branded as a falsehood. Then he went on: "And I can cite to you many, many other examples of rumors that have been started in the same rumor factory—all of them untrue, but every one of them tending to make people believe that this country is going to war. Your President says this country is not going to war." [84]

In what he called his "final national address of the campaign," at Cleveland, November 3, 1940, President Roosevelt summarized again his foreign policy:

There is nothing secret about our foreign policy. . . . I have stated it many times before, not only in words but in action. Let me restate it like this:

82. *Ibid.*, p. 539.
83. *Ibid.*, pp. 540 f.
84. *Ibid.*, p. 543.

The first purpose of our foreign policy is to keep our country out of war. At the same time, we seek to keep foreign conceptions of Government out of the United States. . . .

The second purpose of this policy is to keep war as far away as possible from the shores of the entire Western Hemisphere. . . .

Finally, our policy is to give all possible material aid to the nations which still resist aggression, across the Atlantic and Pacific Oceans. . . .

And through it all [my past record] there have been two thoughts uppermost in my mind—to preserve peace in our land; and to make the forces of democracy work for the benefit of the common people of America.[85]

A Parallel

The reciprocal development of President Roosevelt's and Mr. Willkie's unqualified peace statements to the American people is indicated in the following summary:

President Roosevelt	*Mr. Willkie*
January 3: ". . . nobody expects such an undertaking" as "the sending of American youth to fight on the soil of Europe."	
April 20: "We are keeping out of the wars that are going on in Europe and in Asia. . . ."	
May 16: "Our ideal, yours and mine, the ideal of every man, woman, and child in the country—our objective is still peace—peace at home and peace abroad."	
	June 18: ". . . we must stay out of war. . . . We do not intend to send men from the shores of this continent to fight in any war."

85. *Ibid.*, pp. 546 ff.

President Roosevelt	*Mr. Willkie*
July 10: ". . . we will not send our men to take part in European wars."	

September 7: "When I say [aid to Britain] short of war I mean short of war."

September 13: "If you elect me President I will never send an American boy to fight in any European war."

September 19: ". . . if you elect me President . . . no American boy will ever be sent to the shambles of any European trench."

October 11: "Our boys shall stay out of European wars."

October 17: "And if you elect me President we won't [send boys over there again]. . . . We cannot and we must not undertake to maintain by arms the peace of Europe."

October 22: "If his [President Roosevelt's] promise to keep our boys out of foreign wars is no better than his promise to balance the budget they're already almost on the transports."

October 22: "One difference [between Mr. Willkie and Mr. Roosevelt] is my determination to stay out of war. I have a real fear that this Administration is heading for war, . . ."

October 28: "My most solemn promise . . . is that if you elect me President . . . I

President Roosevelt   *Mr. Willkie*

will so guide your affairs as to keep . . . your boys from ever getting involved abroad."

October 30: "I have said this before, but I shall say it again and again and again: Your boys are not going to be sent into any foreign wars."

October 30: "On the basis of his [President Roosevelt's] past performance with pledges to the people, you may expect we will be at war by April, 1941, if he is elected."

November 1: "I am fighting to keep our people out of foreign wars. . . . And I will not stop fighting."

November 2: "Your national Government . . . is equally a Government of peace—a Government that intends to retain peace for the American people."

November 2: "Your President says this country is not going to war."

November 3: "The first purpose of our foreign policy is to keep our country out of war."

November 4: "I promise . . . not to send your husbands and sons and brothers to death on a European or Asiatic battlefield."

It may be said, however, that this listing of the unqualified peace statements made to the American people by the two candidates lacks proportions. It may be contended that during the same period they also promised on various occasions aid to the Allies at war with the Axis Powers and that such promises in effect offset or canceled their engagements to keep the United States out of foreign wars. Against this interpretation of the record certain facts stand in contradiction.

Repeatedly during the political contest President Roosevelt was accused of pursuing or intending to pursue a policy with regard to the Allies which would lead to war, and he indignantly denied the accusation. On the other side, Mr. Willkie, who often filed this charge against his opponent, again and again limited his promises of aid to the Allies by adding and emphasizing the phrase "short of war."

President Roosevelt's Final Review of Foreign Affairs and Policy for 1940

Although during the campaign President Roosevelt had more than once assured the American people that his foreign policy meant peace for the United States, particularly when he declared on November 2, 1940: "Your President says this country is not going to war," he introduced a new note after his election and before the year closed—a note of doubt on this point. Yet even the doubt did not stand alone, for he coupled with it a positive assertion instructing the people that they could "nail any talk about sending armies to Europe as deliberate untruth."

The new note, accompanied by the old guarantee, appeared in the President's fireside chat of December 29 on "national security." In this radio address to listening millions, he reviewed at length the state of the warring world and the gallant fight of the British people and their allies against the Axis Powers in Europe and the Orient. Then he said with regard to the United States: "Our own future security is greatly dependent on the outcome of that fight. Our ability to 'keep out of war' is going to be affected by that outcome. Thinking in terms of today and tomorrow, I make the direct statement to the American people that there is far less chance of the United States getting into war, if we do all we can now to support the nations defending themselves against attack by the Axis than if we acquiesce in their defeat, submit tamely to an Axis victory, and wait our turn to be the object of attack in another war later on.

"If we are to be completely honest with ourselves, we must

admit that there is risk in any course we may take. But I deeply believe that the great majority of our people agree that the course that I advocate involves the least risk now and the greatest hope for world peace in the future.

"The people of Europe who are defending themselves do not ask us to do their fighting. They ask us for the implements of war, . . ."

Having now warned the American people that there was risk in any course that might be taken and having declared that his course involved the least risk, President Roosevelt still gave them this guarantee: "There is no demand for sending an American Expeditionary Force outside our own borders. There is no intention by any member of your Government to send such a force. You can, therefore, nail any talk about sending armies to Europe as deliberate untruth.

"Our national policy is not directed toward war. Its sole purpose is to keep war away from our country and our people." [86]

Note to Chapter X

IN ADDITION to the addresses the texts of which are given in his *Public Papers*, 1940 Volume, President Roosevelt delivered a few brief speeches during the campaign, which were reported in the press. For example, at Akron, Ohio, on October 11, the President said: "For many years we in the United States have managed to keep out of trouble in other continents and I am confident that in the future we shall be able to avoid being brought into war through attack by somebody else on the Americas." [87]

At New Haven, Connecticut, October 30, he "denounced reports which create the fear that the United States will be led into war," and said: "I think you realize that all this talk about sending American boys to Europe—well, it does not conform with either the facts of the past or the facts of the future." [88]

At Hartford, Connecticut, October 30, the President said: "And you know, too, that we aim to defend only against an at-

86. *Ibid.,* pp. 633 ff.
87. *New York Times,* October 12.
88. *Ibid.,* October 31.

tack from the outside. Almost every year that has passed, sometimes every few minutes, some responsibility has fallen on me to avoid entangling alliances or entangling actions that might lead this country into war. I notice that for seven and one-half years, nearly eight, the United States not only has kept free from any entanglements, but the United States today is at peace and is going to remain at peace." [89]

89. *Ibid.*, October 31.

Index